Empowering Health Care Consumers through Tax Reform

EMPOWERING HEALTH CARE CONSUMERS THROUGH TAX REFORM

Edited by Grace-Marie Arnett

Ann Arbor

THE UNIVERSITY OF MICHIGAN PRESS

Published in the United States of America by
The University of Michigan Press
Manufactured in the United States of America
♾ Printed on acid-free paper

2002 2001 2000 1999 4 3 2 1

A CIP catalog record for this book is available from the British Library.

Library of Congress Cataloging-in-Publication Data

Arnett, Grace-Marie.
Empowering health care consumers through tax reform / Grace-Marie Arnett.
p. cm.
Papers presented at a conference held on Mar. 25, 1996.
Includes bibliographical references and index.
ISBN 0–472–09716–4 (cloth : alk. paper). —ISBN 0–472–06716–8 (pbk. : alk. paper)
1. Insurance. Health—Taxation—United States. 2. Insurance, Health—Government policy—United States. I. Title.
RA395.A3A74 1999
368.38'2'00973—dc21 99–21949
CIP

ACKNOWLEDGMENTS

For their indispensable role in making this volume possible....

Special thanks to John Hoff, co-founder of the Consensus Group, trustee of the Galen Institute, respected health care attorney, astute author, and tireless advisor to the health policy community, for his invaluable contributions to this collection.

Thanks to the early pioneers with a passion for public policy who organized the first meetings of the Consensus Group, including Marty McGeein of the McGeein Group, formerly of the National Council of Community Hospitals.

Thanks to all of those who prepared formal presentations for the 1996 Galen Institute conference for which the papers in this volume were commissioned, and for sharing their unique expertise on health and tax policy during numerous Consensus Group meetings: Bob Helms of the American Enterprise Institute; Mike Tanner of the Cato Institute; Bob Moffit of the Heritage Foundation; Mark Pauly of the Wharton School; Gene Steuerle of the Urban Institute; Mr. Hoff, health care attorney; David Kendall of the Progressive Policy Institute; Steve Entin of the Institute for Research on the Economics of Taxation; Kevin Vigilante of the Brown University School of Medicine; and John Goodman of the National Center for Policy Analysis. Special thanks to Dr. Pauly for his numerous train trips to Washington, D.C., to attend Consensus Group meetings; the group benefited enormously from his expertise and participation. And to Dr. Helms for his dedication in coordinating and facilitating the work of the Consensus Group from 1995 to 1997.

Thanks also to Sewell Dixon for his contributions to this volume and counsel to the Galen Institute and for serving as a valued physician-adviser to the health policy community.

Our appreciation also goes to the keynote speaker for the conference, Senator Robert Bennett, and to Chip Yost, his legislative director, for their early challenge to the health policy community to define core areas of consensus and for their subsequent leadership on health and tax policy. And to Representative Tom Petri and to Joe Flader, his chief of staff and chief policy adviser, for their vision of integrating health, tax, and welfare policy and articulating their ideas during the conference.

Thanks to Jack Faris for speaking at our conference, for agreeing to write the preface to this book, and for working tirelessly as president of the National Federation of Independent Business (NFIB), as a member of the National Commission on Economic Growth and Tax Reform, and through other forums to promote public policy solutions for hardworking businessmen and women. Thanks also to Jean Hudson of the NFIB for her work on the preface to this volume.

We are grateful to labor leader Ed Moffit for illuminating the health policy debate with his real-world experience in negotiating health benefits.

Thanks to health policy consultant Donna Givens for working to expand the Consensus Group, to Brad Belt of the Center for Strategic and International Studies, and to Naomi Lopez, formerly of the Cato Institute and now of the Pacific Research Institute, for their contributions to the Consensus Group and the conference.

Our gratitude to the Robert Wood Johnson Foundation for its support of the conference and for providing the subsequent grant to prepare this publication. Special thanks to Victoria Weisfeld, Senior Communications Director; Nancy Barrand, Senior Program Officer; and Dr. Steven A. Schroeder, President of the Robert Wood Johnson Foundation. This project would not have been possible without their support and counsel.

Thanks to the devoted team at the Galen Institute who organized the conference and supported the work of the health and tax policy communities, especially Elizabeth Kern Terry, Scott Sundstrom, and Brian Pleva.

And special thanks to the team that produced this volume for the Galen Institute: production team leader Ann Klucsarits, text editor

Sheldon Richman, copy editor William Poole, copy editor/designer James Rutherford, designer Michelle Smith, graphics manager Thomas Timmons, and indexer Shirley Kessel. Thanks to Paddy McLaughlin of Paddy McLaughlin Concepts & Design for designing the book jacket and Galen Institute logo.

Our thanks to Rebecca McDermott, editor for Health Policy and Management at the University of Michigan Press, for her tireless work in moving this volume from inception to completion and for the many helpful commentaries provided by the reviewers, including Stephen T. Mennemeyer, professor in the Department of Health Care Organization and Policy, School of Public Health, University of Alabama, Birmingham.

And, finally, special appreciation to Dr. Norman Ture, who authored, with Steve Entin, an important chapter for this book to whom we are indebted for his steadfast guidance on public policy. Dr. Ture died on August 10, 1997, leaving a legacy of lifework that serves as the intellectual underpinning of the ideas that will guide tax and health reform into the next century.

Grace-Marie Arnett
June 1999

CONTENTS

INTRODUCTORY READING

COMMISSIONED CONTRIBUTIONS

INVITED CONTRIBUTIONS

APPENDICES AND INDEX

ABOUT THE CONSENSUS GROUP

The Health Policy Consensus Group is a task force of leading health care economists and health policy analysts, including researchers at the major market-oriented think tanks. The Consensus Group is working to increase public awareness that the tax treatment of employment-based health insurance underlies many of the problems facing the private health sector in the United States.

The incentive-based reforms the group proposes are intended to strengthen and rationalize the health care market. The Consensus Group believes that the competitive marketplace is the most appropriate way to restrain costs and to give Americans more responsibility and opportunity to choose their health insurance and health care arrangements.

The Consensus Group considers different approaches to reform and provides education on their benefits and disadvantages to help the public and policymakers understand the balances that must be struck in any reform effort. The group has been working to provide policy advice since 1993; it endorses basic principles and does not offer specific legislative proposals. The Galen Institute, a not-for-profit health and tax policy research organization, coordinates and facilitates the work of the Consensus Group.

The papers contained in this volume were first prepared by members of the Consensus Group for presentation at a March 25, 1996, conference entitled "A Fresh Approach to Health Care Reform."

This was the first comprehensive conference ever held to explore the impact of tax policy on the health care sector. It provided a forum for experts in the free-market health policy community to present their research and perspectives on this issue in depth. The conference was organized by the Galen Institute and was supported by a grant from the Robert Wood Johnson Foundation.

The ideas in this document are based upon many meetings and exchanges of information by members of the Consensus Group. The views expressed reflect those of the individual authors and not necessarily their organizations.

ABOUT THE GALEN INSTITUTE

The Galen Institute, Inc., was founded in 1995 to promote a more informed public debate over individual freedom, consumer choice, competition, and diversity in the health sector.

The Galen Institute has four core program areas:

- Health Policy Initiative;
- Tax Policy Initiative;
- Center for Health Care Deregulation; and
- Communications Network.

The Institute's primary focus is sponsoring research and educational programs on the crucial intersection of health and tax policy. We believe that health costs can be contained and access to care vastly expanded by joining health reform with tax reform.

Tax policy is the linchpin of the health care reform debate. And the tax treatment of health insurance could be the Achilles Heel of major tax reform. Neither can be solved alone, and both can be solved by addressing the two issues together. We hope that the writings in this book will illuminate the continuing debates over both health and tax reform.

THE GALEN LOGO

The Galen logo is a conceptual depiction of a central problem in the health sector that affects Americans under age 65. The vertical axis of

the graph in the logo represents the value of taxpayer support for health insurance and medical services. The horizontal axis represents individual income.

Those with the very lowest incomes (on the left side of the chart) are most likely to qualify for taxpayer-supported health programs, especially Medicaid. But as an individual moves up the income scale (toward the right side of the chart), the likelihood of qualifying for public programs to receive health benefits drops off. Working Americans with incomes of less than $25,000 are most likely to be uninsured and are caught in the trough which we call the "Galen gap." They earn too much to qualify for public programs but are less likely to have the good jobs that provide health insurance as a tax-free benefit.

As people move up the income scale, they are much more likely to have both the good jobs and the higher incomes to qualify for the generous tax subsidy for employment-based health insurance, worth an estimated $100 billion a year.

C. Eugene Steuerle of the Urban Institute estimates that the value of tax subsidies for health insurance is nearly six times larger for high-income families than for low-income families ($270 a year for families in the lowest quintile vs. $1,560 for the highest income quintile). This is a highly regressive subsidy that drives many of the problems involving cost and access in the health sector today.

It is to those who fall into the "Galen Gap" that the efforts of the Galen Institute are dedicated. The political left has been trying to fill this gap by creating and expanding government programs, such as the $48 billion State Children's Health Insurance Program, and working to expand Medicare to middle-aged Americans.

The Galen Institute works to explore solutions on the right side of the chart by focusing on tax policy. We believe that many more people would have access to medical services and health insurance that would be more affordable and more innovative if the tax treatment of health insurance were reformed—the subject of this volume.

THE ORIGINAL GALEN

The Galen Institute is named after a second-century Greek physician and philosopher, the most important physician of the ancient world after Hippocrates.

Galen served as physician to the gladiators in his native city of Pergamum, where he gained practical experience in the study of human anatomy. He later moved to Rome, where he spoke and wrote prolifically about medicine at the height of the Roman Empire. "Galen absorbed into his work nearly all preceding medical thought and shaped the categories within which his successors thought about not only the history of medicine, but its practice as well," according to Lee T. Pearcy in *Archaeology* (Nov./Dec. 1985). Galen's medical texts were in use for nearly 1,500 years.

The Galen Institute boldly names itself after this philosopher/physician because our ideas are structural, enduring, and controversial, all of which described Galen himself.

CONTACTING US

The Galen Institute is a not-for-profit public policy research organization organized under section 501(c)(3) of the Internal Revenue Code. Trustees are Grace-Marie Arnett, president; Sewell H. Dixon, M.D., treasurer; and John S. Hoff, Esq., secretary.

Comments are welcome at the Galen Institute, P.O. Box 19080, Alexandria, Virginia 22320. You are invited to visit our Web site at *www.galen.org*—a hub for the best ideas from the market-oriented health policy community, with links to the sites and publications of members of the Health Policy Consensus Group, as well as other writings about creating a patient-centered free market in health care.

PREFACE: A FAIR HEALTH INSURANCE SYSTEM

Jack Faris

The tax structure surrounding our health care system is regressive. Just ask any small-business owner who is looking for a way to provide health benefits to his or her employees. The cost and availability of health care continues to rank as a top problem for small-business owners, standing as the number one problem in the National Federation of Independent Business's (NFIB) 1996 study *Small Business Problems and Priorities.* The last time that survey was conducted, in 1991, it also ranked first.

We have known about the problem for some time. What a lot of people do not know, however, is how much of a priority health care is for small business. Think about it this way: The group we want insured most of all is our family, and in the case of small-business owners, their employees are also often their family. But family considerations aside, small employers must provide health insurance in order to remain competitive, and it is a fact that healthy employees are also the most productive employees.

Despite all of this, small-business owners are the group least able to provide health insurance to their employees. Two-thirds of the working uninsured either are in firms with fewer than 500 employees or are self-employed, according to *The State of Small Business,* issued by the Small Business Administration in 1994.

Why have they been left out? Small businesses have created two-thirds of the net new jobs in the U.S. economy since the early 1970s; they account for about 38 percent of gross domestic product and produce 50 percent of private-sector output. Small businesses employ almost 60 percent of the workforce. Yet those businesses are literally punished by the structure of the system.

The self-employed and their employees buy other insurance (such as car and homeowner's policies) under the same set of rules as the people employed by big business. But the ground rules are very different for health insurance. Self-employed businessmen and women get a much less generous tax break if they purchase their own insurance. And the deck is further stacked against small businesses because they have no choice but to buy insurance whose costs are swollen by regulations and mandates.

This just doesn't make sense, and it must be changed.

The NFIB supports a number of reforms that would right some of these wrongs toward small business. There is one crucial reform that would improve our health care system and set our country, as a whole, on a more prosperous, healthy direction: the complete overhaul of our tax code. A seven-million-word mess, the code is confusing, complex, and costly—not just to small business, but to all Americans. Abolishing the IRS tax code and starting fresh with a simpler, fairer system that rewards work and savings would benefit almost every aspect of our lives.

Part of the debate over creating a simpler, fairer tax system involves addressing how the tax code treats the purchase of employment-based health insurance. The Galen Institute and the members of the Consensus Group are providing an important service in proposing new ideas about how to address this problem with important reforms both for the tax code and for the health care system.

THE PROBLEMS THAT FACE SMALL BUSINESS

Small firms' access to health insurance and quality health care is determined largely by affordability. The cost of health insurance can be the greatest non-salary cost for a small business, exceeding the combined cost of workers' compensation and liability insurance. Even when a small employer can afford a group health care plan, many biases remain. The frustration of small-business owners struggling to provide health care is compounded by the many inequities of the current system. Benefits and breaks are given to large businesses which self-insure, while those purchasing insurance in the private or group market bear the burden of high costs and numerous state government mandates.

THE CURRENT THREAT: INCREMENTAL FEDERALIZATION

In a 1993 survey by the NFIB of its 600,000 small-business members, 85 percent said they opposed mandating employers to provide health insurance for their workers. In the fight against the Clinton administration's health care reform plan in 1993 and 1994, these small-business owners drew a line in the sand and warned lawmakers not to cross it. They let the president and lawmakers on Capitol Hill know that they would not accept an employer mandate on health care. Lawmakers backed down, realizing that an employer mandate would kill jobs and force many small businesses to close their doors.

Today, lawmakers have a new, similar lesson to learn: Forcing employers to increase the level of benefits or to comply with a plethora of new regulations does not work, either. This is simply a piecemeal approach to an employer mandate, and it will have the same results and force employers to make painful choices: laying off employees; ceasing to offer health benefits; passing costs on to consumers by raising prices (thereby sacrificing their competitive position in the marketplace); slower growth and, therefore, reduced job creation.

The 104th Congress passed two federal health insurance mandates on employers, the first federal health insurance mandates in history: the mental health parity provision and the 48-hour maternity stay provision. No decent person can make an argument against the need for accessible, affordable mental health care, or against allowing a mother to stay a safe length of time in the hospital after giving birth. But that does not mean the government should impose these mandates. In a freer insurance market, people who wanted policies with this coverage would be able to choose them.

The emotional arguments for insurance mandates have obscured the important issue of *costs*. Here again, we come to the crux of the problem with our health care system: affordability. Mandating health benefits defeats the very purpose of health care reform, which is to lower health care costs and to insure more people. Forcing business to comply with federal and state health care mandates drives up the cost of premiums and provides a disincentive both for employers to offer insurance and for employees to accept the coverage when they have to pay part of the escalating premium costs.

A FROG IN THE POT

As my colleague, Herman Cain, on the National Commission on Economic Growth and Tax Reform pointed out, if you throw a frog in a pot of boiling water, he will try to jump out to save himself. But if you put a frog in a pot of cool water and turn up the heat under him one small step at a time, he won't notice the pain as much, but he also is likely to end up being boiled to death.

Incremental regulation on employers and health insurance is akin to gradually turning up the heat, and it eventually will kill small business. The Clinton health care bill showed Americans the full caldron of boiling water; the incremental reforms passed since then are just turning up the fire. Considering the fact that small businesses employ the majority of the work force, this is a dangerous approach indeed.

THE NEED FOR MORE REFORM —WITHOUT MANDATES

Although Congress has started on a dangerous path of regulation, federal lawmakers also have enacted provisions that directly benefit small businesses. The Health Insurance Portability and Accountability Act of 1996 increased the deduction for health care cost for the self-employed to 80 percent over ten years. The tax bill of 1997 expanded this to 100 percent deductibility phased in over ten years (full deductibility in 2007). This is a significant reform that is good for small business, but it still isn't soon enough.

Congress also set up a test run for Medical Savings Accounts (MSAs), allowing 750,000 employers and self-employed individuals to try out this market-based reform. The NFIB hopes to see the availability of MSAs expanded greatly in the near future. This is a logical plan for a country that is based on individual freedom, giving more families the opportunity to have more individualized health care. Unfortunately, however, MSAs themselves were so tangled in regulation that many small businesses and even insurers find them too cumbersome. Congress should unshackle and expand MSAs to give this free-market option a chance to work.

The next Congress should begin the process of truly reforming our health care financing system by enacting provisions that provide tax benefits to individuals for purchasing their own health insurance.

ON TO ACTION

Too many of Washington's attempts to "reform" our health care system have only made it more complex, more bureaucratic, more expensive, and more hostile to patients and doctors.

Instead of passing more intrusive legislation, Congress would be wise to root out the underlying problem. The tax treatment of health insurance is seriously flawed and discriminates against small-business owners, the self-employed, and individuals who want to purchase their own health coverage.

The health care system will not be able to right itself until we address that fundamental, underlying problem. When everyone has the option to purchase and own his or her own health insurance, we will see a much more vital marketplace for health insurance that provides more choices and is more affordable.

I welcome the debate on this subject that is being launched by the Galen Institute and by the health policy experts from the market-oriented research organizations. Their ideas and research will lead the way to a much fairer, sounder system of quality, affordable health insurance.

INTRODUCTION AND OVERVIEW: EMPOWERING HEALTH CARE CONSUMERS THROUGH TAX REFORM

Grace-Marie Arnett

Reforming the tax treatment of health insurance is essential to creating a more efficient and equitable market for medical care and health insurance in the United States. On this fact, policy experts with vastly different political and economic philosophies agree. For decades, however, the tax treatment of health insurance has been the highly charged third rail of the health care reform debate—a subject that only a few courageous politicians have dared to touch.

Now that is changing. One after another, health care reform initiatives at the federal and state levels have failed to achieve their stated goals of increasing access to affordable health insurance—and sometimes have even exacerbated the problem. As a result, there is growing receptivity to a fresh approach.

In this book, a diverse group of experts, including health policy analysts, economists, employer group and union representatives, physicians, and political leaders, explain the case for changes in current tax policy. They analyze the faults in the current system, offer a variety of arguments for altering the tax treatment of health insurance, and explain their policy prescriptions.

SETTING THE STAGE FOR A NEW DEBATE

The impact of tax policy on the health care system is a sleeping giant that has been awakening in the late 1990s, largely because a few policy experts grew determined in the mid-1990s to focus attention on the problem.

In November 1993, a small cadre of health policy analysts gathered in a conference room in downtown Washington, D.C., to assess the health care reform proposal being advanced by President Bill Clinton. None of those at the meeting was part of the White House Task Force on Health Care Reform, which had been working for months to develop the plan. But all had read the legislation that would create this new health care system, and all feared that the extensive government involvement that it required would seriously harm both the U.S. health care system and the U.S. economy.

Up to then, these health policy experts and others who felt that the Clinton plan was not the right approach had been dismissed by the establishment as largely irrelevant. Their voices had been drowned out by the crescendo of public enthusiasm for health care reform, fueled by excitement in the White House and in Congress that the time finally had come for the United States to join other developed nations in providing government-sponsored universal health coverage. Virtually all of the news coverage at that point centered not on whether this was a proper role for government, but rather on the mind-numbing complexities of how to go about re-engineering the U.S. health care system.

The market-oriented policy analysts at that November meeting, however, believed the evidence was clear: The social welfare programs—including national health insurance—that had proliferated around the world during the twentieth century were bankrupting governments, sending taxes ever higher, and forcing government rationing and other limitations on health services. Yet the Clinton administration was using these failed centralized plans as its models.

A new health care financing system clearly was needed in the United States to meet the challenges of the twenty-first century, but the Clinton plan—which clashed with the needs of an evolving, diversified world economy and the wishes of the American people for individual choice—was not it. The small band who met that day in November knew their views reflected global trends, but not the conventional wisdom in Washington.

HISTORIC TRENDS

Proponents of national health insurance believed the momentum for their cause had been building for most of the twentieth century. The students of history among them looked back and observed that political leaders in developed countries who sought to strengthen the state or to advance their own or their parties' interests had learned they could use insurance against the cost of sickness as a way to turn benevolence into power.[1] Nearly all major European countries had adopted some type of national health insurance program; but throughout the twentieth century, the United States repeatedly had rejected this approach.

Compulsory national health insurance first became a political issue in the United States before World War I.[2] The crusade, led by the Progressive Party, was drowned out by wartime concerns and by the economic boom of the 1920s but rose again during the Great Depression. Debate over national health insurance continued during the 1930s, and President Franklin D. Roosevelt vowed he would push actively for legislation after World War II. President Harry S Truman picked up the legacy after Roosevelt's death, making it part of his 1948 election campaign. The issue, however, became a lightning rod for anti-communists, who used "socialized medicine" as a symbol of the forces they said were infiltrating American society. The national health insurance movement died again.[3]

In 1965, the United States created two huge government health care programs for targeted populations: Medicaid for the poor and Medicare for senior citizens. Proponents saw these programs as a down payment on national health insurance, and liberals began again to advance legislation that would extend government health insurance to all citizens.

A third attempt to achieve a full national health insurance program was associated with concerns in the early 1970s that the United States was headed for a health care "crisis" because of exploding costs in the private health sector and in the growing public health sector. A January 1970 *Business Week* cover story raised alarms about the country's $60 billion health care tab. (Actual figures later set that year's national health expenditures at $73 billion.[4])

In 1970, Senator Edward M. Kennedy (D–Mass.) introduced a bill to replace all public and private health plans with a government-operated insurance system. Even though the national debate over health care led to some incremental changes, the effort to socialize the health care system failed once again.

In the 1990s, the United States continued to stand alone among major developed countries in having more of its citizens insured through private than through public health programs. The last leg of the plan by liberals and progressives to put all citizens under the umbrella of a government-directed health care system remained elusive.

ENTER HARRIS WOFFORD

The seeds of the most recent debate over a national health insurance program for the United States were sown in Pennsylvania in 1991.

Harris Wofford was a self-proclaimed liberal Democrat running against Republican Richard Thornburgh in a special election called to fill the unexpired term of U.S. Senator John Heinz, who had died in a plane crash. The Pennsylvania Senate race was in the national spotlight. Even though Wofford discussed health insurance in his campaign speeches, economic issues were center stage. The country was in a recession, and President George Bush had angered voters the year before by breaking his "no-new-taxes" pledge. Many analysts believed the Pennsylvania race presented voters with an opportunity to retaliate against Bush, under whom Thornburgh had served as attorney general of the United States.

Wofford won the election and concluded that his victory represented not a referendum on taxes and the economy but a call for national health insurance.

As the 1992 presidential campaign began, the economic pain of the recession was exacerbated by anxiety about the lack of health insurance. More than 35 million people then had no insurance (more than 43 million lacked it by 1998). This was something that Democrats had long believed the government could—and should—fix.

Public opinion polls throughout the 1992 presidential election showed broad public support for a major overhaul of the country's health care system. Nearly one-seventh of the U.S. economy was devoted to health care, with an annual price tag that year of $834 billion. The great majority of citizens with private health insurance were (and are) covered through the workplace, receiving a generous, albeit invisible, tax subsidy for doing so. But millions—primarily the self-employed, those without jobs, and those working for smaller firms without group health insurance—were (and are) being left behind.

Candidate Clinton delivered his central health care reform speech at the headquarters of Merck & Co., a pharmaceutical company based in New Jersey, in September 1992, making health care reform a centerpiece of his presidential campaign agenda. With Clinton's upset victory over President Bush in November 1992, the decades-long debate over national health insurance reached critical mass once again. Like Wofford, President Clinton and his advisers attributed their victory largely to their advocacy of health care reform that would provide universal coverage. The newly elected president appointed his wife, Hillary Rodham Clinton, to lead the development of legislation that would implement what they believed was their election mandate.

With Democrats in control of both houses of Congress, and with a focused and determined Democratic president, it seemed inevitable that the United States would adopt a national health insurance system.

COMPETING IDEOLOGIES

In 1993, leaks from the White House Task Force on Health Care Reform appeared daily on the front pages of the *New York Times* and other papers as members wrestled with the technical details of reform: where to cap premiums for small businesses, how to regulate drug prices, where to set geographic boundaries for the new purchasing cooperatives, how to collect tens of billions of dollars to pay for the new system, and so on. But these details obscured the real battle that was taking place.

In fact, the country was engaged in a power struggle between competing ideologies. On the one side were those who believed that the interests of the individual would be served best by strengthening the authority of the state to orchestrate a system that would provide "health security." Judith Feder, then a deputy assistant secretary at the Department of Health and Human Services, explained the philosophy behind the Clinton approach: "What we are doing is replacing the inept, wasteful, and ineffective bureaucracy, if you will, of the unfettered marketplace."

On the other side were those who believed that people would be served best in an open and democratic society by the proper functioning of a free and competitive market for health insurance. The fundamental question at issue was—and is—this: Does the United States want a health care system that gives more power and authority to the government, or one that empowers individual citizens in an open and competitive market?

Concerns about the Clinton plan were raised by many keen observers of Washington policy on the right and the left who said the numbers did not add up—experts like Gail Wilensky, former head of the Health Care Financing Administration under President Bush, and Senator Daniel Patrick Moynihan (D–N.Y.). As the debate reached its crescendo in late 1993, those who supported alternative approaches to health care reform had yet to coalesce around an alternative to the government-controlled approach embodied in the Clinton plan.

FORMING THE CONSENSUS GROUP

A meeting was called on November 30, 1993, by Marty McGeein, a veteran health policy analyst and practitioner; John Hoff, a Washington attorney who had consulted and written on health policy for years; and this writer, Grace-Marie Arnett, then an independent health policy analyst and now president of the Galen Institute. The three of us called the meeting after two Republican senators, Robert Bennett of Utah and Pete Domenici of New Mexico, encouraged the market-oriented think tanks to describe the health care reform principles they held in common.

Health policy experts from three of the leading Washington think tanks agreed to attend that first meeting: Robert Helms of the American Enterprise Institute, Michael Tanner of the Cato Institute, and Robert Moffit of the Heritage Foundation. The meeting took place days after the actual legislation describing the Clinton plan (called the Health Security Act) had been published. All of those around the table had read the entire 1,342-page bill and were eager to discuss its details and policy implications.

Although each of the three think tanks had its own perspective on the proper direction for health care reform, they agreed on one thing during that first meeting: They did not believe that the price controls, premium caps, global budgets, employer mandates, national health board, government-defined benefits package, health alliance monopsonies, criminal penalties, and other elements of the Clinton plan were the proper way to go. They agreed to meet again soon to continue their discussions.

TAX POLICY SHAPES HEALTH INSURANCE SYSTEM

At the second meeting in early December 1993, Helms, Tanner, and Moffit answered the challenge that had been put forth by Senators Bennett and Domenici to describe health care reform principles they held in common. All three agreed that a change in federal tax policy was central to each of their approaches to health care reform.

Their own studies of history convinced them that, even though the United States repeatedly had turned away from an explicit national health insurance system, Washington in fact had directed the organization of the private health insurance market through a key tax provision that had been working its way through the health care sector for 50 years.

Since early in the twentieth century, health insurance increasingly has been linked to the workplace. During World War II, however, employment-based health insurance became more widespread, and the link became much stronger. Factories were pushed to meet wartime production schedules. Competition for good workers was intense but was hampered by wartime wage controls. Some employers wanted to offer health insurance as a benefit in lieu of cash wages so they could compete for scarce workers and boost compensation without running afoul of wage controls.

In 1943, the Internal Revenue Service ruled that employers' contributions to group health insurance would not count as taxable income for employees. That tax ruling, and its codification by Congress 11 years later in 1954, created a strong incentive for the private market for health insurance to be organized around employment-based groups.

This tax preference—a historical accident created to get around temporary wage and price controls—has percolated through the economy for more than 50 years to become the foundation for a system in which 60 percent of all Americans get their health insurance through their jobs.[5] The biggest benefits, however, accrue to those in the highest income brackets who work for employers who offer health insurance; this rich but hidden tax subsidy has little or no value for working Americans at the lower end of the income scale who are least likely to have health insurance.

A NEW VISION FOR REFORM

The market-oriented health policy analysts argued that this regressive tax policy was at the root of many of the problems that the White House was trying to fix in its attempt to re-engineer the U.S. health care system. They felt their voices might be louder together than individually. Therefore, they agreed to continue meeting, calling their informal group the Health Policy Consensus Group.

They often argued for hours about the nuances of health policy. Word by word, line by line, through heated debate, they put together a "Vision for Reform" that stated their common principles and direction for market-based health care reform. Their statement (an updated version of which is reprinted in the appendix) emphasized that "rather than replace the current structure with a government-driven system, we propose a mechanism to achieve genuine reform by creating a competitive, consumer-driven marketplace."

The Consensus Group's vision statement was circulated widely, and its core ideas percolated through the conservative policy community in speeches, media interviews, and papers and articles written by group members. A March 29, 1994, *Wall Street Journal* article (also reprinted in Appendix C) summarized the Consensus Group's views.

The Consensus Group quickly expanded to include other policy experts: Bradley Belt of the Center for Strategic and International Studies, Stephen Entin of the Institute for Research on the Economics of Taxation, John Goodman of the National Center for Policy Analysis, David Kendall of the Progressive Policy Institute, Mark Pauly of the Wharton School at the University of Pennsylvania, Eugene Steuerle of the Urban Institute, Kevin Vigilante of the Miriam Hospital in Rhode Island, and others. Donna Givens, a consultant and former deputy assistant secretary at the U.S. Department of Health and Human Services, helped to expand the group and extend its message to a broader audience.

The work of the Consensus Group spread to the academic community as well. The group developed a petition that Elizabeth Kern Terry, then health policy associate at Arnett & Co., worked tirelessly to distribute, eventually obtaining signatures from about 350 health economists around the country (listed, along with the text of the petition, in Appendix D). This petition describes most concisely the views of the market-oriented health policy community:

Petition Concerning the Tax Treatment of Employment-Based Health Insurance: Diagnosing the Problem

> Reforming the tax treatment of health insurance is essential to creating a more efficient market for medical care and health insurance in the United States.
>
> Employment-based health benefits are actually part of employee compensation. However, these health benefits are not counted as income for tax purposes. This tax policy distorts the health care marketplace. It undermines cost consciousness by disguising the true cost of insurance and medical care to employees. It artificially supports increased demand for medical services and more costly insurance. As a result, inefficient health care is subsidized at the expense of efficient delivery, and cash wages are suppressed. Further, the current tax law discriminates against the self-employed, the unemployed, and those whose employers do not offer health insurance.

> We support reforming the tax treatment of employment-based health insurance to promote a more efficient market in the health sector. We support restraining costs through competition and consumer incentives rather than through destructive methods such as price controls and limits on private spending set by government.

WILL GOVERNMENT OR THE MARKET BE DOMINANT?

The Consensus Group was a pivotal meeting place for the market-based health policy community during the intense national debate over health care reform. Experts at the think tanks analyzed the core ideas and essential details of policy proposals to explore the consequences for people and the economy, elucidating the ideas that launched a meaningful debate over health care reform. Where previously the debate had been about the best mechanisms to implement the Clinton plan, it now addressed the more fundamental issue: a government-driven system versus a market-driven system with individual choice. The Consensus Group brought substance and energy to what had been a one-sided debate.

The Clinton plan was bludgeoned and bloodied throughout 1994. Derivatives followed, including the Mitchell plan, introduced by then Senate majority leader George Mitchell, and the Gephardt plan, introduced by then House majority leader Richard Gephardt.

By then, many interest groups had examined the details of the Clinton–Mitchell–Gephardt plans, and almost all had found something that they were against. Public opposition grew. A series of television advertisements by the Health Insurance Association of America, featuring the now-famous "Harry and Louise," raised serious questions in the minds of average Americans about the price they would pay.

A decisive moment came during a remarkable meeting on August 12, 1994. Senator Paul Coverdell (R–Ga.) had arranged a briefing in a hearing room in the Dirksen Senate Office Building for lobbyists and representatives of a number of interest organizations. So many came that they spilled into the hallway. The briefing turned into an old-fashioned pep rally with cheers, applause, and ovations for opposition leaders. The event energized the troops, who fanned out with a single-minded mission: to defeat the Clinton plan.

Defeat, when it came, came silently. After consuming the country in a historic debate for nearly two years, no vote ever was taken on the floor of either the House or the Senate on any of the health care reform bills proposed by the White House or the congressional leadership, marking once again the failure to enact an explicit national health insurance system for the United States.

Then, in November 1994, Democrats lost control of both houses of Congress, with Pennsylvania senator Wofford among those who were defeated.

THE CONTINUING BATTLE

Although the momentum for health care reform subsided in early 1995, the problems remained. Concerns over health care continued to be among the top issues for voters. Robert Dole, who became Senate majority leader after the 1994 elections, soon appointed Senator Bennett to head the Senate Republican Health Care Task Force, giving him a tangible leadership role to reflect his influence with his colleagues on this issue.

States continued their own march toward reform, but the number of Americans without health insurance continued to creep upward and, by summer 1996, the leadership in Congress felt the need to pass some kind of health care reform legislation to respond to voter concerns.

Republican senator Nancy Kassebaum of Kansas had been working with Senator Kennedy to develop a bill dubbed "incremental reform" of health insurance. Kassebaum, who chaired the Senate Labor and Human Resources Committee, was retiring from the Senate at the end of that year and wanted to leave a legacy. Kennedy, the ranking Democrat on the committee, was ready to join her in any attempt at legislation.

Their joint bill, the Health Insurance Portability and Accountability Act of 1996, introduced federal regulation of the private market for health insurance, new mandates, and expanded regulation of medical practice through criminal law. But it also contained a major provision that conservatives wanted: the first test of Medical Savings Accounts (MSAs), allowing for the creation of 750,000 MSAs, albeit somewhat hamstrung by regulation. (John Goodman's chapter in this book describes the workings and economics of MSAs in detail.)

Forces on both sides of the issue in Washington still are engaged in a tug-of-war. Those who want to see an expansion of publicly supported health care programs have won some battles, as have those who want expanded private-sector options and consumer choice.

In summer 1997, Congress approved a major new federal program to provide health insurance to uninsured children. Although the states were given considerable flexibility in spending the $48 billion in new "KidCare" funds, this represented a significant new federal entitlement. The Children's Defense Fund called it the "biggest step forward for children's health care coverage since the creation of Medicaid in 1965."

But proponents of market solutions also won a partial victory in 1997. Congress approved a gradual phase-in of 100 percent deductibility for health insurance for the self-employed and other individuals (reaching 100 percent in the year 2007) and further expanded the MSA experiment so that Medicare beneficiaries can obtain the accounts.

What was becoming an annual summer debate in Congress over health care reform continued in 1998, this time over "patient protection" legislation. Millions of Americans had been swept into managed care health plans during the 1990s by employers eager to contain health care costs, but some employees had become frustrated with the limitations these plans imposed. In late 1997, a commission that had been appointed by Mr. Clinton proposed a Patients' Bill of Rights that was quickly embraced by Democrats and subsequently introduced in Congress. In this politically charged atmosphere, Republicans huddled and came out months later with their own proposal—which many saw as a watered-down version of the Democrats' bill.

But there was a new element in the debate: Both Republicans and Democrats were quietly beginning to talk about expanding access to health insurance though tax reform, with a variety of measures introduced in both houses by members from both sides of the aisle.

In fact, the only significant health insurance reform legislation to pass in 1998 was a measure included in the omnibus federal spending bill involving deductibility of health insurance for the self-employed; it accelerated the date of 100 percent deductibility of insurance premiums from 2007 to 2003. It was a tiny step in the right direction but, more important, a giant step away from more federal intrusion and regulation in the health sector.

Congress and the states continue to fight over public and private solutions to the high cost and limited availability of health insurance. Each side wins some concessions from the other, but none of the major legislation that has been passed tackles the central problem that lurks in a few lines of the tax code and continues to distort the health care system.

STATES ATTEMPT THEIR OWN REFORMS

While federal policymakers have avoided addressing the tax treatment of health insurance, state lawmakers have been experimenting with hundreds of "reform" measures of their own. Unfortunately, many of these state insurance regulations and mandates are further destabilizing the market for private health insurance.

State insurance rules apply primarily to health insurance purchased by individuals and small groups that are not protected by the federal Employee Retirement Income Security Act (ERISA), which allows employers to self-insure and escape most state regulation. Smaller employers and individuals must either buy policies governed by expensive state mandates and other regulations or go without coverage, as a growing number are forced to do.

ERISA and the tax exclusion have helped to form stable insurance groups around the employment-based setting and have allowed employees to enjoy economies of scale in the purchase and administration of health coverage. But as the economy changes with much more job mobility and worker independence, many policymakers are encouraging a fresh look at the need to modernize these policies to keep pace.

The health care industry now is the most heavily regulated sector of the U.S. economy. Even if consumers were empowered to purchase their own health insurance through tax reform, lawmakers must now untangle the bureaucratic red tape they have created that is crippling the emergence of a competitive, market-driven system for privately purchased health insurance.

A NEW SYSTEM FOR AN INFORMATION-AGE ECONOMY

According to the U.S. Bureau of the Census, more than 43 million Americans lacked health insurance at some point in 1998. Those with insurance fear they will lose it if they lose their jobs and are increasingly angry over managed care restrictions negotiated by their employers. Health care and health insurance costs continue to price millions of people out of the market.

Those without health insurance are primarily working Americans and their dependents who do not get coverage through their jobs and who make too much to qualify for public programs and too little to buy their own expensive health policies. The efforts of the Galen Institute are dedicated to the people who fall into this trough—the "Galen Gap." The Galen Institute was founded in 1995 to stimulate debate on free-market mechanisms to allow millions more Americans access to affordable and innovative health coverage and medical services.

Clearly, public education is needed. The expensive tug-of-war over this issue cannot continue indefinitely. Either the United States will create more federal health programs, like KidCare or Medicare expansion, that extend government-funded health programs to other populations or it will fix the distortions in the private insurance market. Robert Moffit of Heritage believes that "The choice will be between government-run health care—including federal or state financing and rationing—and the free market—including real consumer choice and serious competition."

The Galen Institute and the members of the Consensus Group continue to work to provide research and increase public awareness of the effects of tax policy on health policy. As David Kendall observes,

> The key question for the future of reform is whether the extremes will continue to dominate or a strong center will emerge to move the country toward a universal marketplace for health care.

A FRESH APPROACH TO HEALTH CARE REFORM

On March 25, 1996, the Robert Wood Johnson Foundation supported a conference organized by the Galen Institute in which participants in the Consensus Group presented their views in depth. We believe this was the first comprehensive conference ever held on the impact of tax policy on the health care sector. The major national debate over health care reform in 1993 and 1994 failed, at least in part, because this crucial issue was not addressed.

This book, also supported by a grant from the Robert Wood Johnson Foundation, contains the proceedings of that conference, which was entitled *A Fresh Approach to Health Care Reform*. We hope that publishing and publicizing this collection will promote an intelligent debate about the tax treatment of health insurance. While there is unanimous agreement on the nature of the problem, the reader will find disagreement and occasionally even contradiction among the authors over their policy solutions and recommendations for reform. This represents the best of democracy: agreement on the problem followed by a vigorous debate based upon passionately held convictions about the best solutions. They do not waver, however, from their core belief in the need to reform the tax treatment of health insurance.

Eugene Steuerle says the subsidy for employment-based health insurance is one of the most expensive—by one count, *the* most expensive—of all tax expenditures or subsidies in the tax code. Robert Helms, Mark Pauly, and others estimate that it is worth $100 billion a year. Yet it is highly regressive: It provides a generous subsidy for the chief executive of a company and little or nothing for a young couple working at entry-level jobs and struggling to make ends meet. Steuerle estimates that the value of tax subsidies for health insurance is nearly six times larger for high-income families than for low-income families ($270 a year for families in the lowest quintile vs. $1,560 for the highest income quintile).

Despite this regressivity, politicians have treated any effort to remedy the tax treatment of health insurance as if it were an electrified rail. Advocates of change have been accused of wanting to tax health benefits, raise taxes, and eliminate job-based insurance. All of these allegations are addressed—and refuted—in this book. "Increases in taxes and spending are unnecessary" to solve the problem, as Dr. Pauly explains.

Increasingly, as medical care becomes both more expensive and more effective, a wealthy country like the United States should expect all citizens to have predictable access to medical care, especially to health insurance that covers major medical expenses. This means changing the current system so that more people are getting, not losing, health coverage. The authors of the chapters in this book—academics, economists, physicians, lawyers, and labor leaders—present a variety of views on ways to accomplish this.

The convergence of frustration with the tax system and frustration with the health care system may provide a historic opportunity for change. In 1998, according to the U.S. Bureau of the Census, the average household paid 24.3 percent of its income in federal, state, and local taxes. This high tax rate during peacetime and prosperity, coupled with growing popular disaffection with centralized government, leads many political analysts to believe that the country is ripe for tax reform. A debate over a major simplification or restructuring of the federal tax system would necessarily focus attention on the generous tax benefit provided for employment-based health insurance.

In fact, the reforms we advocate could provide a tax cut to individuals, targeted to those who currently do not have health insurance. It would give individuals more choice as to where and how they obtain medical care, and could create new incentives for a competitive, consumer-driven market for health insurance and medical services. Coupling tax reform with health reform could finally make a win-win political scenario possible.

HOW THE TAX SUBSIDY WORKS

Two important tax terms—deduction and exclusion—are used throughout this book.

Employment-based health insurance is part of the wage package many employers provide their employees—a form of non-cash compensation. Employers take a tax *deduction* for the cost of this health coverage, as they do for most other forms of employee compensation. They write the check for the premiums, and some pay medical bills directly if they self-insure. Businesses can deduct these costs from their earnings since they are part of the total compensation package paid to workers and must be deducted to measure net profits correctly.

What makes health insurance different from cash wage or salary compensation, however, is that workers do not pay taxes on the part of their compensation package that they receive in the form of health benefits. Section 106 of the Internal Revenue Code provides that the value of health benefits is not counted as part of the taxable income of employees—in tax terminology, it is *excluded* from their income. However, workers may receive this tax-favored benefit *only if* their health coverage is provided through an employer. The value of the health coverage, the tax benefit employees receive, and the costs in forgone wages are largely invisible to them.

An example may prove useful. Take a graphic artist whose salary is $35,000. Her company offers health insurance, but the additional $4,000 cost of the policy covering her family and herself is *excluded* from her taxable income. The tax code encourages her to believe that her premiums are paid by her employer and are therefore "free" because her pay stub does not reflect the $4,000 in nontaxable income. In fact, the employer sees the cost of employing her as $35,000 plus $4,000, or $39,000, plus other benefits and taxes. Even if her employer asked her to contribute to the cost of her health insurance, the contribution would represent only a fraction of the full cost of the policy.

A key difference is visibility—one of the core principles stressed as essential to a properly functioning tax system by the National Commission on Economic Growth and Tax Reform[6] and most economists. Deductions are visible, and exclusions are invisible.

In order to take a *deduction* for health insurance, the individual or business must first pay the premium, then subtract all or part of the amount (depending upon tax law) from gross income when paying taxes. The person or business paying the premium knows the full cost of the policy, even though it is subsidized through a reduction in taxes.

In contrast, the *exclusion* is invisible to the recipient of the subsidy. The company must write the check for the premium in order for the employee to receive the tax subsidy. The employee therefore never sees the full cost of the health insurance policy or the cash income that he or she is forgoing in lieu of the insurance policy. The exclusion therefore creates an illusion that the company is providing health insurance as a perk. Employees might well ask why their companies do not offer to pay their mortgages or grocery bills as well. Health insurance has become a job-based perk because of tax policy.

The invisibility of the exclusion provides an incentive for employees to negotiate richer and richer health benefits. But it also puts them in a bind when companies begin to clamp down on health insurance costs—as many have done in the 1990s by instituting managed care plans. Some employees may not like managed care but believe they have little authority to object because many perceive their health benefits as free—or nearly so. If they realized that this was their money and that they had choice in how it was spent, they might very well have chosen a different plan.

Giving a subsidy directly to individuals—as a tax deduction, tax credit, or voucher—would eliminate the invisibility and rectify many other problems the exclusion creates. It also would end the discrimination that gives a generous tax break to people with job-based health insurance and not to others. And by giving consumers more direct control over their choices in health coverage and medical services, it would enable them to force change through market forces rather than the political system.

AN OVERVIEW

As one of the reviewers of this manuscript observed, until now, a reader would have had to search through many journals and books to bring together all of the views and information provided here. The authors who agreed to produce chapters for this book are the top experts in the country on this issue. It is hoped that the reader will be as enlightened by reading their carefully prepared writings as those who have the good fortune to attend Consensus Group meetings are by their lively, vigorous, and congenial debate. What follows is a brief overview of their chapters.

The Importance of Action

In his preface, Jack Faris explains why change is essential. Small business owners continue to rank the cost and availability of health care as their number one problem. The current system is stacked against them, he explains, and many of the so-called reforms passed during the past several decades actually have made the situation worse. Because three out of every five workers in the United States are employed by small businesses, their concerns must be addressed if the United States is to find the path to meaningful health care reform.

The History

In the first chapter, Robert Helms looks at the early history and evidence of the tax treatment of health insurance, focusing on the period from 1940 to 1970 during which the foundations for the current health care financing system in the United States became established. He reviews the early empirical studies that attempt to measure the effects of tax policy on health insurance, the effects of health insurance on medical use and prices, and the effects of higher medical costs on health insurance. He also briefly reviews the history of health markets, emphasizing the changing nature of health insurance in the postwar period. Helms concludes that economic studies over the past 25 years have found that the inefficiencies caused by the tax treatment of health insurance are "real and substantial."

> [H]ealth policy experts, especially health economists, almost unanimously implicate the special treatment of employer-provided health insurance as a major cause of economic inefficiency in medical markets.... [T]he resulting increase in the costs of care touches all consumers and patients, especially those without health insurance who end up paying higher prices.

The Problem Today

Michael Tanner and Robert Moffit describe how tax policy affects—and distorts—the health insurance market today. Tanner looks at the forces that have contributed to rising health care costs and the rising number of uninsured people in the United States: "Workers who must purchase their insurance with after-tax dollars are 24 times more likely to be uninsured than those who are eligible for tax-free employer-provided coverage." He says the system in which consumers are detached from costs distorts the market for health insurance and medical care. "Consumers have little incentive to question costs and every incentive to demand more services," he writes. "Changing the tax treatment of insurance will help solve two of the most important problems facing the American health care system: reduc[ing] health care costs...and extend[ing] coverage to the uninsured."

Robert Moffit details the impact of the current inefficient tax subsidy on individuals and the market, addressing the discrimination against those who are shut out of the job-based market as well as the constraints and limitations on those who do receive health insurance at work. "The tax treatment of employment-based insurance," he writes, "is stunning in its regressivity and constitutes a retention of an odd social policy: from each according to his labor and to each according to the height of his tax bracket. This is America's modern equivalent of the Bourbon dynasty's tax policy." He explores the basic alternatives from which elected officials can choose to redress this imbalance, including a sliding-scale tax credit.

The Vision for Reform

"The goals of health reform never have been controversial," Mark Pauly begins. "Reformers have wanted what polls keep telling us citizens want: a society in which everyone has access to appropriate and efficient medical care." This also concisely sums up both the goal of this book and the work of the Consensus Group.

Agreeing that the current tax subsidy for purchasing health insurance is "mistargeted, miscalibrated, and open-ended," Pauly presents a vision of an efficient and equitable alternative. He explores options under which the current subsidy could be distributed more equitably to assure that everyone has access to appropriate and efficient medical care. This involves specifying the amount of insurance regarded as appropriate for each citizen and offering fixed-amount assistance for people to buy it. "If the tax exclusion for employment-based health insurance premiums were abolished," Pauly asserts,

> tax collections at all levels of government would rise by up to $100 billion. That money should be returned immediately to citizens as a reward for purchasing adequate amounts of health insurance.... The reason to seek adequate coverage is not only that it is the right thing to do, but also that it would make the transfers already occurring more efficient and dignified.[7]

Implementing the Vision

Eugene Steuerle and Gordon Mermin then detail how to structure a better subsidy to provide more widespread access to health care, encourage the purchase of health insurance and efficient spending for health care, and distribute benefits in a way deemed equitable. Their prescription has three legs: cutting back on the value of the existing exclusion, providing a credit for health insurance, and creating "carrot-and-stick" incentives for those who can afford to buy insurance but do not do so.

John Hoff further explores the implications of capping or eliminating the tax exclusion for job-based insurance. He discusses problems in the individual market for health insurance, then analyzes the alternatives for targeting subsidies to individuals, including providing a tax deduction for insurance premiums, a tax credit, and vouchers. He looks at the costs of continuing to deliver the subsidy through employers, the implications of change for high-risk populations, and the cross-subsidies buried in the current system. Hoff concludes that "severing the link between subsidy and employment is likely to expand coverage.... The trick is to try to set up the right structure first and then modify it as the subsidy competes honestly for money with other social needs."

David Kendall says that overall tax reform would provide the ideal opportunity to remedy the inequities in the tax treatment of health insurance. He explains his prescription to expand coverage and individual choice through tax credits and to restrain medical inflation through a tax cap: "Reforming the tax treatment of health insurance offers the opportunity to buttress the fight against medical inflation, expand coverage to the uninsured, and broaden individual choice. The combination of a tax cap and tax credits would steel the employment-based system by creating a competitive alternative."

The fundamental principles of "real insurance" are elucidated by Stephen Entin and Norman Ture in a paper co-authored before Dr. Ture's death in 1997. They analyze the distortions created by government intrusion and policy errors and offer their prescriptions for a better health insurance system based on free-market proposals. They explain the benefits of real insurance in a market truly free of government interference and offer a series of tests for health insurance governed by market forces. They also agree that the tax provisions pertaining to health insurance should be revised to transfer the tax favor to the individual. Their conclusion: "A free market could provide the vast majority of the people affordable insurance, vested in the individual, portable from one job to the next, and with acceptable provisions regarding existing conditions."

Policy Innovations

John Goodman presents a detailed description of medical savings accounts, including plans for individuals, employment-based groups, and Medicare and Medicaid beneficiaries. He discusses studies and data to answer critics' concerns about adverse selection, timely access to medical treatment, and the ability of MSAs to reduce excessive health care costs. He then explores the implications for the design of MSAs, including combining these accounts with managed care. Goodman concludes that changes in tax policy are essential to create MSAs, provide tax fairness, and create more explicit, equitable subsidies for health insurance.

After John Goodman presented his paper at the conference, Congress enacted two limited experiments with MSAs, one for the self-employed and others without access to employment-based health insurance and another for Medicare beneficiaries. Supporters of MSAs say the regulatory restrictions that Congress attached to these accounts are inhibiting the sale of policies and that mandates in many states make it virtually impossible for would-be MSA buyers to obtain the accompanying catastrophic insurance policy. They therefore continue to work for legislation that will expand and unshackle MSAs to give additional millions of Americans genuine freedom in their choice of the MSA option.

Physician Kevin Vigilante offers a front-line perspective on the special challenges of reaching the chronically uninsured poor, with whom he works everyday. He concludes that existing public programs fail this group, and he explores a practical proposal to target subsidies so that individuals can obtain coverage while enhancing the efficiency and equity of the overall health care financing system. "Although it is true that the poor are vulnerable in many ways," he posits, "the argument that they cannot make prudent medical decisions for themselves is demeaning and excessively paternalistic. The uninsured who are poor are every bit as capable of discerning disrespect and neglect as the rich and well-insured. The problem is that there is little they can do about it right now."

Policy, Political, and Medical Perspectives

Several other presentations offered at the conference provided policy, political, and medical perspectives that are important to the debate.

Senator Bennett ties together his experience as a successful businessman and politician to describe the benefits of health insurance that is owned and controlled by individuals and provides protection against the risks of catastrophic illness or accident.

Representative Tom Petri (R–Wisc.) throws the health care reform debate into a new light by exploring the broader implications for welfare and tax reform. "If we look at all of these related problems and focus on making all the pieces fit together," he says, "we can accomplish far more." With the aid of Chief of Staff Joe Fladen, Mr. Petri focuses on the benefits and policy implications of a universal tax credit.

Edward Moffit presents his front-line experience in trying to alter the status quo to provide MSAs to labor union members. A local union president in Bucks County, Pennsylvania, Mr. Moffit details the bitter fight he waged to negotiate MSAs for his members so that they will "know what they are getting and what they will be paying [and will have] the right to spend their own money on medical services they need without being dictated to or restricted by management."

Finally, Sewell Dixon offers another physician's perspective on how dramatically third-party payment has affected the practice of medicine, including the physician–patient relationship, in the United States. "Doctors had no incentive to learn to control costs over the past three decades," he says. "For the best of American medicine to survive and provide inclusive, scientific, and effective health care for the next century, an amalgamation must be forged between ethical and scientific medical practices and efficient and sustainable business practices." Dixon plans to continue his work on how this amalgamation can be achieved.

SOLUTIONS FOR A NEW CENTURY

The key to reform of the health care system is giving individuals freedom of choice in an open and competitive marketplace. Whoever controls the money also controls the choices. Will it continue to be private-sector bureaucracies through employers, health insurance companies, and managed care organizations? Will it be through expansion of government bureaucracies? Or will the resources be controlled by individuals with the resources and the authority to transform the health care system into one that caters to millions of individual needs?

It is no coincidence that the United States offers the highest-quality health care in the world and that, during the twentieth century, it repeatedly has turned its back on socialized medicine. The challenge for the twenty-first century is to modernize tax policy decisions made more than 50 years ago so that this high-quality health care is accessible and affordable for all Americans. That will come not through the collective solutions that have been attempted again and again this century, but through solutions that focus on individual authority, competition, diversity, and freedom of choice that will drive the rest of economy in the twenty-first century.

Ultimately, the road to health care reform will run through tax reform. The invisible and regressive tax break for health insurance will be brought to light when the country debates a major overhaul of the tax code. As a result, the route to the health care reform that has eluded policymakers for decades may very well be through a simpler, fairer, and flatter tax system.

NOTES

[1] Paul Starr, *The Social Transformation of American Medicine* (New York, N.Y.: Basic Books, Inc., 1982), p. 235.

[2] *Ibid.*, p. 236.

[3] *Ibid.*, p. 280.

[4] Health Care Financing Administration, Office of the Actuary.

[5] U.S. Bureau of the Census, Current Population Survey, March 1996.

[6] National Commission on Economic Growth and Tax Reform, *Unleashing America's Potential: A Pro-Growth, Pro-Family Tax System for the Twenty-first Century* (New York, N.Y.: St. Martin's Griffin, 1996), pp. 24–25.

[7] Dr. Pauly devoted his recent sabbatical to researching and writing *Health Benefits at Work: An Economic and Political Analysis of Employment-Based Health Insurance* (Ann Arbor, Mich.: University of Michigan Press, 1997). He investigates the confusion among employers and political leaders over who really pays for employer-arranged health insurance, provides a comprehensive assessment of the economic theory bearing on this central question, and offers assessments of the implications for policymakers and business.

1

THE TAX TREATMENT OF HEALTH INSURANCE: EARLY HISTORY AND EVIDENCE, 1940–1970

Robert B. Helms, Ph.D.

Can there be any doubt that a tax policy that directly affects the financial well-being of 157 million Americans[1] and that has been in existence for over 50 years has made a substantial difference in the performance and efficiency of the U.S. health market? The answer is yes. But that doubt is very unevenly distributed across the American population. The complex way in which tax policy has affected the growth of health insurance and the behavior of consumers and providers is understood by a small number of health economists and other health policy specialists who have studied health markets and examined the empirical evidence. The rest of the population, including most politicians and policymakers, sees little connection between the arcane rules of the Internal Revenue Service and the policy problems we are experiencing in the health care marketplace.

Health care economists and other analysts have been writing about the effects of tax policy on health care markets for over 40 years.[2] Even though the effects of tax policy on the growth of private health insurance and the effects of health insurance on the behavior of consumers and providers are well understood by a few health policy specialists, it has not been easy to disentangle those effects from other

Figure 1

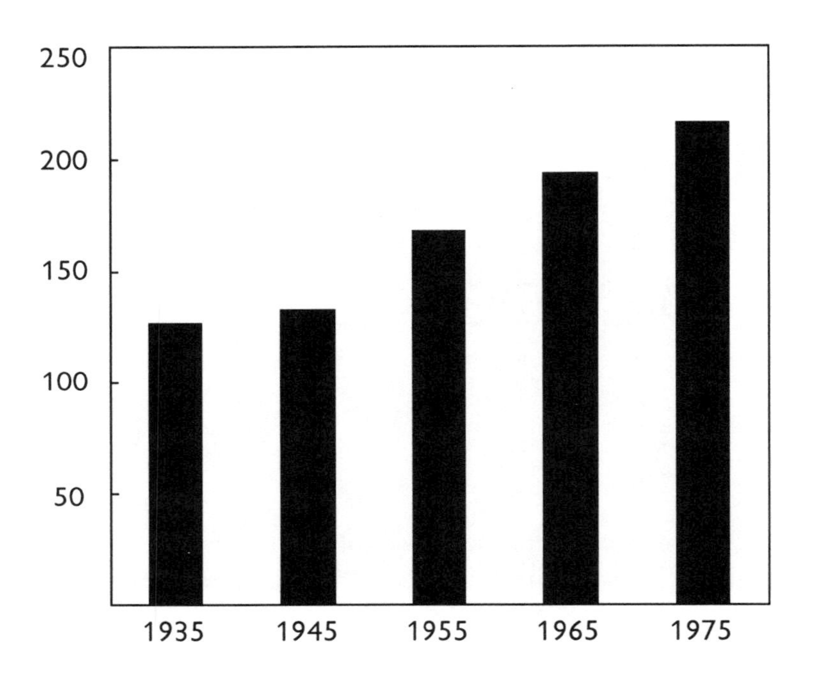

Source: *Statistical Abstract of the United States, 1990,* Table 2.

forces affecting health markets in order to present unambiguous measurements. This has left room for academic skeptics, special interests, and some politicians to argue against tax changes designed to improve the performance of health markets. The purpose of this chapter is to review the early history and principal studies undertaken to measure the effects of tax policy on health insurance and economic behavior in health markets.[3] To help understand those studies, the next section briefly reviews the history of health markets with emphasis on the changing nature of health insurance in the post–World War II period.

Figure 2

Per capita national income, 1935–1975, in constant 1982 dollars

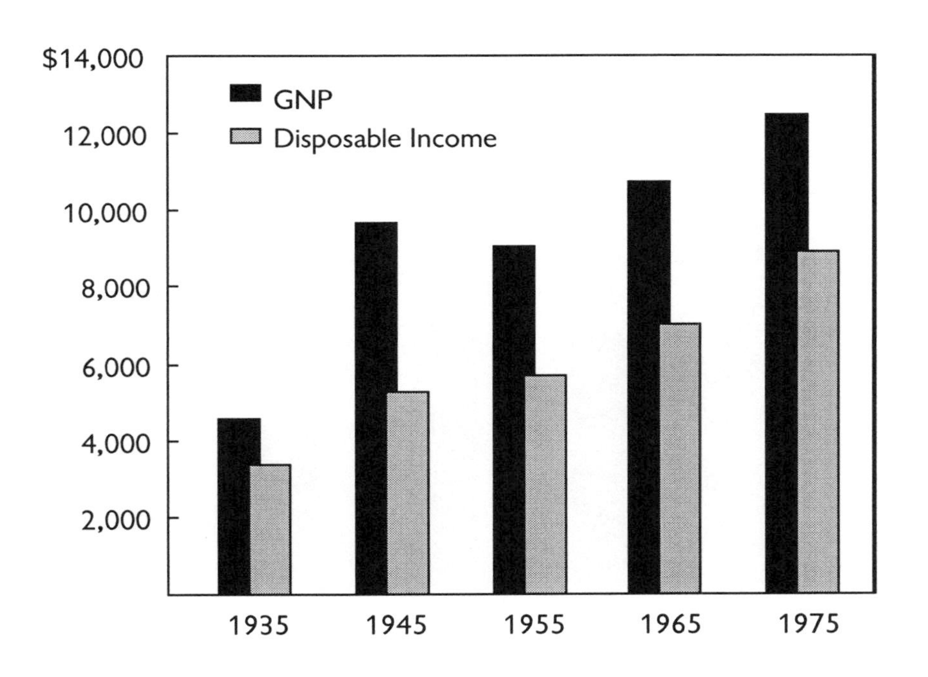

Source: *Statistical Abstract of the United States, 1990*, Table 695.

THE CHANGING POSTWAR HEALTH MARKET

To understand the effects of tax policy on health markets, it will be helpful to consider the rapid rate of change in almost all aspects of medicine and insurance after World War II. Historical accounts of the history of medicine and health care delivery all point to the nineteenth century and early twentieth century as a period of major change in the knowledge of medicine, in the role of hospitals and physicians, and in the financing of health care.[4] All the major changes we associate with the period after World War II—the change in medical technology, the growth of employment-based insurance, and the changing nature of the hospital—had their antecedents in the period before World War I. What distinguishes the post–World War II period is the rapid rate of

Figure 3

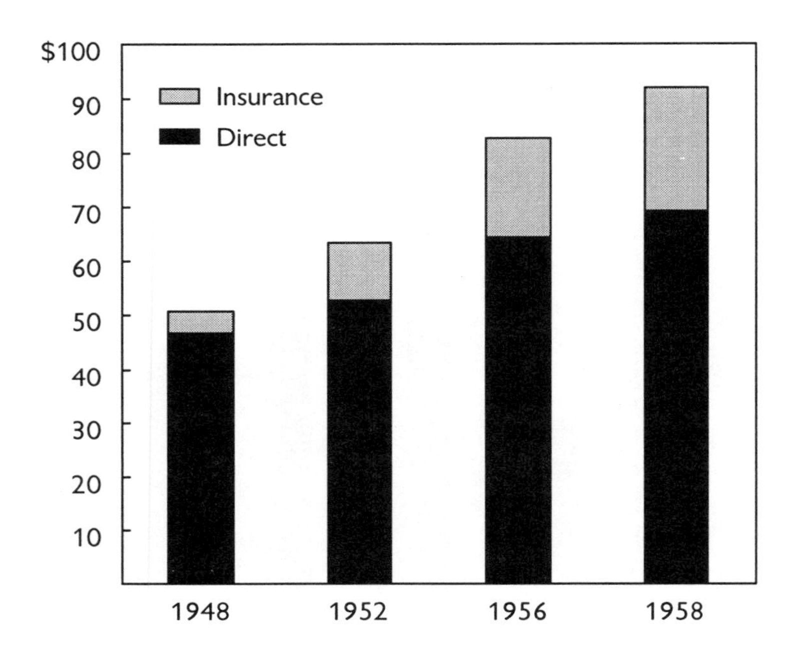

Source: Herman M. Somers and Anne R. Somers, *Doctors, Patients, and Health Insurance,* Table A-10.

change of these factors. A look at some of the available data can help illustrate the magnitude of the changes.

The period following World War II is regarded generally as one of unprecedented growth and prosperity. Figure 1 shows the growth of the population after World War II. That bulge became known as the baby-boom generation. It was accompanied by a growth in national and personal wealth, as illustrated in Figure 2 by the growth of per capita gross national product and disposable personal income in 1982 constant dollars. It is not surprising that some of that growth in personal income went into the purchase of medical care and health insurance. Although we do not have comparable data for prewar and postwar per capita expenditures, Somers and Somers present data on per capita expenditures for medical care and health insurance for 1948

Table 1

Admissions to hospitals by diagnostic category

	Admissions per 1,000 Population	
	1923–43	1957–58
Mental and Nervous	2.6	5.6
Heart Diseases	1.0	3.2
Other Digestive	1.3	4.4
Deliveries	10.2	24.1
Accidental Injuries	4.6	8.2
Total Admissions	56.7	99.4

Source: Herman M. Somers and Anne R. Somers, *Doctors, Patients, and Health Insurance*, p. 65.

through 1958.[5] Figure 3 illustrates the rapid growth in per capita total expenditures, payments made out of pocket by consumers, and those made through insurance. While total per capita expenditures went up 82 percent, consumers' out-of-pocket payments went up 49 percent and payments by the relatively small but growing insurance sector went up 442 percent.[6]

There was substantial progress in medical knowledge and the ability of health professionals to affect medical outcomes in the early half of the twentieth century, but the development of modern drugs and surgical and other medical procedures made possible a much more rapid increase in the application of scientific knowledge to medicine after World War II.[7] The increased ability of medicine to provide valuable medical services and the public willingness to purchase those new services are reflected in the data on both expenditures and utilization. Table 1 is a partial reproduction of a Somers and Somers table showing a comparison of admission rates to general hospitals by diagnostic category for 1928–1943 versus 1957–1958. Considering that new technologies allowed some conditions to be treated in an outpatient setting, the increase in total admissions reflects the increase in hospital care for serious medical conditions requiring more intensive and expensive technologies and personnel. Looking at expenditures, Somers and Somers report that "In 1929 the proportion of disposable

Figure 4

Private health insurance enrollment in millions, by type of coverage, 1940–1959

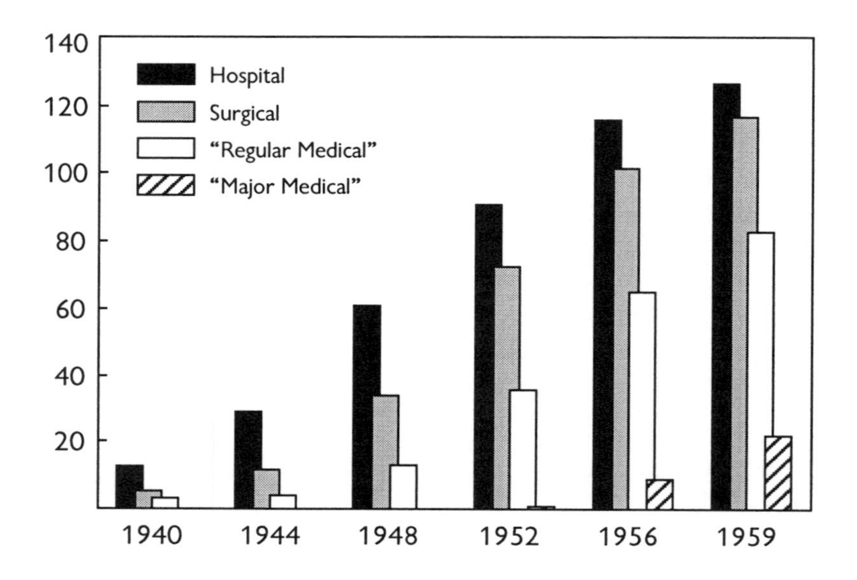

Source: Herman M. Somers and Anne R. Somers, *Doctors, Patients, and Health Insurance*, Table A-12.

personal income spent for medical care was 3.5 per cent. In 1946 it was 3.8 per cent; by 1956, 4.9; and in 1958, 5.2. The increase between 1946 and 1958 was thus 37 per cent."[8]

This increase in the demand for medical care elicited a response from every sector of the health industry, including hospitals, physicians and other personnel, pharmaceutical and other medical product suppliers, and the health insurers. William White reports that "Between 1940 and 1965 the total number of general hospitals in the country increased by nearly 40 percent, while the number of beds increased by over 85 percent."[9] During the same period, the number of physicians increased 74.2 percent (from 133 to 153 physicians per 100,000 population) while the number of nurses increased 115.8 percent (from 216 to 319 nurses per 100,000 population).[10]

The large and relatively rapid growth of the health care industry in the postwar period raised the cost of care for the average consumer and created the conditions that were conducive to the growth of the health insurance industry. In discussing the history of hospitals in the early years of this century, White makes the point that "new technologies sharply increased the cost of care, so that in the absence of health insurance, a major illness spelled financial crisis for all but the most wealthy members of society."[11]

The financial risk faced by a few consumers in the early part of the century was becoming increasingly important to the vast majority of postwar consumers. For the average consumer, the probability of having a major medical expenditure was relatively small, but if a serious medical problem developed, the costs of hospital and physician care could impose a significant financial burden. This concern among several million Americans with rising incomes about the potential costs of medical care helped create the desire to spread the risk of sudden financial loss.[12]

Looked at in this way, it is not difficult to understand why conditions after World War II were ripe for a rapid growth in the health insurance industry. At the same time, however, other types of insurance, such as fire, life, and automobile insurance, also were facing expanding consumer demand. To anticipate the following discussion, we will point out that these other forms of insurance expanded primarily through sales directly to consumers, while health insurance expanded primarily through provision by employers. The difference in the development of health insurance has had major effects on the performance and efficiency of health markets compared to other insurance markets, a topic discussed in more detail below, but first we will look at some characteristics of the growth of private-sector health insurance.

As the absolute growth in health insurance increased, there was increased enrollment not only in the traditional hospital coverage that dominated the prewar period, but also in coverage for surgery, physician services, and major medical expenses.[13] Figure 4 presents the enrollment in health insurance plans by type of coverage from 1940 through 1959.

While individual purchase of health insurance was increasing during the postwar period, the major growth in enrollment was occurring in group policies being purchased through employers. Figure 5 shows the growth of Blue Cross/Blue Shield and group insurance policies sold directly to employers relative to the growth of individual policies

Figure 5

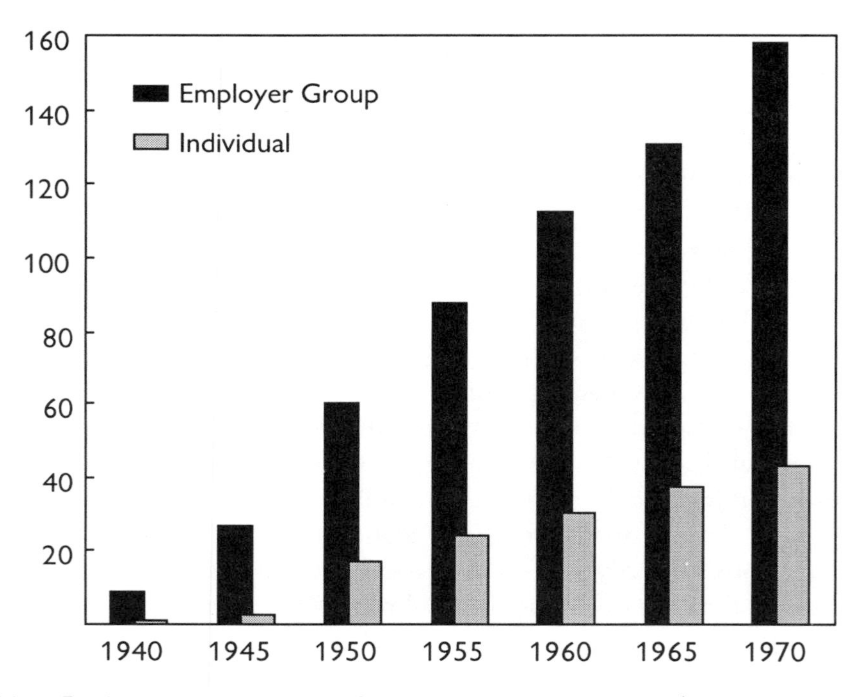

Note: Employer group is the total of persons covered by Blue Cross/Blue Shield plus insurance company group policies.
Source: *Historical Statistics of the United States — Colonial Times to 1970,* Series B 401–412.

before and after World War II. Somers and Somers point out that only 2 percent of the labor force (1 to 2 million employees) and their dependents (another 1 to 2 million) had any protection for health services in 1930. In contrast, by 1958, 123 million Americans had hospital insurance and 75 percent of them were enrolled through their employer.[14]

The absolute growth in the size of the health care sector obviously was affected by the rapid growth of population and wealth after the war. At the same time, the development of penicillin during World War II and more modern medicines in the next two decades led to an increase in the effectiveness of medical care and in consumer demand for medical services. The higher cost of more advanced medicine stimulated the demand for medical insurance. As a result, the rapid growth of employer-provided insurance after World War II set the U.S. health care system on a different course from most other developed countries. While Canada and the European "welfare states" adopted various forms of public health care delivery and financing, the United States relied on public programs for the elderly and the poor while retaining private-sector financing for the majority of working Americans. Compared with most other systems, those developments enabled the American health care system to perform better in terms of personal choice and technological and scientific progress but more poorly in terms of cost and number of people covered.[15]

THE TAX TREATMENT OF HEALTH INSURANCE

A poll of Americans about the causes of high medical costs probably would elicit many answers regarding "greedy physicians" and "waste, fraud, and abuse," but almost no mention of tax policy. Yet health policy experts, especially health economists, almost unanimously implicate the special treatment of employer-provided health insurance as a major cause of economic inefficiency in medical markets. Those experts also believe that the special treatment explains the historical development of these markets in the postwar period.

One reason tax policy is so misunderstood is that it works in an indirect way through health insurance. The pioneering work explaining the complex and indirect effects of tax policy on medical market behavior was done in the early 1970s by Martin Feldstein in conjunction with Elisabeth Allison and Bernard Friedman.[16] The following summary starts with their studies and then adds information from some more recent studies. To facilitate understanding of both the economic effects and the empirical estimates, the summary will be presented in three sections: (1) the effects of tax policy on health insurance; (2) the effects of health insurance on medical use and prices; and (3) the effects of higher medical costs on health insurance.

Table 2

Effects of tax rates on the cost of health care insurance (HI)

	20% MTR	30% MTR
Wages w/o HI	$20,000	$20,000
Taxes w/o HI	4,000	6,000
After-tax wages	16,000	14,000
Wages w/ $2000 HI	18,000	18,000
Taxes w/HI	3,600	5,400
After-tax wages w/HI	16,400	14,600
After-tax cost of $2000 HI	1,600	1,400
Tax subsidy (lost rev.)	400	600

Source: Sherry Glied, *Revising the Tax Treatment of Employer-Provided Health Insurance*, p. 4.

The Effects of Tax Policy on Health Insurance[17]

Tax policy subsidizes the purchase of health insurance in two ways: first, by allowing the deduction of a limited amount of medical expenses and health insurance premiums from taxable income; and second, by excluding the value of employer-provided insurance from the employee's taxable income for the income tax and Social Security and Medicare payroll taxes.[18] Like wages and other costs, the cost of health insurance to the employer is deductible as a business expense.

The tax exclusion is the more important.[19]

Both aspects of federal tax policy had their origins during World War II. The medical deduction of health expenses started in 1942. The exclusion of employer-provided health insurance from taxable income also started during the war as business firms offered fringe benefits as a way to compete for scarce labor under wartime wage controls.[20] This practice was recognized by a special ruling of the Internal Revenue Service (IRS) in 1943.[21] In 1953, the IRS ruled that employers' contributions to individual policies were to be included in taxable income. Congress overturned the ruling the next year.[22]

Tax policy increases the demand for health insurance by providing a government-funded discount for health expenditures and employer-provided health insurance. The higher the marginal tax rates (MTR) faced by an individual, the greater the amount of the discount.[23] Table 2 presents an example developed by Glied to explain how tax policy makes additional health insurance benefits more valuable than additional wages.[24] Because the tax subsidy lowers the net cost of a given level of health insurance, an employee rationally would prefer additional dollars spent on health insurance rather than on wages. An employee would have to pay taxes on the additional wages (at his or her MTR) but not on the health benefits. Under the assumption that employees value health insurance at least as much as an equal amount of wages, the employee with a 20 percent MTR is better off when the employer provides health insurance because the employee has the health insurance and $400 in additional after-tax income.

How high are MTRs and the resulting discounts on health insurance purchased by the employer? According to Feldstein and Allison, the effective MTR for 1969 ranged from 13 percent for incomes under $1,000 to 36 percent for incomes over $25,000.[25] They estimate that the total tax subsidy in 1969 was $2 billion, including $1.63 billion in reduced revenue and $339 million from individual insurance payments. This is a 15 percent discount from the $15.7 billion total health insurance premiums in 1969.[26] Writing in 1981, Feldstein reported that updates of these estimates indicate that the tax subsidy for 1978 exceeded $10 billion on insurance premiums totaling $42 billion, which implies a 24 percent discount.[27]

Tax policy has several other implications, some of which are discussed by Feldstein and Allison, and others that follow from the history given above. For example:

- The value to the individual taxpayer and the cost to the government of the tax subsidy are greater when a person's income (MTR) is higher.
- Rising incomes and MTRs have increased the amount of the subsidy over time.
- The tax exclusion creates incentives to expand the scope of medical benefits (e.g., more coverage for dental, eyeglasses, and weight reduction programs) and to reduce the degree of cost sharing (smaller co-payments and deductibles).
- Tax policy was not the only factor affecting the rapid growth of health insurance and medical costs in the postwar period, but the distortions it created in labor and medical markets magnified the effects of the other factors, such as income, population, and medical technology.[28]

Feldstein and Allison conclude their study by saying that the subsidy "causes a substantial revenue loss, distributes these tax reductions very regressively, encourages an excessive purchase of insurance, distorts the demand for health services, and thus inflates the prices of these services."[29]

The Effects of Health Insurance on Medical Use and Prices

One of Feldstein's major contributions was his explanation of the effects of health insurance on the performance of medical markets. His analysis of the tax treatment of health insurance was preceded by his two large studies of the effects on hospital and physician markets.[30] Because conditions in physician markets made it difficult to estimate the demand for services, his study of health insurance concentrated on the hospital market.[31] Feldstein argues that the effects are complicated by the special nature of nonprofit hospitals and by insurance.

As noted, the discount for employer-provided health insurance could be expected to increase the demand for it. The expansion of health insurance took three forms: an expansion in the absolute amount of insurance (more employees covered); an increase in the types of coverage (more extensive hospital and nonhospital coverage); and a reduction in cost-sharing (deductibles and/or coinsurance rates). For typical insured employees, expanded insurance reduced the observed price of a hospital stay or a physician visit, inducing them to increase their demand for these services.

But, as Feldstein argues, that is not the end of the story.[32] Nonprofit hospitals (which were more prevalent in the 1960s than today) responded to the increase in demand not only by raising their prices, but also by investing in more technology and labor to improve their services. That was how they competed for physicians and patients. Feldstein also noted that "this response does not depend on the usual mechanism by which increased demand raises price through higher profits and higher input costs. It is primarily by inducing a change in the hospital's product that insurance raises its price."[33]

After measuring the welfare losses from excess health insurance, Feldstein uses his model to estimate the potential gains that could be achieved by higher coinsurance rates.[34] After allowing for the effects of changing hospital quality, and assuming a reasonable range of elasticity and risk-bearing values, Feldstein compared the welfare gains from reducing price distortion (raising the coinsurance rate) with the welfare losses of increased risk-bearing. Arguing that his estimates are likely to understate the net welfare losses, he anticipated "net gains in excess of $4 billion per year."[35] In 1969, this net welfare gain was 32 percent of the $12.6 billion in private hospital care expenditures.[36] This led Feldstein to conclude that

> an increase in the average coinsurance rate would increase welfare and that the net gain would probably be quite substantial. Moreover, a more general restructuring of the form of health insurance, reducing its role as a method of prepaying small and moderate hospital bills, and increasing its role in protecting against the major financial risks of very large health expenses, could produce even greater gains.[37]

The Effects of Higher Medical Costs on Health Insurance

Incorporated into Feldstein's estimates of the consequences of tax policy are the feedback effects of an increase in medical costs on the demand for insurance. As explained above, the discounts made possible by the tax treatment of employer-provided health insurance increased the amount and type of coverage. That, in turn, increased both the demand for and the cost of hospital and physician services. The tax-induced rise in medical costs increased the risk of financial loss for the typical consumer. The desire to protect against this risk is the principal

Table 3

Health-related tax expenditures, 1969–2000, in billions of dollars

			Principal Federal Tax Expenditures		
	Total	State	Total Federal	Employer Paid Ins. Premiums	Medical Expense Deduction
1969	3.9	0.3	3.6	1.5	1.7
1970	4	0.4	3.6	1.5	1.7
1975	8.7	0.8	8	3.5	2.3
1980	21.6	1.9	19.7	12.4	3.2
1985	35.9	3.7	32.2	21.7	3.6
1990	50.4	6.3	44.2	32.9	2.8
1995	86.8	9.9	76.8	58.4	4.2
2000	144	16.2	127.8	96.3	8.2

Source: CBO, *Projections of National Health Expenditures*, p. 56. Not included in these figures are untaxed Medicare benefits, deductibility of charitable contributions, and interest on state and local bonds for nonprofit hospitals.

reason a rational consumer buys insurance. The result of rising medical costs was a further increase in the demand for insurance that, like the original tax-induced increase in demand, resulted in even higher medical costs and even more demand for insurance. Feldstein concluded that insurance is used more than it would have been and medical costs are higher than otherwise because the two are interdependent. The effect of any outside factor is magnified by that interdependence.[38]

In historical terms, Feldstein pointed out that this two-way relationship between hospital behavior and the growth of insurance led to an "explosively unstable" period from 1958 through 1965, but that the system became more stable after 1966 even though hospital prices continued to rise at a rapid rate.[39]

Figure 6

Private insurance premiums, 1965–93, in billions of current dollars,

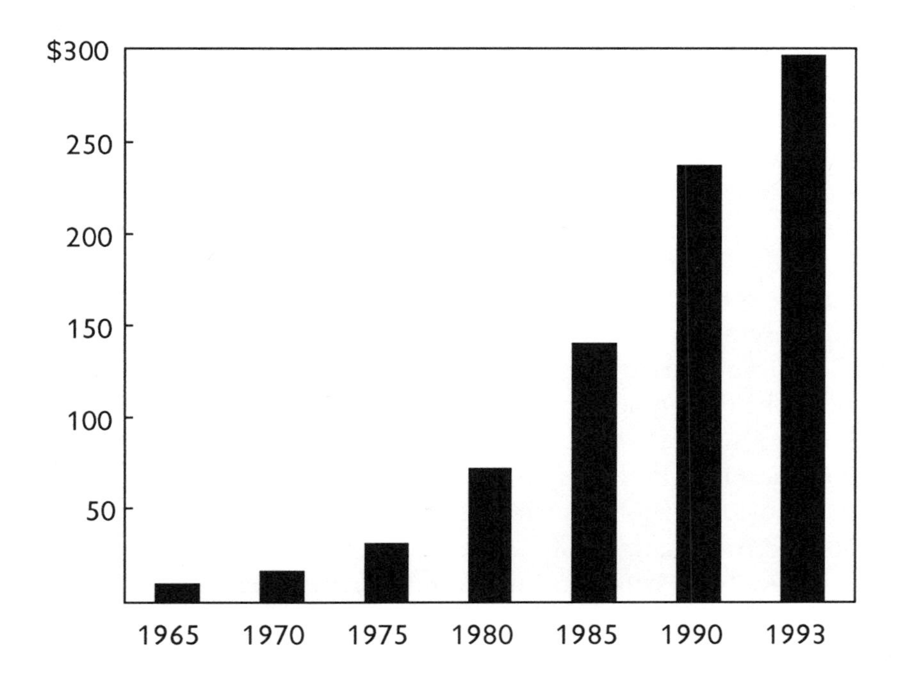

Source: *Statistical Abstract of the United States, 1995,* Table 150.

MORE RECENT STUDIES AND EVIDENCE

The purpose of this chapter has been to look at the early history and evidence of the tax treatment of health insurance. A brief look at some data on tax policy and health insurance premiums, as well as a review of more recent studies, will help put the historical discussion into perspective.

The revenue lost by the federal and state governments because of the tax policy under discussion is computed annually. Table 3 presents the Congressional Budget Office (CBO) version of these so-called tax expenditures, compiled from annual budget documents as well as projections by the Joint Tax Committee.[40] The table covers selected years including 1969, the year of the Feldstein and Friedman estimates.

Comparing the composition of "tax expenditures" in 1969 and 1995, medical expense deductions have declined in importance (from 44 percent to 4.8 percent) while employer-paid premiums have increased (from 38.5 percent to 67.3 percent). The loss in state tax revenue has increased slightly (from 7.7 percent to 11.4 percent), reflecting the general increase in state taxation. As a result of higher federal income and payroll taxes, tax expenditures from the exclusion of employer-provided health insurance from federal taxation have grown, both in absolute terms and in relative importance, since 1969.

Another measure of the growth of private health insurance is total premiums paid. The available data covering the late 1960s, when Feldstein made his estimates, to the present are for total private insurance premiums paid by employers and individuals to commercial insurance companies and Blue Cross and Blue Shield. Because the data include premiums paid for individual policies, the amount is larger than the total premiums employers paid for group policies. Figure 6 displays the growth in private health insurance premiums from $10 billion in 1965 to $296 billion in 1993, a growth rate averaging 12.9 percent annually. If we assume that Feldstein's estimate of welfare loss as a proportion of total private insurance premiums remained constant at 30 percent (an admittedly crude assumption), welfare losses in 1993 would have been $89 billion and could be expected to have increased with the growth of insurance costs.

To my knowledge, we have no sophisticated update of Feldstein's estimates that accounts for changes in health and insurance markets and more recent estimates of the elasticity of demand and risk preferences of consumers. But the studies by Feldstein, Allison, and Friedman did elicit a number of follow-on studies and critiques of their methodology and results. This literature, much of it dealing with the medical industry and health insurance response to price changes, has been reviewed separately by Pauly, Morrisey, and Glied.[41] The two most recent attempts to provide empirical estimates of the effects of these subsidies have been by the CBO in 1994 and, in preliminary work, by Gruber and Poterba.[42]

The CBO study uses the 1987 National Medical Expenditure Survey (NMES) and its own tax model to estimate the distribution of tax benefits for 1994. For families with employment-based health insurance (61 percent of the population), CBO estimates that the tax subsidy averages 26 percent of health insurance premiums (which average $4,310). The subsidy increases with income, going from 11 percent for those with family incomes under $10,000 to 33 percent for those with incomes over $200,000.[43] When the subsidy is compared with after-tax income, the CBO finds that it averages 2.4 percent for families with employment-based health insurance but only 1.9 percent when taxpayers without such health insurance are included.[44] The CBO percentages can be compared roughly with Feldstein's and Allison's 1969 estimates of the tax reduction per family. When those estimates are expressed as a percentage of the midpoints of their family income ranges, the results range from 2.4 percent for families with incomes under $1,000 to 0.14 percent for families with incomes over $25,000.[45] The lower percentages reflect the lower MTRs and less extensive provision of health insurance by employers in 1969 than in 1994.

Gruber and Poterba use new data sources to show that previous studies have overstated the tax subsidy of employer-provided health insurance. Their data and methodology correct for two changes in the health insurance market: the growth in the proportion of employer-provided health insurance paid for by employees and changes in the use of the medical deduction for large medical expenses. Yet even with these new findings, their results seem to verify the large effects of the tax subsidy and the order of magnitude of the previous studies.[46]

CONCLUSION

Milton Friedman has said that economists may not know much, but they know that if the government sets the price of any product below the market rate, a shortage will result. On the basis of this review of the tax treatment of health insurance, the noneconomist may be inclined to agree only with the first part of Friedman's statement. The natural doubt that most noneconomists have about the influence of tax policy on health care markets has not been helped by the highly technical and confusing literature on the subject. Working through the markets for labor, health insurance, hospitals, and physicians, the effects have been indirect and difficult to understand or measure.

Understanding the effects of tax policy and measuring these effects have been complicated further by a number of other strong forces impacting health care markets. Increases in population, income, and medical technology all have worked to increase the demand for both medical care and health insurance. The special tax treatment for health insurance purchased through employers has not been the only influence on those markets, but it has helped magnify the expansionary effects of the other forces. It has increased the demand for health insurance, reduced consumers' perceived cost of medical care, and induced the medical sector to supply a level and style of health care far beyond what consumers would value in the absence of this tax policy.

In what Clark Havighurst has called "flat-of-the-curve medicine," medical care markets operate beyond the point of maximum efficiency.[47] This obviously has left some people better off, but at the cost of leaving almost everyone else worse off. Economic efficiency means using valuable inputs for the goods and services most valued by consumers. "Net welfare losses" is what economists call their measurement of inefficiency after allowing for the offsetting effects of consumer gains and losses. It is a measure of what society loses from a known distortion—or, to turn it around, what society could gain if it eliminated the cause of the inefficiency.

Economic studies conducted over the past 25 years have found that the inefficiencies caused by the tax treatment of health insurance are real and large. Even though the tax exclusion directly affects those with employment-based insurance, the resulting increase in the cost of care touches all consumers and patients, especially those without health insurance who end up paying higher prices. Taxpayers also are affected because of the higher taxes they have to pay to make up for the lost revenue and the diversion of tax dollars from other uses. But, as Havighurst has argued, the effects are even more pervasive because of the politics of health care. The tax-induced expansion of health insurance lowers the perceived cost of medical care and insurance and, in the process, helps to create a "pervasive entitlement mentality" among consumers. Those who receive the subsidies see no direct personal costs and thus would be happy to have additional subsidies. There is little reward for any politician who looks to tax policy as a solution to the long list of complaints about our system.[48] In one especially telling passage, Havighurst says that a "tax subsidy is insidious precisely because, in addition to being an off-budget public expenditure, it can misallocate huge amounts of society's resources, yet be entirely painless at the level of individual producers and consumers."[49]

The effects of the tax treatment of health insurance on health care markets are real and substantial, but they are also complicated, indirect, and difficult to separate from other influences. This creates the ironic situation in which we turn to direct control of prices and utilization to correct the problems of health care costs and access. It is indeed time for a fresh approach to health care reform. Empowering health care consumers through tax reform would be a good start.

NOTES

[1] Employment Research Benefit Institute, *Sources of Health Insurance and Characteristics of the Uninsured* (Washington, D.C.: EBRI, February 1996), Table 1, p. 5.

[2] The principal studies and references to this literature will be presented subsequently.

[3] For some previous reviews of this literature, see Ronald J. Vogel, "The Tax Treatment of Health Insurance as a Cause of Overinsurance," in Mark V. Pauly, ed., *National Health Insurance: What Now, What Later, What Never?* (Washington, D.C.: American Enterprise Institute, 1980), pp. 220–249; Mark V. Pauly, "Taxation, Health Insurance, and Market Failure in the Medical Economy," *Journal of Economic Literature* 24 (June 1985), pp. 629–675; Congressional Budget Office, *The Tax Treatment of Employment-Based Health Insurance* (Washington, D.C.: U.S. Government Printing Office, March 1994); Sherry Glied, *Revising the Tax Treatment of Employer-Provided Health Insurance* (Washington, D.C.: AEI Press, 1994).

[4] For reviews of the history of American medicine and health care, see Paul Starr, *The Social Transformation of American Medicine* (New York, N.Y.: Basic Books, 1982); Herman M. Somers and Anne R. Somers, *Doctors, Patients, and Health Insurance* (Washington, D.C.: Brookings Institution, 1961); Randall R. Bovbjerg, Charles C. Griffin, and Caitlin E. Carroll, "U.S. Health Care Coverage and Costs: Historical Development and Choices for the 1990s," *Journal of Law, Medicine & Ethics*, Vol. 21, No. 2 (Summer 1993), pp. 141–162; William D. White, "The American Hospital Industry Since 1900: A

Short History," in Richard M. Scheffler and Louis F. Rossiter, eds., *Advances in Health Economics and Health Services Research,* Vol. 3 (Greenwich, Conn.: JAI Press Inc., 1982); and Marilyn J. Field and Harold T. Shapiro, eds., *Employment and Health Benefits* (Washington, D.C.: National Academy Press, 1993), pp. 49–86.

[5] Somers and Somers, *Doctors, Patients, and Health Insurance,* Table A–10, p. 546.

[6] *Ibid.*

[7] For one discussion of the change in medical technology, see *ibid.,* pp. 17–24. Writing in 1961, the authors say (p. 24), "It is estimated that 90 per cent of the drugs prescribed in 1960 were introduced in the previous two decades; 40 per cent could not have been prescribed in 1954." For a discussion of the effects of technology on hospitals, see White, "The American Hospital Industry Since 1900," p. 162.

[8] Somers and Somers, *Doctors, Patients, and Health Insurance,* p. 213.

[9] White, "The American Hospital Industry Since 1900," p. 162. Hospital growth was also affected by the passage of the Hill–Burton Act, introduced in 1948. For an assessment of Hill–Burton, see *ibid.,* pp. 162–163, and Judy Lave and Lester Lave, *The Hospital Construction Act* (Washington, D.C.: American Enterprise Institute, 1974).

[10] *Historical Statistics of the United States, Colonial Times to 1970, Part 1* (Washington, D.C.: U.S. Bureau of the Census, 1975), Series B275–290, pp. 75–76.

[11] White, "The American Hospital Industry Since 1900," p. 159.

[12] For readable explanations of the basic economics of insurance, see Mark A. Hall, *Reforming Private Health Insurance* (Washington, D.C.: AEI Press, 1994), esp. chapter 2, and Mark V. Pauly, "Overinsurance: The Conceptual Issues," in *National Health Insurance,* pp. 201–219.

[13] Somers and Somers, *Doctors, Patients, and Health Insurance,* Table A–12, p. 547. "Regular medical expense" was the term used to refer to coverage of outpatient physician expenses and physician services not covered under hospital insurance. "Major medical" refers to supplemental and catastrophic coverage not covered by other policies.

[14] Somers and Somers, *Doctors, Patients, and Health Insurance,* pp. 228 and 230. *Historical Statistics of the United States,* Series B 401–412, the source for Figure 5, gives the total of persons covered in 1958 by Blue Cross / Blue Shield and group policies by insurance companies as 103.1 million.

[15] For a sample of the rather extensive literature on international health systems, and for additional references, see Health Care Financing Administration, *Health Care Financing Review, 1989 Annual Supplement,* Vol. 11, No. 1 (Fall 1989), and Robert B. Helms, ed., *Health Care Policy and Politics: Lessons from Four Countries* (Washington, D.C.: AEI Press, 1993).

[16] Their articles are conveniently reprinted in Martin Feldstein, *Hospital Costs and Health Insurance* (Cambridge, Mass.: Harvard University Press, 1981), chapters 6–8. For additional explanations by economists of the role of tax policy, see Glied, *Revising the Tax Treatment of Employer-Provided Health Insurance,* pp. 2–4; Congressional Budget Office, *The Tax Treatment of Employment-Based Health Insurance,* March 1994, pp. 5–27; and Vogel, "The Tax Treatment of Health Insurance Premiums as a Cause of Overinsurance," pp. 228–233. For explanations by a legal scholar, see Clark C. Havighurst, *Deregulating the Health Care Industry* (Cambridge, Mass.: Ballinger Publishing Company, 1982), pp. 388–391, and Clark C. Havighurst, *Health Care Choices* (Washington, D.C.: AEI Press, 1995), pp. 100–103.

[17] Because the above material has relied extensively on the comprehensive historical analysis and data presented by Somers and Somers, it is interesting to note that, to the best of my knowledge, they at no time explicitly acknowledge tax policy as a contributing factor in the growth of health insurance in the postwar period. They

come close to acknowledging it in their explanation for the reason that 75 percent of those with hospital coverage received it through employee benefit plans when they say that, "*For numerous reasons* most Americans now appear to prefer the extension and improvement of 'fringe benefits' to direct wage increases." Somers and Somers, *Doctors, Patients, and Health Insurance,* p. 228; emphasis added. They place major emphasis on the growth of unions and collective bargaining; *ibid.*, p. 226.

[18] For a study of the role of the medical deduction, see Bridger M. Mitchell and Ronald J. Vogel, *Health and Taxes: An Assessment of the Medical Deduction* (Santa Monica, Cal.: RAND Corporation, R–1222–OEO, August 1973).

[19] See Table 3.

[20] Sherry Glied points out that the exclusion of health benefits "existed implicitly since the inception of the federal income tax in 1913" but grew in importance due to the expansion of fringe benefits to avoid wage controls beginning in World War II. Glied, *Revising the Tax Treatment of Employer-Provided Health Insurance,* p. 5. See also Congressional Budget Office, *The Tax Treatment of Employment-Based Health Insurance,* p. 5.

[21] Vogel, "The Tax Treatment of Health Insurance Premiums as a Cause of Overinsurance," p. 223. Vogel's cite is Special Ruling, October 26, 1943, 433CCH, Federal Tax Service, paragraph 6587. The IRS ruling apparently followed a ruling by the War Labor Board that health and pension benefits did not count as wages. See Field and Shapiro, *Employment and Health Benefits,* p. 70.

[22] Congressional Budget Office, *The Tax Treatment of Employment-Based Health Insurance,* p. 5. The exclusions of the employer's contribution for health insurance from the federal income tax and payroll taxes are contained, respectively, in Sections 106 and 3121 of the Internal Revenue Code.

[23] The marginal tax rate refers to the ratio of the additional tax burden for an additional dollar of income.

[24] Glied, *Revising the Tax Treatment of Employer-Provided Health Insurance,* p. 4.

[25] Feldstein and Allison, in Feldstein, *Hospital Costs and Health Insurance,* Table 7.2. Their estimates do not include the effects of state taxes.

[26] *Ibid.,* pp. 174 and 208–215. Feldstein and Allison argue that these estimates are likely underestimates of the actual subsidies due to limitations of their data and model.

[27] *Ibid.,* p. 174. Some additional updates are discussed later.

[28] A number of analysts identify medical technology as the leading cause of the rapid rise in medical costs. Technology obviously added to the cost of medical care (and, it is hoped, improved outcomes), but the tax-induced rise in the demand for insurance increased the demand for medical technology and resulted in a larger effect on medical costs than would have existed without the subsidy. Health insurance induced hospitals, physicians, and consumers to adopt a more intensive use of technology, and insurance companies to pay medical claims without questioning whether technology was used efficiently. For discussions of the role of technology in explaining medical-cost increases, see Joseph P. Newhouse, "An Iconoclastic View of Health Cost Containment," *Health Affairs,* Supplement 1993, pp. 152–171, and Burton A. Weisbrod, "The Health Care Quadrilemma: An Essay on Technological Change, Insurance, Quality of Care, and Cost Containment," *Journal of Economic Literature,* Vol. 29, No. 2 (June 1991), pp. 523–552.

[29] Feldstein and Allison, in Feldstein, *Hospital Costs and Health Insurance,* p. 216.

[30] Martin S. Feldstein, *The Rising Cost of Hospital Care*; Martin Feldstein, *Hospital Costs and Health Insurance*, chapters 1–5; and "The Rising Price of Physicians' Services," *Review of Economics and Statistics,* Vol. 52, No. 2 (May 1970), pp. 121–133.

[31] Feldstein, *Hospital Costs and Health Insurance,* p. 179.

[32] See Martin Feldstein, "Hospital Cost Inflation: A Study of Nonprofit Price Dynamics," *American Economic Review,* Vol. 61, No. 5 (December 1971), pp. 853–872, reprinted in *Hospital Costs and Health Insurance,* chapter 3.

[33] Feldstein, *Hospital Costs and Health Insurance,* p. 187.

[34] In any economic change there usually are winners and losers. In its simplest meaning, welfare losses (sometimes referred to as dead-weight losses) refer to net losses from a change. If the gainers cannot compensate the losers, then it can be said that there is a net loss in welfare for society. For Feldstein's discussion of five aspects of the welfare effects of health insurance, see *Hospital Costs and Health Insurance,* pp. 97–98.

[35] Feldstein, *Hospital Costs and Health Insurance,* p. 203.

[36] In a review article published in 1974, Feldstein summarizes his estimates of welfare losses by saying that the "estimated welfare cost for 1969 was about $2.4 billion, or 30 percent of total insurance benefits and 20 percent of total private hospital expenditure." Feldstein, *Hospital Costs and Health Insurance,* p. 99.

[37] *Ibid.,* p. 203.

[38] *Ibid.,* p. 173.

[39] *Ibid.,* p. 18.

[40] Congressional Budget Office, *Projections of National Health Expenditures,* October 1992, p. 56.

[41] Pauly, "Taxation, Health Insurance, and Market Failure in the Medical Economy"; Michael A. Morrisey, *Price Sensitivity in Health Care: Implications for Health Care Policy* (Washington, D.C.: NFIB Foundation, 1992); Glied, *Revising the Tax Treatment of Employer-Provided Health Insurance.* For a criticism of Feldstein's assumptions about hospital behavior, see Peter Temin, "An Economic History of American Hospitals," in H. E. Frech III, ed., *Health Care in America*

(San Francisco, Cal.: Pacific Research Institute for Public Policy, 1988), pp. 92–97.

[42] Congressional Budget Office, *The Tax Treatment of Employment-Based Health Insurance,* and Jonathan Gruber and James Poterba, "Tax Subsidies to Employer-Provided Health Insurance," National Bureau of Economic Research *Working Paper* No. 5147, June 1995.

[43] Congressional Budget Office, *The Tax Treatment of Employment-Based Health Insurance,* Table 4, p. 30.

[44] *Ibid.,* Table 4, p. 31.

[45] Calculated from Feldstein and Allison, *Hospital Costs and Health Insurance,* Table 7.2, p. 208. They use $40,000 to represent all incomes over $25,000.

[46] Gruber and Poterba, "Tax Subsidies to Employer-Provided Health Insurance."

[47] Havighurst, *Health Care Choices,* pp. 92–96.

[48] *Ibid.*, pp. 101–103. At one point (p. 103), Havighurst says that "capping the tax subsidy is a notion that only a policy wonk could love, a meritorious policy idea with no natural political constituency."

[49] *Ibid.,* p. 102.

2

WHAT'S WRONG WITH THE PRESENT SYSTEM

Michael Tanner

After nearly a year and a half of debate, tens of millions of lobbying dollars, and smothering media attention, the debate over President Bill Clinton's plan for health care reform finally died not with a bang, but a whimper. But there remain significant problems in the health care system in the United States that must be addressed.

Most important, health care continues to cost too much. In 1995, Americans spent nearly $1 trillion on health care, amounting to 14.2 percent of gross domestic product. That is a 7.4 percent increase in health spending over 1994.[1] Although recent trends indicate that the increase in health care costs is moderating, both the relative price of medical care and real health care expenditures per capita continue to increase at a rate higher than the average increase over the past 30 years.

At the same time, almost 40 million Americans still lack health insurance, and millions more worry that if they lose their jobs, they will lose their insurance. Although most Americans are uninsured for only a short time, a method must be found to enable more Americans to obtain and keep health coverage.

As bad as these problems are, however, they are merely symptoms of a much larger flaw in the health care system in the United States: the link between health care and a misguided tax policy.

Current federal and state tax laws exclude the cost of employer-provided health insurance from taxable wages. Therefore, the vast majority of Americans—those who receive health insurance through their employers—do not pay federal or state income taxes or Social Security taxes on the value of their policies. Moreover, the employer can deduct the full premium cost as a business expense. Employers do not even pay Social Security payroll taxes on these benefits. In short, the entire cost of employer-provided health insurance is financed with before-tax dollars.[2]

Those Americans not fortunate enough to receive employer-provided health insurance, however, face entirely different tax laws. Part-time workers, students, the unemployed, and others—including most employees of small businesses—receive little or no tax benefit for purchasing health insurance. (Until recently, individuals were able to deduct out-of-pocket medical expenses only if they itemized deductions and these expenses exceeded 7.5 percent of their adjusted gross income (AGI). Less than 5 percent of American taxpayers were eligible for this deduction.)[3] Self-employed workers received a tax deduction for a portion of their premiums.

For everyone else, except for the 7.5 percent AGI deduction for which few people qualify, out-of-pocket spending on health care outside of insurance policies is at a tax disadvantage relative to out-of-pocket spending under health insurance policies.

The difference in tax treatment effectively doubles the cost of health insurance for people who must purchase it themselves. For example, the family of a self-employed person earning $35,000 per year, paying federal and state taxes with only a 30 percent deduction, and paying Social Security taxes must earn $7,075 to pay for a $4,000 health insurance policy. A person working for a small business that offers no health insurance would have to earn $8,214 to pay for that $4,000 policy.

As a result, Americans increasingly have been driven to pay for their health care through third-party insurers and to purchase that insurance, when possible, through their employers. This, in turn, has led to rising health care costs while making it harder for Americans without employer-provided insurance to obtain coverage.

There are many reasons that Americans spend so much on health care. They include:

- **Demographics.** The population of the United States is growing older rapidly. Because the elderly require more—and more costly—health care, the U.S. system must absorb costs that the other systems avoid.

- **Lifestyle.** The United States has much higher rates of such social problems as AIDS, drug abuse, teen pregnancy, and violent crime, all of which lead to increased health care costs. Costs also are affected by such lifestyle decisions as smoking, diet, and exercise.
- **Significant U.S. investment in medical technology.** This includes significant investment in both research and development.

Only recently, however, has serious attention been given to another major reason for rising health care costs in the United States: third-party payment.

HOW THIRD-PARTY PAYMENT INCREASES HEALTH CARE COSTS

Most Americans do not pay directly for most of their health care. The overwhelming majority have health insurance that pays the bills. On average, for every dollar of health care services purchased, a third party pays 76 cents.[4] As a result, consumers have little incentive to question costs and every incentive to demand more services.

Compounding this problem is the fact that most Americans do not pay even directly for their health insurance. Nearly 85 percent of working Americans receive health insurance through their employers. By shielding consumers from the consequences of their health care purchasing decisions, the third-party payment system encourages excessive use of medical services and drives up health care costs.

The concept of "excessive" medical use has a very precise meaning in economic analysis. When the marginal value of the resources used in a medical treatment is greater than the marginal value provided to the patient by that medical treatment, the treatment is classified as "excessive." (It should be noted, however, that this economic concept does not require that the treatment be entirely without value.)

Under normal conditions, an individual will purchase treatment when the cost equals the actual value (determined most easily by the average price that all individuals are willing to pay) plus the individual's idiosyncratic value of the treatment.[5] This idiosyncratic value may be positive or negative. Not all patients assign the same value to a given procedure. How they view it includes many factors, such as peace of mind, threshold for pain, concern over missing work, and so on. Also relevant are "physician-induced demand" (a physician's ability to talk a patient into having a procedure) and even a patient's reaction to advertising.

Thus, under optimal conditions, a treatment would be purchased if $V_a + V_i = C$, in which V_a is the average amount that individuals are willing to pay, V_i is the idiosyncratic value to the patient, and C is the cost of the treatment.

Most Americans, however, are insured for a substantial portion of treatment costs. Therefore, most patients are not dealing with the cost (C); rather, they are dealing with the perceived cost (I x C), in which I is the fraction of the total cost actually paid by the patient. A patient will tend to purchase treatment whenever $V_a + V_i > I \times C$. Therefore, whenever $I \times C < 1$, there will be a tendency on the part of the patient to overconsume. As we have seen, the proportion of costs actually being paid by the purchaser has been declining rapidly. Thus, the value of I x C has been decreasing. It is no surprise, therefore, that patients have been overconsuming health care and driving up total health care spending.

To cite a practical example, assume a patient had a headache. If aspirin cost $1,000 per pill, the patient would be likely to decide to live with the pain. On the other hand, if it cost a penny per 1,000 pills, he might well treat not only the headache, but every other ache and pain as well. Now assume that every person had a magnetic resonance imaging (MRI) brain scan as part of his or her annual physical. Relatively little value would result: A handful of brain tumors might be caught earlier. But if insurance paid for an unlimited number of MRIs, thereby eliminating the cost to the patient, more patients might choose to have the procedure. Because MRIs cost nearly $1,000 each, health care costs would rise considerably.

Some of the most compelling evidence that third-party payments alter the use of medical resources comes from a study performed under the auspices of the RAND Corporation in the late 1970s.[6] The study assigned families to four health insurance plans with differing coinsurance provisions and deductibles. Coinsurance is the percentage of medical bills paid out of pocket by the patient; the deductible measures the maximum dollar amount that a family must pay out of pocket before the plan will drop the coinsurance requirement and pick up the remaining medical bill. Some families had no coinsurance, meaning that the plan paid all of their medical bills, while others had to pay up to 95 percent of their medical bills until they reached a deductible of $1,000 in 1973 dollars (approximately $2,850 in today's dollars).

The RAND researchers observed how the different coinsurance rates influenced the use of medical resources by 2,500 families for three to five years. They concluded that "The data from the Health Insurance Experiment clearly show that the use of medical services responds to changes in the amount paid out-of-pocket."[7] In particular, families with no coinsurance used 30 percent more hospital services (measured in dollars) and 67 percent more visits to doctors, drugs, and the like than did the group that paid 95 percent coinsurance. Overall, the total use of medical resources was 46 percent greater for the group with no coinsurance.

Even smaller coinsurance rates produced savings. The study found that an individual with a 50 percent co-payment spent 25 percent less on health care than an individual with no co-payment. It also found no measurable difference in health status observed between these groups during the course of the experiment.[8]

The RAND study essentially confirms earlier studies by Martin Feldstein and others.[9] In addition, studies of specific health care services such as mental health[10] and prescription drugs[11] have shown that consumers will make cost-conscious decisions.

There also is evidence that prices will be reduced in response to cost-sensitive purchasing by consumers. For example, a study by Joseph Newhouse and Charles Phelps found that a 10 percent increase in out-of-pocket expenditures resulted in a 2 percent reduction in the price of physician services.[12] Several additional studies also have found that increased third-party payment led to price increases.[13]

There are only three ways to limit health care spending. Government can do it, insurance companies can do it, or individual consumers can do it. Take the MRI example described above. Government can prevent people from having MRIs with their annual physicals either by directly prohibiting them or by limiting the number of MRI units available. Insurance companies can do it through managed care, with a "gatekeeper" to ration the availability of MRIs.

The final alternative is for the individual consumer to do it for himself. But that will occur only when the cost to the consumer reflects the value.

If out-of-pocket health care payments and individually purchased health insurance received the same tax treatment as employer-provided insurance, people would be more inclined to purchase insurance with high deductibles. They would reserve insurance for the type of risk-based catastrophe for which it was intended and reduce reliance on third-party payment for routine, low-cost expenditures.

JOB-BASED INSURANCE AND THE UNINSURED

A second serious problem with our current health care system is that insurance is linked so closely to employment. If you lose your job or change jobs, you are in danger of losing your insurance.

Of the estimated 40 million Americans without health insurance at any given time, half are uninsured for four months or less, and only 15 percent are uninsured for more than two years.[14] Essentially, these are people who have lost their jobs and, therefore, their insurance.

Yet these people did not lose their homeowners insurance or their auto insurance. The reason they lost their health insurance is that it alone is linked to employment through the tax code. If the tax code did not give preference to health insurance purchased through an employer, people would be more inclined to purchase insurance individually, with employers acting as little more than brokers, or through nonemployer groups. In that case, the individual, not the employer, would own the health insurance policy, making it fully portable.

Moreover, the difference in tax treatment influences who receives insurance in the first place. Workers who must purchase their insurance with after-tax dollars are 24 times more likely to be uninsured than those who are eligible for tax-free employer-provided coverage.[15] Significantly, the poor and minorities, who are less likely to have employer-provided insurance, are most likely to be left without access to health insurance.[16] Thus, the perverse impact of our tax policies is to penalize those least able to afford health insurance.

The lesson is clear: Changing the tax treatment of insurance will help solve two of the most important problems facing the health care system in the United States. By encouraging Americans to move away from first-dollar third-party insurance, changing the tax code will help reduce health care costs. Moreover, it will break the link between insurance and employment, thereby helping to extend coverage to the uninsured.

NOTES

[1] Health Care Finance Administration, *Health Care Finance Review,* Vol. 16, No. 4 (Summer 1995), p. 235.

[2] *Federal Tax Policy and the Uninsured: How U.S. Tax Laws Deny 10 Million Americans Access to Health Insurance* (Washington, D.C.: Health Care Solutions for America, January 1992).

[3] Internal Revenue Service, *Statistics of Income Bulletin,* Spring 1991, p. 1.

[4] John Goodman and Gerald Musgrave, *Patient Power: The Free-Market Solution to America's Health Crisis* (Washington, D.C.: Cato Institute, 1993), p. 77.

[5] David Dravone, "The Five W's of Utilization Review," in Robert Helms, ed., *American Health Policy: Critical Issues for Reform* (Washington, D.C.: AEI Press, 1993), p. 241.

[6] Joseph Newhouse et al., "Some Interim Results from a Controlled Trial of Cost Sharing in Health Insurance," *New England Journal of Medicine,* Vol. 305, No. 25 (December 17, 1981), pp. 1501–1507.

[7] Willard Manning et al., "Health Insurance and the Demand for Medical Care: Evidence from a Randomized Experiment," *American Economic Review,* Vol. 77 (June 1987), pp. 251–273.

[8] *Ibid.*

[9] See, for example, Martin Feldstein, "Econometric Studies of Health Economics," in D. Kendrick and M. Intrilligator, eds., *Frontiers of Quantitative Economics* (Amsterdam: North Holland Press, 1974); Richard Eichhorn and LuAnn Aday, *The Utilization of Health Services:*

Indices and Correlates: A Research Bibliography, NTIS No. PB–211 720 (1972); and Avedis Donabedian, *Benefits in Medical Care Programs* (Cambridge, Mass.: Harvard University Press, 1974).

[10] Richard Frank, "Pricing and Location of Physician Services in Mental Health," *Economic Inquiry,* Vol. 23, No. 4 (October 1985), pp. 115–133, and John Wallen, Paul Roddy, and Michael Fahs, "Cost Sharing, Mental Health Benefits, and Physical Complaints in Retired Miners and Their Families," a paper published by the American Public Health Association, 1982.

[11] Alan Liebowitz, Willard Manning, and Joseph Newhouse, "The Demand for Prescription Drugs as a Function of Cost-Sharing," *Social Science and Medicine,* Vol. 21, No. 10 (1985), pp. 1063–1069.

[12] Joseph Newhouse and Charles Phelps, "New Estimates of Price and Income Elasticities," in Robert Rosset, ed., *The Role of Health Insurance in Health Sector Services* (New York, N.Y.: National Bureau of Economic Research, 1976), pp. 261–320.

[13] See, for example, Frank Sloan, "Effects of Health Insurance on Physician Fees," *Journal of Human Resources,* Vol. 17, No. 4 (Fall 1982), pp. 533–557.

[14] Bureau of the Census, Current Population Reports, Series P70–37, and unpublished data.

[15] Jill Foley, *Uninsured in the United States: The Nonelderly Population Without Health Insurance* (Washington, D.C.: Employee Benefits Research Institute, April 1991).

[16] *Ibid.*

3

HIGH ANXIETY: WORKING FAMILIES NEED MARKET-BASED HEALTH CARE REFORM

Robert Emmet Moffit, Ph.D.

INTRODUCTION

Many American workers and their families are in a state of high anxiety. They are insecure in their jobs, and many fear that losing their jobs also could mean losing their health insurance. There is an attraction to public policies that would reduce their insecurity. Meanwhile, surveys show that the majority of Americans are unfriendly to health care reform measures that would compromise what they feel are the best features of the health care system. The pharmaceutical, medical device, and biomedical research communities give Americans access to an astonishing level of rapidly advancing medical technology. At the same time, however, more Americans are uneasy about the quality of the medical care they get from managed care arrangements made by their employers. The growing popular concerns about "quality" are relatively new.[1]

Nonetheless, there is still broad popular dissatisfaction with the health care system, echoing President Bill Clinton's 1993 description of it as "badly broken." The number of Americans with no health insurance at all is growing, reaching approximately 44 million at any one time. Even though recent annual declines in corporate insurance premiums are welcome, both business leaders and employees harbor a residual fear of a significant rise in future costs. Moreover, physicians still are frustrated with unreformed and costly medical malpractice laws, and employers and employees remain dissatisfied with the paperwork and cumbersome administration of insurance claims processing.

TWO CHOICES

In reforming the health care system, it is important for policymakers at the federal and state levels to recognize that the universe of policy options is shrinking. The United States has a health care system that is best described as a "mixed economy" with a cumbersome and interlocking system of public and private arrangements. The public (meaning taxpayer-funded) sector of the health care economy is growing rapidly. Today, huge and rapidly growing government health care programs, primarily Medicare and Medicaid, make up almost half of all health care spending. The public portion of the health care dollar is projected, even under the most conservative reform proposals in Congress, to grow substantially in the foreseeable future. Beyond the government programs, moreover, the private health insurance market itself is one of the most highly regulated sectors (if not *the* most highly regulated sector) of the U.S. economy.

Over the past half-century of intermittent debate over government involvement in financing health care, Americans have traveled a very long and controversial road. It is not clear what the outcome will be, but the choice will be between government-run health care, including federal or state financing and control, and the free market, including real consumer choice and serious competition.

Regrettably, the current trajectory of health care policy in the United States and the evolution of the health care market are not in a direction that would be recognizable to Professor Adam Smith, the father of modern political economy and author of *The Wealth of Nations* (1776). Current trends, particularly in financing, point to something far less liberal, in the very best and noblest sense of that ancient word, and far less humane.

The problem certainly is not that members of Congress and state legislators suffer from any lack of market-based reforms from which to choose. If anything, their problem is sorting out the most prudent policies from among a wide range of conservative and libertarian proposals for reforming the health care system. The Heritage Foundation's comprehensive tax credit proposal is just one of the most prominent contributions to the national debate,[2] but there are many others as well.

UNFINISHED BUSINESS

Americans who think that the current system is structurally unsound have one thing in common: They are right. While federal and state policymakers speak in the largely unintelligible jargon of complex cost-control methodologies and arcane insurance market rules, workers and their families are anxious about the deficiencies of the current system. They suffer from these deficiencies in concrete and often painful ways.

First, there has been no portability in the employment-based health insurance system.[3] If a worker loses or changes his job, he does not lose his life insurance or his auto insurance or his homeowner's insurance. But he does lose his health insurance: the insurance that protects him and his family in case of serious illness or accident. The reason: It does not belong to him. Considering that Americans live and work in an information age characterized both by rapid technological advances and a high degree of mobility in the work force, the current system of employment-based health insurance not only is outdated, but also represents absurd social policy.

The absence of portability often confounds workers and their families. It is not immediately clear to them why they can change jobs or move from job to job without losing any insurance except health insurance. But there is, of course, a specific reason for it: Unlike every other type of insurance that American workers and their families buy, they do not buy their own health insurance, at least not directly, and therefore do not own it. Instead, the employer owns the policy.[4]

There are specific historical and economic reasons for this arrangement. Employment-based policies conveniently spread risk over the employees' group. As Robert Helms of the American Enterprise Institute, my colleagues at the Heritage Foundation, and many others have shown, the current structure of the employment-based health insurance system is also deeply rooted in the wartime economic conditions and compensation and tax policies of the 1940s.[5] Even though those wartime policies of price controls and rationing long since have disappeared in the mists of memory, and even though the compensation requirements of workers entering the twenty-first century are radically different from those of the 1940s, the basic tax policy and its dominance over our health insurance remain virtually unchanged: American workers can get meaningful tax relief for the purchase of health insurance only if they get their insurance through their employers.

For a variety of reasons, the impact on workers and their families of this federal tax treatment is dramatically disparate. There are big "winners" and "losers" in the current system. If, on the one hand, a worker is employed in a large corporation (often self-insured) with a large benefits package, the tax benefits are likewise generous, and the worker and his family receive a substantial portion of income tax-free. If, on the other hand, a worker is middle- or low-income and is employed in a smaller company with a smaller benefits package, the tax breaks are proportionately less generous. Low-skilled workers often do not command a wage that enables them to buy health insurance, and they get little if any government assistance in purchasing it.

Fortune plays a decisive role. For American workers and their families, much depends on the size of the company; large companies generally have a higher proportion of their personnel covered by health insurance and offer a richer benefits package. If a company offers workers and their families no health insurance at all, their options are severely limited. Workers can purchase individual policies, assuming they are not disqualified because of medical status, but these policies are likely to be prohibitively expensive. There are several reasons for this.

- First, the price of a policy may include the price of politically ordained health benefits, providers, or procedures mandated by the legislature of a particular state, ranging from mandatory coverage of chiropractic services and mammography screening to in-vitro fertilization, speech therapy, and rehabilitation for alcohol or substance abuse. This drives up the cost of premiums.

- Second, it also includes the cost of marketing individual policies, which obviously is more expensive than the cost of marketing group insurance.
- Finally, and even more important, workers must purchase their individual policies with after-tax dollars, which makes them even more expensive. Even though recent legislation has rectified this to some extent with deductibility for part of the costs of health insurance for the self-employed, it is far from the 100 percent exclusion from taxation enjoyed by workers in company-based plans.

For most middle-income workers and their families, today's purchase of an individual health insurance policy simply is not realistic financially. In good times or in bad, American workers have every reason to be concerned about health insurance costs.

RESTRICTED ALTERNATIVES

The basic economic consequence of the federal tax treatment of health insurance is that it severely constrains the market. Workers and their families, as consumers, are operating in an economic environment in which the only realistic option available to them is employer-based insurance. The economic effect of federal tax policy, therefore, is to confine Americans to one kind of health insurance: employment-based insurance. Naturally, the effect of this restriction on the supply of alternatives is like the effect of restricting supply in any market: Normal market efficiencies are frustrated or forgone, and the normal competitive pressures to control costs or moderate prices are lessened or lost altogether. It takes little imagination to picture what life, auto, or homeowner's insurance would be like if Congress subjected them to the same type of tax policy. Imagine, for example, what the housing market would be like if a homeowner could deduct his mortgage only if his employer selected the real estate agent or purchased the home. Needless to say, any attempt by Congress to apply the restrictive federal tax treatment of health insurance to the housing market in this manner would be dismissed as madness.

The paradox of this "New Deal" tax policy is its perverse impact on low-income working families. Tax policy in the United States historically has been "progressive," meaning that the rate of taxation rises with income; the higher one's income, the higher one's tax liability. But the tax treatment of employment-based health insurance is stunning in its regressivity. The more a person makes, the more valuable the tax treatment of employment-based health insurance.

This regressivity has been studied many times by economists in both the public and private sectors. A 1998 analysis by the Lewin Group, a leading econometric firm, revealed that families making less than $15,000 a year received an average tax break of about $63 a year.[6] For families making over $100,000 a year, it was over $2,000. Lewin and others have shown that the biggest tax breaks—the largest bloc of tax-free income—goes to upper-income families, while relatively little goes to lower-income families. On the basis of the earlier Lewin analysis, my colleagues at the Heritage Foundation have calculated that approximately 25 percent of the total tax relief for company-based health insurance in the United States goes to families making $75,000 a year or more.

For members of Congress, the stubborn insistence on the current tax treatment reflects their commitment to an odd and enduring social policy: from each according to his labor and to each according to the height of his tax bracket. In other words, the premise of federal tax policy seems to be that while health insurance is a "social good," its tax benefits are to be distributed disproportionately to upper-income workers and their families—the very people who need them the least. This is modern America's equivalent of the Bourbon dynasty's tax policy.[7]

Policymakers at the federal level who want to reform health care by building on the current "free-market" private-sector model, thus retaining the current federal tax treatment, logically must insist, therefore, on retaining this regressive tax structure and all its odd inequities.

ACCESS, EXCESS, AND DUPLICATION

The paradox of regressivity in the federal tax treatment of employment-based health insurance gives rise to other inequities. Yet another paradox in the health insurance market is that workers and their families often lack insurance in the traditional sense—that is, insurance against real risk or a catastrophic event. Instead, they have tax-subsidized prepaid medical care, obtained almost exclusively through the place of work. Workers at large profitable companies may have access to a generous package of benefits; those who command low wages or who have the misfortune of working for companies without great financial resources, however, will be among a growing minority of Americans—approximately 18 percent at the present time—with no health insurance at all.[8] Or they will have company-based coverage but with significant and financially devastating gaps, such as the absence of catastrophic coverage. Or they will have generous, even excessive coverage, which they do not purchase but nevertheless pay for indirectly. Some Americans are overinsured by being enrolled in costly "Cadillac" health plans that they would not think of buying if they were spending their own money directly on such coverage. Some families, including retirees, have two or even three policies with duplicative coverage.

THE BROKEN MARKET

The ultimate paradox, of course, is that members of the business community often defend private-sector health insurance arrangements as models of the market and identify the various rapid and recent changes, including managed care, as "triumphs of the free market." But the health insurance market is not a "free market" in the normal sense.

Although the health care system in the United States still is largely private, it does not operate on the free-market principle of consumer choice. As noted, the competition that does exist is largely competition among employment-based plans: Corporate insurance executives bargain with corporate benefits managers, there is no normal collision between the forces of supply and demand at the consumer level, and the customer is distinct from the consumer. Most consumers of health care—the majority of American workers and their families—do not purchase health insurance; it is purchased for them by the companies that employ them. These companies are the real insurance customers. For them, offering a good health benefits package is sound compensation policy, and their payments for employee health insurance, like wages, are tax-deductible. For workers, health insurance often is perceived as an added benefit on top of wages, and sometimes even as a "free good" that automatically comes with the job. They often think the company pays for it, but appearances disguise the true nature of the economic transaction. Company health insurance is not free to workers and their families, and companies, no matter how generous or beneficent, *give* their workers nothing. Too many Americans still do not understand either this relationship or how much the company actually pays them in the form of health care benefits.[9]

Employers spend the money of their employees. On this central point, regardless of ideological persuasion or political bias, economists overwhelmingly agree. For every increase in company-based health benefits, there is a proportionate decrease in wages and other benefits. Health benefits, like wages, are compensation. American workers, not employers, bear 100 percent of their own and their families' health care costs.[10] But the trade-offs are not always clear to them.

Within the framework of company-based health insurance, the economic problem of health care costs has been generated by both appearance and reality. It is fair to say that the problem is broadly psychological rather than narrowly economic. To the extent that workers think health insurance is an "add-on" or a free good, they have no natural economic incentive to curtail this demand for health care services. Free goods invite high utilization.

This brings us to another paradox of the federal tax treatment of health insurance: A worker who indulges in an unrestrained demand for "free" medical services is acting in an economically rational manner. It would be irrational for him to do otherwise under traditional employment-based arrangements, because any immediate savings from cost-effective health care decisions will go into the coffers of the company, not into his own pocket.

Thus, within the context of tax-favored, employer-based insurance, one cannot expect traditional fee-for-service medicine to control costs. The incentives on the demand side to increase costs are complemented by similar incentives on the supply side. Among liberal health policy analysts, a dominant theme has been that the health care market is "supply-driven," and thus that the key to cost control invariably is the tough application of various complicated fee schedules or government price controls on doctors and hospitals.[11]

Under the traditional fee-for-service model that prevailed until recently in employment-based health insurance, doctors and hospitals normally were paid on a cost-plus basis. They obviously had no incentive to control costs or curtail services, including services that might be of only marginal benefit to workers and their families. If physicians are paid on a cost-plus basis, the more services they provide, the more money they make. It is easy to see the reason that doctors have a different kind of relationship with patients who do not pay directly for their own health care or insurance. If doctors had to deal with patients as consumers—as individuals seeking the best value for each medical dollar—they would enter into a different economic relationship with them. Under fee-for-service, the doctor is deeply committed to the welfare of his patients, but the patient also happens to be the doctor's point of entry into the lucrative third-party payment system. It is a system in which a corporate bureaucracy, executing the indemnity contract with the patient's employer, is ready and able to pay the "usual and customary" or reasonable charges—in other words, the highest fees the physician can charge the third party without appearing outrageous. It is easy to see why that traditional arrangement is disappearing so rapidly.

Without the normal collision of supply and demand that characterizes other sectors of the economy, and considering that consumers and suppliers of medical services are largely insulated from the economic decisions they make, it is no surprise that health care costs have been difficult to control. The supply and demand incentives built into the very structure of the system have been set to increase rather than constrain health care costs.

THE FORCED MARCH TO MANAGED CARE

During the 1980s, as the cost of traditional fee-for-service medicine was increasing by double digits, an increasing number of companies responded by offering managed care plans, such as health maintenance organizations (HMOs). The result has been nothing less than a breathtaking transformation of the health insurance market in a relatively short period. The percentage of workers enrolled in employer-sponsored fee-for-service plans dropped from 71 percent to 49 percent between 1988 and 1993 alone.[12] Today, more than three-quarters of all employees in the private sector are enrolled in some form of managed care plan. Promising to protect the business community's bottom line, managed care companies dominate employment-based insurance.

Managing patient care is what managed care insurance companies do. Physicians are members of a network, governed by internal rules and guidelines designed to ensure "appropriate" medical care. Although a patient may or may not have the choice of doctor, the ratio of doctors to patients in the typical HMO is about half that found in other plans. Generally, doctors in HMOs must spend less time with patients compared with doctors in fee-for-service medicine. Not surprisingly, waiting times in excess of one month for nonemergency services are "twice as prevalent" among HMOs as they are among traditional indemnity plans.[13]

Managed care organizations have different structures, attributes, and deficiencies and are evolving constantly, but their rapid rise to "market" dominance is the latest variation of tax-supported employment-based insurance. Thus, the rise of managed care, whatever its benefits, is no triumph of free-market forces. Consumer choice in employment-based insurance still is limited, frustrated, or nonexistent. The key decisions still are made by employers, corporate benefit managers, and insurance executives, not by consumers. Decision-making by doctors is similarly constrained.

Unlike a genuine free market, managed care involves an unusual distinction between consumer and customer. The interests of each are rarely the same. In choosing the managed care plan, the employer, not the worker, is the customer. The consumer (worker), for all practical purposes, has no property rights in health insurance. The insurance seller does not compete with other sellers for the consumer's dollars, and the consumer cannot realize any savings from cost-conscious buying. The rise of managed care, therefore, is anything but a triumph of the free market: In most instances, there is neither consumer demand nor a consumers' market.

Corporate benefits managers are moving to managed care because companies no longer can afford traditional indemnity insurance. In many instances, this amounts to a reduction in workers' compensation. Companies could avoid this problem by paying workers the clear and specific difference between the higher-cost traditional plan and the lower-cost managed care plan. Based on the preliminary evidence, it is fair to say that, even though managed care invariably yields transitional savings for employers, it is disputable whether it will be able to maintain high quality and consumer satisfaction while containing costs.[14] Employment-based coverage can improve to the degree to which employers offer a broader range of health care choices, possibly through the use of a "defined contribution" system for health insurance.

Even managed care insurance options can flourish under consumer choice and competition. Perhaps the best example is the current Federal Employees Health Benefits Program (FEHBP), a unique consumer-driven health system with over 300 options nationwide that serves 9 million Americans, including members of Congress and their staffs.[15] Within the FEHBP, members of Congress and federal workers and retirees can choose for themselves what types of plans and benefits they want and what they are willing to pay for them. Currently, approximately 40 percent of subscribers are enrolled in various managed care plans, and surveys of federal workers and retirees report a very high degree of satisfaction with the system. This satisfaction may well be a reflection of the crucial difference between FEHBP enrollees and workers enrolled in most private health insurance arrangements: If federal participants do not like a plan or service, they can fire the insurance company.

Without the pressure of consumer choice and competition, managed care will be plagued by perverse incentives that are the opposite of those found in traditional health insurance. Where a fee-for-service system enables physicians and other providers to make more money by rendering more services, managed care rewards physicians for providing fewer services. This is akin to importing the absurdities of federal agricultural subsidies into the health care sector of the economy.

From the standpoint of the market, the future of managed care, and the personal freedom of workers and their families, much depends on the broader direction of health care reform. HMOs under the "managed competition" regimes proposed by some members of Congress and several state legislators will curtail, not enhance, consumer choice. If consumers are given a "choice" of as many as two dozen HMOs in any region of the country, with all offering the same government-standardized benefits plan and only one (or even no) fee-for-service plan, the inevitable result will be to foreclose the possibility of any meaningful range of options for American workers and their families.

THE FUTURE DIRECTION OF REFORM

The American people once again are at a critical juncture in health policy. Ultimately, members of Congress have only two choices: They can adopt a government-run health care system along the lines of the British, Canadian, or Clinton-style model or they can eliminate the distortions in the U.S. health insurance market and recreate a sound market in the financing and delivery of health care. There is no third way. Indeed, close examination of the various incremental reforms in Congress invariably reveals a structural bias toward one or the other of these two diametrically opposed options.[16]

If members of Congress refuse to open up the health care market, thereby allowing people more freedom of choice and compelling insurance companies into genuine competition for consumer dollars, they probably will wind up attempting to build on the current system. But if they insist on doing that, they must recognize that the current system is characterized by severe distortions in the health insurance market. They will have to compensate for these distortions and their accompanying problems and paradoxes by imposing various mandates and regulations, largely under the rubric of insurance reform, to accomplish what otherwise would be accomplished by market forces through a tax reform that empowers the consumer.

Building on the current system, therefore, inevitably means restricting the health care system even more and increasing the role of bureaucracy in the activities of doctors, hospitals, and the insurance industry. It means barring real consumer choice and genuine competition, and reducing doctors and hospitals to the status of highly regulated public utilities.

THE CLINTON PLAN

President Clinton's health plan was perhaps the best example of comprehensive reform within the framework of the current system. It proved to be a heavy mixture of government and private employer-based insurance. The president's plan simply expanded the direct control of the federal government over an already highly regulated private sector.[17]

President Clinton and members of his administration persist in claiming that critics "misrepresented" his plan as a government-run health care system. In promoting it, the president initially employed the language of consumer choice and competition, condemning bureaucracy as "wasteful and inefficient" and calling for "simplicity" in the health care system. But the specifics he presented to Congress in 1993 in a 1,342-page bill portrayed an entirely different system: a national health board with vast regulatory powers, hundreds of government-sponsored "regional health alliances" to control the "market" in every sector of the country, and a mandate on employers and individuals that amounted to a hefty new federal payroll tax on labor and business.

MANAGED COMPETITION

Another variant of government control of health care is the "managed competition" model, produced by a group of scholars associated with the prestigious Jackson Hole Group and currently a prominent model for health care reform at the state level. Combining the elements of market competition and government management, this model has proven to be politically attractive. But "managed competition" is a politically unstable platform for health care reform. Even though its proponents correctly diagnose the key weakness of the current system—an absence of price competition that undermines the efficiency of the health care system—they prescribe a regulatory infrastructure that will be even more restrictive, more bureaucratic, and perhaps even more costly than today's.[18]

CONSUMER CHOICE

There is no lack of options for market-based health care reform. If anything, Congress confronts a veritable inflation of ideas and proposals. John Goodman of the National Center for Policy Analysis, Robert Helms of the American Enterprise Institute, Mark Pauly of the Wharton School at the University of Pennsylvania, John Hoff of the Galen Institute, and Michael Tanner of the Cato Institute, among many others in the market-based health care community, have advanced innovative proposals for reform.[19] Likewise, my colleagues at the Heritage Foundation have developed a comprehensive health care proposal based on consumer choice and competition.

Under the Heritage proposal, every American family, regardless of employment status, would receive a voucher or tax credit in place of the current tax exclusion. Families could use that tax relief for health insurance, out-of-pocket medical costs, or a tax-free medical savings account from which they could pay medical bills directly. The tax relief would be targeted at need. Using a sliding scale of refundable tax credits, more help would go to families with low incomes or high medical bills.

As a condition for receiving a credit or voucher, the head of every family would be required to purchase at least a basic package of catastrophic coverage. By shifting tax breaks directly to families, the Heritage plan would change the health insurance market from an employer-based to a consumer-based market. It would stimulate intense competition among insurance carriers and set off an explosion of group insurance outside the workplace, enabling trade associations, unions, professional associations, and even church groups and religious institutions to sponsor health insurance, as well as community-based clinics and other health care services. The intense competition for consumers' dollars would control costs, much as it controls the cost of other goods and services everywhere else in the economy.[20]

As noted, an econometric analysis of the Heritage plan conducted by the Lewin Group shows that virtually every income group in the United States would be better off under a tax credit system. Families making $30,000 to $40,000 per year would be helped most.[21]

It is worth noting that the superiority of a tax credit approach to health care financing was underscored by a March 1994 study by the Congressional Budget Office, which observed that "by providing a larger subsidy for low income families, a credit would encourage more people to secure health insurance, reduce adverse selection, and discourage free riders."[22]

CONCLUSION

Congress has neglected the fundamental problems of the health care system in the United States. This system cannot be improved unless policymakers reform the health insurance market, and the health insurance market cannot be reformed until Congress changes the tax policy that governs it. Serious health care reform, therefore, depends on serious tax reform. Legislative manipulations of a distorted insurance market are no substitute for genuine reform.

Congress can be assured that, without genuine reform, matters will get worse. For workers and their families, this is still a time of high anxiety. The reasons are obvious. Far too many people are uninsured, and the number is rising and will continue to rise. Far too many people still have gaps in their coverage that leave them vulnerable to catastrophic illness and its financial devastation. Moreover, the enactment of the Health Insurance Portability and Accountability Act of 1996 (Kassebaum–Kennedy) has not substantially addressed, let alone resolved, these problems. Congress has imposed an unprecedented level of regulation on the individual insurance market to mitigate the problem of workers losing their health insurance when they change jobs, but this is merely regulatory compensation for a failure to address the tax-related distortions in the health care sector of the economy. There still is no true portability in health insurance, and there never will be true portability until people can own their own policies.

Finally, the good news about health care costs is not likely to last. Even though corporate premiums are down, the dip is only temporary. Health care costs can be expected to rise once again after managed care arrangements have done everything feasible to restrain the supply of medical services. One major reason is that the United States has a rapidly aging population, and the volume and intensity of the demand for medical services is bound to increase.

Economics cannot solve every social problem, and the market does have its limits. But it is a masterful engine of efficiency and pricing. It would be unfortunate if health care costs increased without benefit of the happy collision of supply and demand. The discipline of the market chastens the demand for goods "somebody else" pays for and roots out inefficiencies of supply with a vengeance. If we do not rely on the free market for health care services, American workers and their families will not be able to afford the consequences.

NOTES

[1] Public opinion during the 1994 debate on health care reform is summarized in *American Attitudes Toward Health Care, Health Care Reform and The Clinton Plan,* prepared for the Heritage Foundation by

Fabrizio, McLaughlin and Associates, January 19, 1994. The public's view of the "quality" of health care has become less favorable since the debate on the Clinton plan.

[2] For a discussion of the Heritage Foundation's Consumer Choice Health Plan, see Stuart M. Butler, "A Policy Maker's Guide to the Health Care Crisis, Part II: The Heritage Foundation Consumer Choice Health Plan," Heritage Foundation *Talking Points,* March 5, 1992. See also Stuart M. Butler and Edmund F. Haislmaier, eds., *A National Health System for America* (Washington, D.C.: The Heritage Foundation, 1989).

[3] The Health Insurance Portability and Accountability Act of 1996 is designed to give workers who leave their jobs the opportunity to take their health insurance with them; but as will be described below, the tax system still discriminates against them in a way that makes the policy much more expensive.

[4] As analysts for the Congressional Budget Office have noted, "Workers who are sick or have a sick family member can get trapped in their jobs because most new insurance policies will not cover the preexisting condition. Finally, because insurance is tied to one's job, it is inherently insecure. Employees can lose their insurance if they lose their jobs or if their employers stop carrying insurance." Congressional Budget Office, *The Tax Treatment of Employment-Based Health Insurance* (Washington, D.C.: U.S. Government Printing Office, March 1994), pp. xii–xiii, 3.

[5] See, for example, *A National Health System for America;* see also Stuart M. Butler, "A Policy Maker's Guide to the Health Care Crisis, Part I: The Debate over Reform," Heritage Foundation *Talking Points,* February 12, 1992.

[6] "Distribution of Federal Health Benefits Tax Expenditures by Family Income in 1996," the Lewin Group, 1998.

[7] The Congressional Budget Office notes that "Families with higher incomes receive larger tax subsidies because they are in higher income tax brackets. Thus, the reduction in taxable income that the

exclusion produces is worth more to them on average than it is to families in lower tax brackets. Because the income tax is progressive, people with relatively high incomes (and high tax rates), who may need the least assistance in getting health insurance, benefit the most from the tax exclusion." Congressional Budget Office, *The Tax Treatment of Employment-Based Health Insurance,* pp. xiv, 4.

[8] Carolyn Pemberton and Deborah Holmes, eds., *EBRI Date Book on Employee Benefits* (Washington, D.C.: Employee Benefits Research Institute, 1995), p. 243.

[9] According to the Washington-based Employee Benefits Research Institute, a 1994 survey of American workers with company-based health insurance revealed that 28 percent thought they paid nothing for it; 50 percent had no idea of the true cost of their package.

[10] Analysts at the Congressional Budget Office have noted how the structure of employment-based health insurance arrangements tends to hide the true cost of the commodity and disguises the way in which working families bear the full cost of health insurance benefits: "An often overlooked point is that the employer share of the cost of 'employer provided' health insurance is ultimately passed on to workers in the form of lower wages and reductions in fringe benefits other than health insurance.... This study calls health insurance that employees receive at work 'employment based' rather than 'employer provided.'" Congressional Budget Office, *The Tax Treatment of Employment-Based Health Insurance,* Introduction.

[11] For an account of the application of these fee schedules in the Medicare system, see Robert E. Moffit, "Comparable Worth for Doctors: A Severe Case of Government Malpractice," Heritage Foundation *Backgrounder* No. 855, September 23, 1991, and Robert E. Moffit, "Back to the Future: Medicare's Resurrection of the Labor Theory of Value," *Regulation,* Fall 1992, pp. 54–63.

[12] Jack Tawil and Frederick Bold, *Reinventing Health Care* (Richland, Wash.: Research Enterprises, 1994), p. 26.

[13] *Ibid.*, p. 8.

[14] See Erik Larson, "The Soul of an HMO," *Time,* January 22, 1996, pp. 44–52.

[15] For a general discussion of the FEHBP, see Robert E. Moffit, "Consumer Choice in Health: Learning from the Federal Employees Health Benefits Program," Heritage Foundation *Backgrounder* No. 878, February 6, 1992.

[16] For an example of the problem of incremental reform, see Stuart M. Butler, John C. Liu, and Robert Rector, "How Incremental Health Care Reform Would Make Things Worse: The Rowland–Bilirakis Bill," Heritage Foundation *Issue Bulletin* No. 203, September 26, 1994.

[17] For a comprehensive description of the Clinton health plan, see Robert E. Moffit, "A Guide to the Clinton Health Plan," Heritage Foundation *Talking Points,* November 19, 1993; see also Stuart M. Butler, "What the Lewin–VHI Analysis of the Clinton Health Plan Really Shows," Heritage Foundation *F.Y.I.* No. 7, January 7, 1994.

[18] For a general discussion of the theory of "managed competition," see Robert E. Moffit, "Overdosing on Management: Reforming the Health Care System Through Managed Competition," Heritage *Lecture* No. 442, April 15, 1993; see also Peter J. Ferrara, "Managed Competition: Less Choice and Competition, More Costs and Government in Health Care," Heritage Foundation *Backgrounder* No. 948, June 29, 1993.

[19] See, for example, John C. Goodman and Gerald L. Musgrave, *Patient Power: Solving America's Health Care Crisis* (Washington, D.C.: Cato Institute, 1992), and Mark Pauly et al., *Responsible National Health Insurance* (Washington, D.C.: AEI Press, 1992).

[20] Beyond these tax changes, the Heritage Foundation plan also includes several key health insurance reforms, including guaranteed renewability of policies, restrictions on exclusions for preexisting conditions, limited underwriting, and the provision of insurance

premium discounts for individuals and families who enroll in preventive health or health promotion programs.

[21] Butler, "A Policy Maker's Guide to the Health Care Crisis, Part II." In a second iteration of the Lewin–VHI econometric analysis, American families did better under the Heritage approach than under the Clinton plan. When the distribution of "winners" and "losers" is broken down by income category, the tax credit approach leads to more "winners" in virtually every income category, including the working poor. See Stuart M. Butler, "How the Clinton and Nickles–Stearns Health Bills Would Affect American Workers," Heritage Foundation *Issue Bulletin* No. 188, April 11, 1994.

[22] Cited in John C. Liu, "What the Congressional Budget Office Says About the Tax Treatment of Employment-Based Insurance," Heritage Foundation *F.Y.I.* No. 16, May 26, 1994.

4

AN EFFICIENT AND EQUITABLE APPROACH TO HEALTH REFORM

Mark V. Pauly, Ph.D.

The goals of health reform never have been controversial. This was true before the Clinton plan, before the Nixon mandate, before Harry Truman's intended completion of the New Deal social agenda—even as far back as World War I and the American Medical Association's brief flirtation with socialized and universal coverage. It is no less true today. Reformers have wanted what polls keep telling us citizens want: a society in which everyone has access to appropriate and efficient medical care.

The problem, then, is not choosing the neighborhood. Rather, the problem is choosing the precise destination and, even more, how we should get there. Some differences over destination arise from different views on which imperfections are tolerable or necessary in this imperfect world. Most differences over means deal with the question of who should win and who must lose in the transition.

This chapter has three objectives. First, I want to argue in favor of a particular vision, which I hope will command some assent. Second, I will argue that extricating ourselves gracefully from the current situation will be much easier if we think of reform as a reformulation of the rules by which we govern ourselves—rules made to benefit everyone in the long run. Third, I will describe how achieving the objectives I propose, via the rules I suggest, eventually will benefit not only citizens as consumers and taxpayers, but also the owners and employees of America's businesses.

OBJECTIVES AND DEFINITIONS

The goal of a health care system is to ensure that people consume adequate amounts of medical care without inappropriately reducing their ability to obtain other things they need and enjoy. Because some medical services are expensive to provide but needed only rarely, insurance is the most sensible way to hedge against some (but not all) medical care costs. One social objective, then, is to assure that each citizen has insurance that leads to the use of appropriate amounts of care.

Those commonsense statements are not much help without further definition of "appropriate." Because we are discussing social choice, it should be obvious that the definition must be a social definition: It must take into account both the individual's own desires and resources and the concerns of others in society. The appropriate amount of care, then, is that amount at which citizens equate marginal benefit to marginal cost; the benefit includes both the person's own value and any additional value others might place on that person's medical care.[1]

While medicine as a science (or art) can provide necessary information on the effectiveness of medical services, this information by itself is insufficient to define appropriateness, because medicine cannot translate effects into benefits or value. Instead, the valuation process must be collective or political, at least in part. In the final analysis, the definition of socially appropriate amounts of care really depends on our attitudes toward unrelieved but treatable illness-related suffering in our fellow citizens. If we believe that additional care will alleviate enough illness to justify our paying for it through taxes or subsidies, the initial level of care obviously was "inappropriate" and inadequate. If, on the other hand, the value of additional care to the individual and to other citizens is not as great as its cost, failure to receive that care does not constitute inappropriateness.

The proper social objective is to achieve appropriate or adequate care and adequate financing as efficiently and equitably as possible. "Efficiency" in economics carries two meanings. One is the commonsense notion of lowest cost; in medical care and insurance, it would mean finding methods that are most likely to approximate the lowest-cost production and sale of adequate insurance. The other, less obvious meaning of efficiency is the satisfaction of different desires or demands. In effect, we want a system that not only minimizes costs, but also produces the amounts and types of products that people most value and then gets them to the right people. Private competitive markets are most "efficient," relative to government provision, because they do a better job of catering to people's different needs and demands, even when markets cannot be proved to have lower costs than the government in the production of some product.

When it comes to medical care and insurance, different Americans want different things. They want different kinds of medical plans, from the restrictive but inexpensive to the open but costly; they attach different values to convenience versus cost; and they differ on how far they want the system to go, both in providing heroic measures and in limiting their choices of treatments and doctors. An efficient system allows these differences to be expressed. But the key element is that, except for people who otherwise would use inadequate care, people's choices should proceed only from their own values and the true cost of alternative ways of achieving their objectives; they should face neutral incentives when choosing between one kind of health insurance and another, when choosing between insuring a medical expense and paying for it out of pocket, and when choosing whether to spend their money on medical care or other goods.

The second part of the social objective is what might be called "general equity." There is no commonly accepted economic definition of the ideal amount of equity. Equity is a social judgment that must be made through the political process established to judge what distribution of rights to general consumption (as opposed to consumption of particular goods about which there is social concern, such as medical care) is fair. So far, this political process has not rendered an unequivocal verdict about how it (or "we") would define equity. It does seem to have ruled some things out as inequitable. A system that allows otherwise similar people with the same income to pay different amounts of taxes is usually regarded as horizontally inequitable and therefore undesirable. Equity judgments about what people at different income levels should pay are more controversial and often represent decisions about trade-offs between redistribution and the distorted incentives that often accompany it. There is good evidence that some methods of distribution would sacrifice growth in total income, and I believe there is general agreement that we should not redistribute income from those with less to those with more.

WHAT WE DO NOW ABOUT HEALTH INSURANCE AND WHAT WE SHOULD DO

The objective of helping people to obtain adequate health insurance certainly accounts in part for public intervention into the medical insurance markets, such as explicit public spending for the elderly and disabled under Medicare and for the poor under Medicaid. Although the vision I will outline for better medical financing also can be applied to these programs, I will concentrate on a less visible but equally important way by which we help people buy insurance: the exclusion from taxation of health insurance premiums paid by employers.

Surely, part of the reason the exclusion exists is that people correctly believe it helps some to afford insurance. The new vision embraces the objective of assisting and encouraging people to buy adequate insurance. This is a desirable goal, but the current system is too inefficient and inequitable to achieve it effectively. There is a better way. The tax exclusion is mistargeted, miscalibrated, and open-ended. Specifically, it is available only to employees at firms with group coverage; it offers stronger incentives to persons at higher tax rates, usually persons earning higher incomes; and insurance is encouraged even when it is in excess of a socially adequate amount. The vision entails abolishing the exclusion and replacing it with a better system to encourage the purchase of insurance.

Removal of this tax distortion could increase the amount of funds government extracts from the private sector. Ordinarily, any sensible person would look upon attempts to increase the flow of funds to the government with skepticism. There is reason for skepticism, even if we thought that the government was going to spend the money wisely: Taxes distort the private sector. Taxation has compliance costs, but as Hall and Rabushka note, those costs are dwarfed by the "indirect economic losses from disincentives" (what economists call the "excess burden" of transferring a dollar from the private to the public sector).[2] However, raising tax funds by removing an existing distortion, as abolition of the tax subsidy would do, is a different proposition altogether. In this case, private-sector distortions actually can be reduced by a transfer of funds to the public sector.

Of course, one must be careful not to take this argument too far. The negative excess burden can occur only because some initial high tax imposed a positive burden on the private sector, and any gain will be wasted if the government uses the money in a way that causes more distortion. Nevertheless, financing a new subsidy to the uninsured by removing the old inefficient tax subsidy means that this is a legitimate exception to the general proposition that higher taxes slow growth or do other bad things to the economy. The additional tax collections are hardly free, but they do represent one of the lowest-cost sources of money for public purposes.

THE BARE ESSENTIALS AND THEIR RATIONALE

If the tax exclusion of employment-based health insurance premiums—including so-called employer-paid premiums and Section 125 plans—were abolished, tax collections at all levels of government would rise by up to $100 billion. That money should be returned immediately to citizens as a reward for purchasing adequate amounts of health insurance. In addition, the method of reward should be efficient, offering no distortive incentives and permitting diversity. The resulting pattern of disposable income should be regarded as generally equitable.

The best way to accomplish those objectives is to return a fixed amount of money to citizens if, and only if, they buy appropriate insurance. There are, as we shall see, several ways to do that, but they all share the goals of rewarding the purchase of appropriate coverage and turning off the subsidy once appropriate coverage has been reached for each person. This fundamental notion allows us to cut through the intellectual clutter that has accumulated as health insurance reform has been discussed and analyzed: If we want people to buy appropriate coverage, we should define appropriate coverage and offer them financial incentives to obtain it.

That simple idea can help us keep our way when we take up the more complicated question of how to implement a public plan in our diverse society. Diversity can be broken down into two parts: variations among persons as to how much coverage is needed for adequate medical services and variations among them as to how large the subsidy should be.

WHO NEEDS WHAT, AND WHAT WILL IT TAKE TO GET HIM THERE?

The level of insurance needed to assure that a poor person will use some amount of medical care is greater than that needed for a wealthier person. The willingness to pay cost-sharing, the valuation of health and health care, and skill in navigating the system all mean that, faced with equal coverage at equal illness levels, higher-income people will surpass lower-income people in the use of health services. To offset this initial inequality, many proposals would vary the level of coverage with income. At a minimum, there is usually some "step" below which very generous coverage is provided to poor people and above which coverage can be less comprehensive and less extensive and still be appropriate.

In a rough-and-ready sense, appropriate coverage could be defined by policies that limit the maximum out-of-pocket payment for medical services to some percentage of income. Whether that percentage should be 10 percent or 12 percent, and whether it might rise slightly as income rises, ultimately is a political decision. It can be informed by evidence indicating how a different percentage might affect the use of services and health, but ultimately it is a social judgment about how much unrelieved suffering we are willing to tolerate.

While the question of optimal coverage can best be formulated by defining and adding up citizen values, there is an undoubted difference between medical care and other goods. When a person gets sick, some medical care is provided in our society, even when he cannot pay. Crude data indicate that, even after adjusting for differences in illness levels, those who pay nothing because they are uninsured use medical care that is 25 to 50 percent less costly than the average insured person's care—but the care still does cost something. Whatever our social judgments about appropriate care, there already are many devices (both public and philanthropic) by which some services are provided to those who cannot pay. We can make charitable care larger or smaller in many ways, but sometimes we cannot refuse it if the need is great. Thus, the reason to seek adequate coverage is not only that it is the right thing to do, but also that it would make the transfers already occurring more efficient and dignified.

ADEQUATE FINANCING FOR ADEQUATE CARE

Although the issues sometimes are combined, level of subsidy and the requirement for adequate insurance coverage really are separate questions. To take the most extreme case, we could decide in theory that poor people need complete coverage but then require them to pay the entire premium themselves. Practicality and equity usually suggest, however, that lower-income people should receive larger subsidies than higher-income people. Of course, the subsidy can be combined with rules or mandates, more or less binding, that also affect behavior. If the subsidy varies with income, it may reduce the incentive to earn.

Another problem is that the subsidy at different incomes required to encourage coverage, along with existing taxes and transfers, also might be regarded as unfair. That is, there may be a clash between effectiveness and equity. In principle, both depend on the aggregate pattern of taxes and transfers. The analysis of health insurance cannot be conducted independently of those other factors. Also in principle, inefficiency can be avoided by mandating insurance; subsidies would be used primarily for distributional objectives, although they also may facilitate enforcement of the mandate.

ELEMENTS AND EXAMPLES OF THE VISION

The vision involves only two actions: specifying the amount of insurance regarded as appropriate for each citizen and offering predetermined-amount incentives to get people to buy it. That approach minimizes government involvement in citizens' lives and yet ensures that all have the opportunity to obtain appropriate coverage.

The fundamental idea, then, is to remove the present distorted incentives, recycle the money the government collects, and target it to those who most need help. But what form should the new incentives take? That is a serious design question that requires a social choice.

Think of taxpayers with lower-middle pretax incomes. Imagine that adequate insurance for this group can be obtained for P dollars and call this the "P policy." How can we act efficiently to induce them to buy that policy?

One way—in many senses the theoretically perfect way—would be simply to mandate purchase. If almost all people at that income level already were purchasing the policy, perhaps a "mandate" to round up the stragglers would be a good idea. After all, that most already buy the policy shows that everyone with this income can afford it; any subsidy would add to the government's expenditures and probably create distorted incentives. Moreover, the minority who fail to obtain coverage and cannot pay for their care are irresponsible free riders who unfairly impose costs on others. They should no more be allowed to go without health insurance than to drive uninspected cars with bad brakes.

The fewer who would buy at least P coverage on their own, the less attractive the "mandate." Enforcing it would be more costly because more people would violate it. Therefore, we may want to consider a subsidy instead. If so, there are two further design questions: (1) should there be a mandate along with the subsidy, and (2) what form should the subsidy take?

A subsidy would make it easier to enforce a mandate, so perhaps the answer to the first question is yes. But the real answer has to do with an overall social judgment about how close to universal coverage we want to be. In the waning, silly days of the Clinton health reform debate, there were serious proposals that 90 or 95 percent coverage be rounded up to "universal coverage" and labeled good enough for government work.

The more serious question is how to pay and structure the subsidy. It could be paid either as an explicit public expenditure in the form of a voucher or as a refundable credit against taxes. From an economic viewpoint, the two are identical. From a political-economic viewpoint, the explicit expenditure often is seen as more conducive to rational decision-making, precisely because explicit expenditures are easier for voters to see than "tax expenditures" (and we need go no further than the tax subsidy for employer-paid insurance to see the confusion caused by back-door methods of financing). There may be some advantages to "spending" public money by netting the voucher against taxes rather than by collecting money on April 15 and giving it back on April 16. If the value of the voucher could be reasonably stable or bear some stable relationship to tax collections (e.g., grow at the same rate), the tax credit might work. If not, perhaps making it explicit would be better.

Designing the subsidy is fairly simple. Suppose the subsidy is S. The rule would be: "You get S dollars only if you obtain at least the P policy"—with no partial subsidies, escalators, or adjustments.

The reason it is best for the subsidy to be fixed is that only then would it not distort decisions about the type and amount of coverage purchased. We expect most people to buy more than the P coverage, but we do not want to subsidize them or distort their additional purchases.

ADJUSTING TAXES TO THE SUBSIDY

A mandate by itself would require no adjustment of the tax system; but when a subsidy is paid, there is an additional question that cannot be avoided: Because a subsidy costs something, how should other taxes be adjusted to remain (or become) equitable and efficient?

The most commonly proposed way is to use credits for the purchase of adequate coverage.[3] Some proposals place more emphasis on limiting the subsidy to a fixed amount, whereas others would increase it somewhat with total spending on insurance to adjust for variation in risk. (More on this below.) However, the fundamental idea was quite similar.

Another possibility is to integrate the vision with a flat tax. The flat tax, as originally proposed by Hall and Rabushka, would tax all income above a personal allowance at a uniform rate. The allowance ideally would be fixed, although it could vary according to, say, family size. Hall and Rabushka do not give a detailed rationale for the allowance other than to say that it would allow the system to be progressive (in the sense that taxes rise more than proportionately with income) and yet have relatively low marginal rates; their plan "limits the burden on the poor. The current federal tax system avoids taxing the poor, and we think it should stay that way."[4] For them, employment-based health benefits and other fringe benefits violate tax neutrality and erode the tax base. They would tax benefits by not allowing them to be deducted from business income as wages are. Presumably, they expect employers to substitute cash for benefits and allow workers to pay their own health insurance premiums (which would not necessarily deprive workers of the advantages of group insurance, since employers still could arrange insurance groups at much lower administrative cost and even withhold cash for what is now erroneously labeled the "employer's share" of the premium).

The report of the National Commission on Economic Growth and Tax Reform gives a fuller explanation of the allowance: "Americans must first be able to feed, clothe, and house their families before they are asked to feed the federal spending machine."[5] I would add the ability to obtain medical insurance to that list. Americans must be able to afford medical care before we call on them to pay taxes. This observation is relevant to the design of the flat tax. Because the design of the flat tax is likely to cause employers to convert insurance into wages for employees, the personal allowance needs to rise by the amount of the insurance cost.

If one is willing to use taxes as well as expenditures to influence behavior, the personal allowance could be helpful. It could be increased if people buy adequate insurance and reduced if they do not. To make the incentives to buy insurance as neutral (or undistorted) as possible, the additional allowance must be fixed and should grow no larger if someone chooses to buy more coverage. In the strongest version, it should not be offered at all if the individual buys either no coverage or less than the socially determined appropriate amount.

How high would the additional allowance have to be? At a minimum, it should equal the cost of a policy. For families, that would be approximately $5,000. But because the income tax base would be increased by the current "employer-paid premiums," tax rates would not have to go up as much. (Hall and Rabushka apparently take the additional revenue into account in estimating the tax rate, so the rate would have to be a little higher if the allowance is higher.) It may be, however, that the tax incentive for coverage would be too small for people with incomes just above the allowance because the reward would be only the tax rate times the cost of the policy. If we think a stronger incentive is needed, and if we are not going to have a mandate, the only alternatives are a larger additional allowance or an explicit subsidy. Either way, the tax rate would have to be higher.

HOW TO GET THERE FROM HERE

One distressing aspect of the reaction to the Tax Reform Commission report is how quickly and blatantly various interest groups calculated their short-term financial pain or gain. This venality is understandable, however: Taxes do have major effects on how much people gain or lose from their interaction with the government. The obvious problem in moving to a fairer distribution of insurance subsidies is that some current gainers will lose in the transition.

The classic theoretical solution to this problem is both elegant and irrelevant: Pay off those who are getting the break. Say that I (as an upper-middle-class person) estimate my tax subsidy—employer payment for premiums and cafeteria plan—to be $2,000 per year. To achieve this large subsidy, I buy the most costly insurance plan my employer offers, deposit the maximum amount in my medical flexible spending account, and have the largest family collection of designer prescription sunglasses on my block. A theoretically ideal solution would be to remove the subsidy in return for a $2,000 tax cut. The problem is that such a tax cut would be seen as unfair, both to people with less income and to people with the same income who spend less extravagantly. So the current inequity and inefficiency persist.

One approach to reform might be to tell people that in 2005 (or some other future date) they will get a tax cut in return for giving up various tax loopholes and exclusions, most especially those related to medical care. The cut for any income group would equal the average tax exclusion in that group.

A person might prefer that arrangement if it became law today, even if it would cost him money, because he is uncertain about his future benefit from the exclusion; after all, his income might fall, his employer might change benefits policy arbitrarily, tax policy might change, or health benefits costs might change. A far-sighted person, however, might realize the good of sacrificing current advantage for a well-designed system that would help him when he needs it most, minimize the tax distortion of his other activities, and lead him to purchase health insurance that delivers the most value for the money. On top of that, the system—unlike the current one—would be fair and stable. It would allow him to plan confidently for the future and feel good in the process.

Two other possible changes, one technical and one political, would be useful. The technical fix, suggested by John Goodman and me, would permit people to surrender their tax breaks in return for the voucher discussed above.[6] I would not expect all to do so, but those whose net benefit from the current system is small relative to the average benefit will gain from taking the money. Careful design could make such a "trade-in" policy revenue neutral.

The political change would be to make the tax structure more difficult to change than the level of public expenditures. Proposals to require supermajorities on tax votes and to replace indirect taxes like the corporation income tax with direct income taxes move in that direction. Such changes would correct what James Buchanan calls the "fiscal illusion," the delusion that government can give people benefits at no cost. In a perfect world, we would not need such devices as a fiscal constitution (nor, for that matter, would we need the real Constitution); all would come together to make rational political choices. But in the real world, it may be better to specify simple rules that determine how government extracts money from the private sector. Then the public, having a clearer recognition of the trade-offs, can decide how much to spend and how to divide that spending among various activities.

If the tax system were operated in this way, there would be no place for a tax subsidy, but there would be a place for a health insurance voucher whose value would be determined by the political process after comparing it with other uses for that tax money. Perhaps the benefits of such a system will be so apparent that the loss of the insurance exclusion would more than be offset by the gains in efficiency.

SOME SPECIAL POPULATIONS

The vision I propose would improve the well-being of the average citizen substantially and also would make people more comfortable with the political process and the medical care financing system. Two groups, however, may feel that movement toward this vision could harm them. The first comprises unusually high-risk people who may believe they are receiving, and stand to lose a subsidy from, the current system. The other comprises employers who are making the payment that is shielded from taxation.

The extent to which high-risk people actually are subsidized may not be large. Moreover, the best way to subsidize those people is not through the tax exclusion, but through explicit government transfers, either by vouchers or a high-risk pool.

Firms or groups that provide health insurance typically do not charge employees premiums that vary with age, likelihood of foreseeable medical expenses, or chronic condition. There is indirect but strong evidence, however, that their wages may be affected by such risk indicators. Wage offsets of 100 percent or more of the additional premium cost have been associated with the likelihood of using pregnancy benefits and with age.[7] Low-risk workers can and do avoid subsidizing high-risk workers by taking jobs at firms that do not offer insurance. They also may go to firms that have relatively few high-risk workers.

In any event, if the current system does subsidize high-risk workers, it will continue to do so to some extent even without the tax subsidy. For medium-sized groups (perhaps 100 workers), the administrative cost advantage of group insurance would be strong enough that it could be expected to emerge even without the tax subsidy. Because the subsidy does not depend on the extent of community rating in the group, the demise of the subsidy should not affect it.

However much the current system subsidizes high-risk people, it does so in an inefficient and unfair way. Subsidies resulting from pooled premiums in employment-based insurance are, as noted, affected by wage levels; they are much larger for those fortunate high-risk employees who are in firms in which low-risk employees pay high marginal tax rates (and in which there are relatively few other high-risk employees).[8] Likewise, high-risk individuals unable to work, or unable to get work in groups with generous insurance, do not receive subsidies. Finally, some subsidies are from young to old or from men to women, regardless of income level; those do not necessarily improve equity. In short, the current system offers the same haphazard subsidy to community rating in the employment group as it does to group insurance in general. High-risk workers still participate in a benefits lottery that may be as variable as risk-rated insurance premiums would have been.

Finally, and most important, there are better ways for society to achieve its presumed objective. One way is to allow insurers to risk-rate premiums and make vouchers higher for low- and moderate-income persons with high-risk conditions. The other is to create pools for high risks, ideally financed with explicit, direct income taxes (not assessments on insurers). Either way, the subsidies could be targeted more precisely at those for whom they are intended.

Employers who now make tax-deductible payments for insurance on behalf of their employees also fear loss of the exemption. Many versions of the flat tax would tax employer payments, as would some of the health reform proposals from 1994. The alternative proposal is to permit employer payments to be deductible for purposes of computing business taxes, but to make those payments part of employees' taxable income. From an economic viewpoint, the two approaches are identical as long as the same tax rate is applied to personal income and business income (as would occur under the flat tax) and as long as each worker receives the same allowance under either system.

The main distinction between the two approaches is not in terms of the economic consequences, but in terms of the perceptions employers and employees are likely to have. If employer premium payments must be declared as part of employee taxable income, it will be much easier for employees to see them as part of their compensation and to value them as such. From the employers' perspective, having all business expenses (including noncash compensation) treated the same makes it easier for them to understand what taxes they are paying out of their net business income.

Even in that case, however, some for-profit employers may oppose removal of the tax subsidy because they believe the premium payments would reduce their profits and not their workers' wages. Economic theory and empirical studies are as conclusive as they can be: Almost all employer-paid benefits come out of wages. If that is true, then the only sense in which an employer should object to taxing benefits as income is as an agent for his workers—and then I hope that the arguments for why such a tax is efficient and equitable will be persuasive. Employers should not think they will bear the tax. They will not.

CONCLUSION

Removal and recycling of the upper-middle-class tax subsidy for excessive health insurance would be both efficient and fair. Recycling the subsidy could reduce free-rider behavior by people who will not or cannot buy health insurance. It would improve the production and financing of health services. It would help simplify the tax system. Thus, it must be an integral part of any large-scale attempt to restructure the tax system.

The argument for removing the subsidy is independent of how much the cost of medical care would change. Even if the savings should be in the 10 percent range for those affected, that would be better than what the Congressional Budget Office estimates is achieved by the rapidly growing Independent Practice Association (IPA) and network forms of HMO. More important, if the subsidy makes little difference, why have it? Why not use the funds for those lower-income families who need help?

This vision, combined with ways to provide good information on health care and insurance, can minimize political interference with and influence on the health care delivery and financing systems. Because of history and error, government has tangled itself in the financing and control of what ought to be an individual's most personal choice: what to do to protect his and his family's health. As a result, the federal and state governments have borne substantial fiscal burdens that have affected how they perform their other legitimate functions. The vision proposed here would permit us to discharge our social obligation to assure adequate health care for all while also cutting the knots and letting the bonds fall away.

NOTES

1 Mark V. Pauly, *Medical Care at Public Expense* (New York, N.Y.: Praeger Publishers, 1971).

2 Robert E. Hall and Alvin Rabushka, *The Flat Tax,* 2nd ed. (Stanford, Cal.: Hoover Institution Press, 1995).

3 See, among others, Pauly, *Medical Care at Public Expense.*

4 Hall and Rabushka, *The Flat Tax,* p. 53.

5 National Commission on Economic Growth and Tax Reform, *Unleashing America's Potential: A Pro-Growth, Pro-Family Tax System for the Twenty-First Century* (New York, N.Y.: St. Martin's Griffin, 1996), p. 21.

6 Mark V. Pauly and John Goodman, "Tax Credits for Health Insurance and Medical Savings Accounts," *Health Affairs,* Vol. 14 (Spring 1995), pp. 125–139.

7 Jonathan Gruber, "The Incidence of Mandated Maternity Benefits," *American Economic Review,* Vol. 84 (June 1994), pp. 622–641, and

Louise Sheiner, "Health Costs, Aging, and Wages," Federal Reserve Board, processed 1995.

[8] Jonathan Gruber and James Poterba, "Fundamental Tax Reform and Employer-Provided Health Insurance," Brookings Institution Conference on Fundamental Tax Reform, February 1996.

5

A BETTER SUBSIDY FOR HEALTH INSURANCE?[1]

C. Eugene Steuerle, Ph.D., and Gordon B. T. Mermin

WHY THE ISSUE WON'T GO AWAY

Both the health policy and tax reform debates often play out at a superficial level, with little public attention to the building blocks required to achieve reform. This approach has confused issues considerably, as any major reform tends to involve hundreds of very important policy changes, each of which deserves separable, serious consideration. A major item in most health reform and tax reform proposals that misses the headlines but nonetheless plays a significant role behind the scenes is the treatment of the existing tax exclusion of employer-provided health insurance. This exclusion has become so important and so rich—at least $70 billion in annual costs, much more by some accounting[2]—that no health reform or tax reform is complete without deciding what to do with it.

Almost all recent extensive health reform proposals have scaled back the exclusion to finance new health policy. Even in proposals where the exclusion is not explicitly changed, its value is often reduced through the substitution of alternative means of attaining insurance or through hoped-for reductions in future costs of health care.

In many tax reform efforts, in turn, an attempt is made to tax in full all compensation, including that received in the form of health insurance. Indeed, Robert Hall and Alvin Rabushka—two well-known promoters of the flat tax—state explicitly that the taxation of employee and fringe benefits is a major source of the improvement they seek under comprehensive tax reform.[3] Health and pension benefits together comprise the vast majority of all nontaxable employee benefits, yet pension benefits would remain deferred from tax under most consumption taxes, just as they are under current law. Therefore, it is primarily the taxation of health benefits to which attention is turned when reformers speak about restricting tax preferences for employee benefits.

Cutting back on the exclusion for employer-provided health benefits came up several other times during the 1980s and 1990s. For example, President Ronald Reagan proposed it to finance deficit reduction in the early 1980s, and the Department of the Treasury proposed it to finance tax rate reduction in the early rounds of tax reform in 1984.

Just why is there so much focus on the exclusion, and why do most proposals pare or eliminate it? First, it has become one of the most expensive—by one count, the most expensive—of all the tax expenditures or subsidies in the tax code.[4] It is difficult not to attract attention when you're the big kid on the block. Second, many feel the tax exclusion is a poor way to subsidize health insurance. To evaluate the exclusion on that score, we need a set of criteria for judging health insurance subsidies.

SUBSIDIZING HEALTH INSURANCE

The goal of subsidizing health insurance is to increase coverage as equitably and efficiently as possible.[5] Increasing coverage provides greater access to health care and insures families against major financial loss due to health expenses. Many treatments for health problems are too expensive for individual families unless they pool their resources through insurance. Increasing coverage also reduces the number of people who ride free on the health care system. If they become seriously ill, the uninsured may fall back on public medical programs or receive free medical care from providers, who often shift the cost to private and public insurers.[6]

If benefits are to be distributed equitably, individuals in similar circumstances should be treated the same way. For example, those with the same resources and health status should receive equal subsidies. Also, it is generally accepted that the overall government benefit and tax structure should be progressive. Government efforts then will serve disproportionately to help, on net, those with greater needs and fewer means. A health insurance subsidy, by the nature of insurance, will achieve some redistribution from the healthy to the nonhealthy, especially when there is a stable pool of insured individuals.[7] It should not be distributed in a manner that provides greater subsidies at higher income levels at which they may be less needed.[8]

To be efficient, a health insurance subsidy should distort as little as possible the trade-off individuals face between health insurance and other goods and services. Likewise, government policymakers should weigh the trade-off between subsidizing health insurance and meeting other social needs. If a tax or spending subsidy is an open-ended entitlement, the government no longer has a level playing field for deciding how to allocate its revenues. In this case, it is likely to devote too many public resources to subsidizing health insurance as opposed to educating children and other worthwhile goals.

The public finance literature sometimes suggests that cash transfers are more efficient than transfers of particular goods and services. The argument is that those who receive benefits are free to use them as they see fit: low-income families might prefer to use the money spent on health insurance subsidies for food or housing. They might be better off moving to a safer neighborhood than receiving medical services. Also, in-kind benefits are inefficient to the extent providers of the subsidized service or good capture benefits (for example, doctors receive higher salaries than otherwise would be the case).

In the case of health insurance, however, some amount of in-kind benefit may make more sense because of the free-rider problem.[9] A cash benefit would allow recipients to buy things other than health insurance and then fall back on society when they become sick. Many also believe that redistribution should concentrate only on selective, more "meritorious" goods and services.

PROBLEMS WITH THE EXISTING EXCLUSION

How well does the exclusion meet these objectives and deal with the inevitable trade-offs? Although it does increase health insurance coverage to some extent, it meets almost no equity or efficiency goal well.[10] Much of its benefit is used in a way that actually works against most of the goals sought by the country's health policy.

Figure 1

Percentage of U.S. population covered by employer-provided health insurance, calendar years 1990–1992, by family income

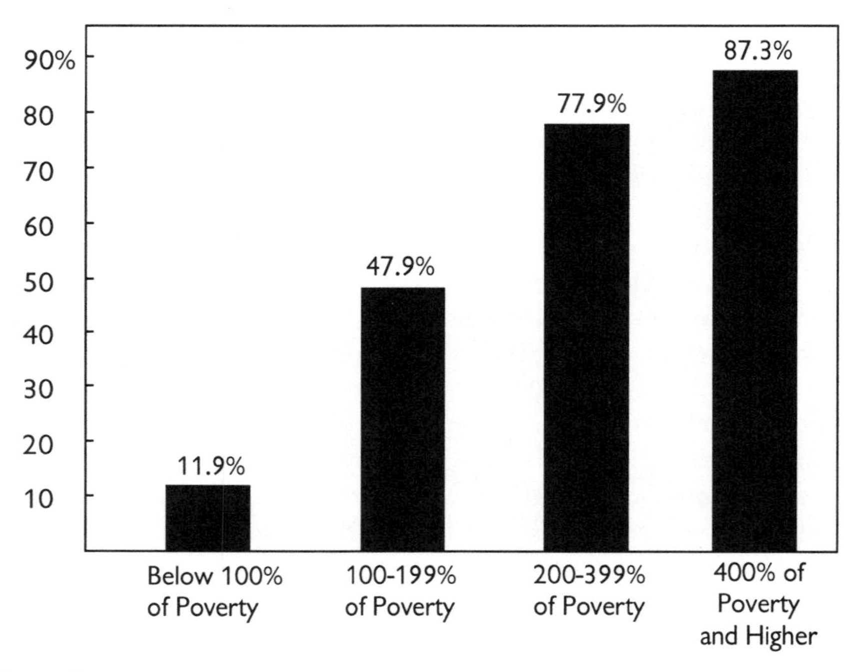

Note: Calculations exclude those over age 65, living in institutions, and families with active military service members.
Source: Winterbottom, Liska, and Obermaler (1995). Data from the March 1991, 1992, and 1993 Current Population Surveys.

Equal Treatment of Equals

First, the exclusion violates almost any reasonable interpretation of treating individuals in equal circumstances equally. It is available to those who buy insurance through their employers but not to those who are not in the labor force or to those working for an employer who does not provide health benefits. It also is more valuable to those with generous plans than to those whose employers offer lower-cost plans.

Figure 2

Estimated value per capita of federal tax subsidies for employer-provided health insurance, calendar year 1996, by family income quintile

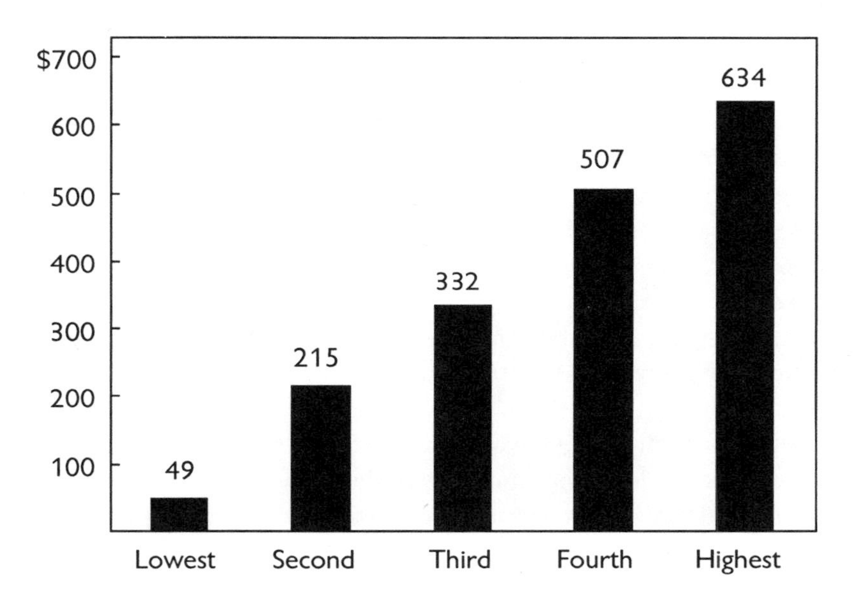

Note: The calculations exclude persons over age 65, families receiving cash welfare benefits, and persons living in institutions.
Source: Based on calculations from Zedlewski, Holohan, and Winterbottom (1994). Zedlewiski, Holohan, and Winterbottom used the Urban Institute's TRIM2 model and the March 1992 *Current Population Survey.*

Regressivity

The exclusion is regressive in a way that serves no public policy purpose. High-income families are more likely to receive employer-provided health insurance and therefore benefit from the exclusion. Eighty-seven percent of individuals with family income over 400 percent of the poverty line receive employer-provided insurance, as contrasted with only 12 percent of those below 100 percent of the poverty line and 48 percent of those between 100 and 200 percent of the poverty line (see Figure 1). Also, high-income families are likely to receive more generous policies and face higher tax rates, both of which increase the value of the exclusion. As a result of these three factors, the exemption is worth much more to high-income families. By one estimate, the exemption is worth $634 per capita and $507 per capita for families in the highest and second-highest income quintiles but only $49 per capita and $215 per capita for families in the lowest and second-lowest income quintiles (see Figure 2).[11]

Traditional Efficiency Issues

Perhaps worst of all, the exclusion is a poor and inefficient way to provide health benefits. Because all insurance costs are subsidized, it encourages people to purchase more insurance than otherwise. Because savings on federal and state income taxes and the Social Security tax are often worth 30 to 45 cents on the dollar, a person is encouraged to spend $1 to buy insurance that is worth only 55 to 70 cents to him. The government (that is, other taxpayers) contributes the shortfall.

The inefficiency stretches beyond the purchase of excess insurance. Many economists believe that the current design of health insurance weakens normal market incentives to control costs. The argument is that you and I do not bargain with the hospital or doctor once we know that insurance will cover our costs. We are willing to demand a continuing array of services because we always can shift costs to other persons. Where no copayments are required, we can pay zero for each dollar of cost imposed on other members of the insurance group.[12]

Bargaining over the Cost of Insurance

Even though these traditional efficiency arguments are fundamentally sound, they miss an important market constraint: We can pay only so much for the insurance in the first place. That is, we may have difficulty bargaining over costs when health services are delivered, but we surely can bargain over the design and cost of the insurance policy itself. The amount we collectively put into those insurance policies will determine, both directly and indirectly, what comes out. Insurance companies, in effect, can become our regulators if the plans are not open-ended, assuring that we or our employers pay all shortfalls. Insurers can regulate the services allowed, reduce fees paid to providers to meet budget constraints, and bargain with health care providers to keep salaries within bounds.

The market, therefore, can be made to work better at the point of insurance purchase, but only if the cost of the insurance is an item of bargain. When that cost is hidden, the bargain is seldom engaged effectively because we are less likely to recognize that spending more on health insurance reduces the amount we have available for other goods and services.

The exclusion for employer-provided insurance works against this recognition of cost. For the employee, the cost really comes about in the form of reduced wages. The cost of health insurance is too huge to come primarily out of profits. Even to this day, however, few employees receive regular statements with their paychecks telling them how much their health insurance costs them. They thus have little understanding of how to bargain with employers to receive higher wages in lieu of a still more generous health plan. Even if they received that information, the current exclusion requires them to bargain away additional subsidies from the government when they bargain to reduce health insurance costs, thus reducing substantially their net private gain.

Most items of income that are taxable require individual accounting for benefits received. Because the exclusion applies like a blanket to all health insurance costs, no matter who gets them or at what level, it does not require individual accounting. People, moreover, cannot receive a comparable tax benefit if they buy health insurance individually or through any other group. Thus, the employer exclusion discourages the very type of accounting that would make costs more apparent. For example, in 1994, before taking account of the tax savings, families with employer-provided health insurance paid only 14 percent of the cost of their premiums directly through employee contributions. They paid much of the rest without knowing how much they gave up in wages.[13]

Not only are the costs of employer-provided health insurance hidden, but so too are most of the costs of the health care system in general. For 1996, we estimate total health care spending per household to have been almost $11,000, of which only $2,800—about one-quarter of the total—was paid directly. Approximately $5,700 was paid indirectly through higher federal, state, and local taxes to fund government health efforts and to compensate for revenue lost due to

Table 1

How households pay for health care, without recognizing costs (estimated total health care spending in the U.S., FY 1996)

	Average Per Household[1]	Percent of GDP	Percent of Personal Income	Percent of Money Income	Total Spending in Billions
Paid Indirectly:					
Taxes: Federal Hospital Insurance Payroll Tax	$1,033	1.40%	1.60%	2.20%	$102.40
Taxes: Other Federal, State, & Local[2]	$4,701	6.40%	7.40%	10.10%	$465.90
Reduced Wages: (Paid by Employers)[3]	$1,959	2.70%	3.10%	4.20%	$194.20
Other[4]	$490	0.70%	0.80%	1.10%	$48.60
Paid Directly					
Personal Contributions: to Private Health Insurance[5]	$843	1.10%	1.30%	1.80%	$83.50
Out-of-Pocket Payments	$1,769	2.40%	2.80%	3.80%	$175.30
Premiums: Medicare	$204	0.30%	0.30%	0.40%	$20.20
TOTAL	$10,999	14.90%	17.30%	23.60%	$1,090.10
Addendum					
Mean GDP per Household	$73,605				
Mean Personal Income per Household	$63,409				
Mean Money Income per Household	$46,556				

Source: Author's calculations based on data from the Congressional Budget Office, the Office of Management and Budget (1995), and the Joint Committee on Taxation (1995).

Notes:

1) We estimate 99.1 million households for 1996.
2) Includes taxes needed to finance direct government health spending out of general revenues, plus the amount by which general taxes must be raised in order to compensate for tax subsidies for certain health-related income. All tax subsidies are measured in revenue-loss terms. Tax subsidies for private health expenditures are subtracted out of their corresponding private categories and added to government expenditure accounts; thus, they do not alter total national health expenditures. Tax subsidies for such public health expenditures as Medicare are not subtracted from any other accounts; thus, they are treated as additions to total net national health care expenditures.
3) Employer contributions for health insurance, less government tax subsidies.
4) Consists primarily of non-patient revenue, which includes philanthropy, hospital parking, gift shops, and interest income.
5) Includes both employee contributions to private group health insurance plans and individual's policy premiums.

special tax treatment of certain health-related income; around $2,000 was paid indirectly through lost wages for employer-provided insurance;[14] and nearly $500 was paid through such nonpatient revenue as charitable donations, hospital parking, and gift shops (see Table 1).

In recent years, employers have been taking on a larger intermediary role in trying to control health costs. One reason may be that in years of modest economic growth, the price of health insurance has risen so exorbitantly that it has been difficult to offer even modest cash wage increases to many workers from year to year. As the cost of health care has risen, therefore, new private mechanisms for trying to control spending have come into place.[15] Their ultimate impact has yet to be determined.[16] Nonetheless, even if the growth in health care costs should level out, the share of national income is still likely to be much too high so long as costs remain hidden from those really paying for them.

The Exclusion and Budget Policy

The exclusion is inefficient at the government level as well. Because it is open-ended, its total cost is determined by employers, employees, insurance companies, and health providers, not by government. Government therefore cannot rationally allocate spending for the subsidy and weigh the trade-offs with other social needs. As the cost of health insurance has rapidly grown, government subsidy of health insurance has had to follow suit automatically, regardless of how pressing other needs have been.

DESIGNING AN ALTERNATIVE

For the reasons discussed, the tax subsidy should be reduced gradually and replaced by a better, yet still imperfect, alternative. By "better," we mean it is possible to design a subsidy that will be a considerable improvement over current law on all the counts covered. By "imperfect," we confess up front that we do not believe it possible to design a subsidy that will meet all or even most of the goals that health care reformers seek. Indeed, the failure to recognize the extraordinary and often conflicting nature of these many goals often prevents improvements in health policy. We also recognize that changes cannot be implemented without some friction. What we suggest here, therefore, is only that there is a much better way to spend the more than $70 billion now involved with the exclusion. Spending that significant sum well, however, must be put in the context of a health care market with expenditures of over $1 trillion and nearly $11,000 per household.

An appropriate proposal would do three things. First, it would limit—and, ideally, eventually eliminate—the existing exclusion for employer-provided insurance. Second, it would substitute a credit of equal value per person and require employers to offer insurance plans on which the credit could be used.[17] Finally, this new subsidized market would contain an income-based penalty on households that did not buy insurance. The penalty would take the form of a surtax on income or the denial of personal exemptions.

The first suggestion—capping or eliminating the employee exclusion for employer-provided health care—might be achieved through several mechanisms. The key is to try to design something that can be administered by both the private sector and government. Perhaps the most straightforward way to limit the value of the existing exclusion is simply to impose a tax at a flat rate on the total amount of employer payments for health care except in cases in which the money already has been taxed or paid out to employees as taxable compensation. Indirectly, this is how the current broad-based flat tax proposals insure that compensation in the form of health benefits is subject to tax. In this case, exactly the same rate of tax is imposed on all compensation. Partial or complete substitution of value-added taxes (VATs) for income taxes—the VAT has a tax base similar to that of most flat tax proposals—would reduce or eliminate the exclusion.

Within the existing tax structure, there are many ways to impose a flat rate on health benefits. For example, some amount of Social Security tax might be imposed. To simplify matters, it might be done in a way that does not involve attributions to individuals and recalculations of benefits for Old Age, Survivors, and Disability Insurance. Without a benefit adjustment, of course, a tax rate of less than the full 15.3 percent might be in order. Although an incomplete alternative, it could be administered with some ease.

A more complex alternative is to cap the exclusion. Unlike a flat rate tax, a cap requires some calculation of insurance costs per employee (an administrative issue we discuss below). From an economic standpoint, a cap has many advantages. By setting a maximum amount, it forces the taxpayer to pay all excess costs. Thus, the subsidy would be concentrated on the first, not the last, dollars of insurance purchased, thereby greatly reducing the incentive for individuals to purchase additional insurance at a social cost greater than the value they place on it and bringing taxpayers into fuller recognition of that cost. In the end, a cap also would make the subsidy per employee somewhat more equal by restricting the maximum tax benefits that can be received.

The second leg of this stool is to offer a fixed credit to individuals for the purchase of insurance. To preserve their efficient administrative role in the health insurance market, employers would be required to offer insurance on which the credit could be used (discussed below). If a cap produces revenue and gradually becomes tighter relative to the growth rate provided by an uncapped exclusion, more dollars might be available for the credit. We repeat a suggestion one of us has made for a number of years: A 100 percent subsidy should be provided on the first dollars of most types of insurance, even catastrophic policies.[18] That would induce almost everyone to buy some insurance, which is the primary goal of the subsidy.

A credit that covered only part of each dollar of cost would be inferior. For example, rather than a $1,000 credit for insurance costing $1,000 or more, a partial credit might pay 20 percent for insurance costing up to $5,000. The problem with partial credits and subsidies is that many individuals never use them. The subsidy for individual retirement accounts, even when available to all workers, never induced more than a few to make deposits.

A credit would be distributed more equitably than the current exclusion. Individuals would be treated the same regardless of employment status, the generosity of their insurance plans, or whether their employers provide health insurance. The credit would be modestly progressive because individuals in poor health often have fewer means and higher health costs and would benefit more than those in good health. Also, poorer people would benefit more than richer people because the latter would pay more in taxes while getting a credit of equal value. Indeed, this type of credit is more progressive on the spending side than many expenditures made by government.[19]

The credit would encourage efficiency as well. By not subsidizing the last dollars of insurance, it would encourage individuals to recognize and confront the cost of insurance directly. They would keep all the benefits of bargaining for a lower-cost plan instead of just a portion of the savings as when the entire cost is subsidized. The subsidy would require people to be more involved in the purchase of health insurance than they currently are, thereby making its cost more explicit. If health insurance costs are explicit, individuals will put more pressure on the system to control premiums. Some of the pressure that consumers would place on the industry would benefit them in turn in the form of lower prices for health care.

Finally, the credit promotes better creation of budget and expenditure policy because it is not open-ended. The government can choose the appropriate amount of public resources to devote to subsidizing health insurance by weighing the trade-off between health and other social needs, such as education.

Some proponents of a credit would phase it out as income rises. Although an equal-dollar credit is more progressive than the current exclusion, a phased-out credit is more progressive still. Our concern here is that these proposals go far beyond health care policy and suggest a welfare and tax policy that we do not believe has been thought out thoroughly.

For example, if the credit is phased out, it will be difficult to know how much to pay taxpayers during the year. As with the earned income tax credit, few payments are likely to be claimed during the year, and it would be hard to reflect this type of credit in some regular schedule like withholding or in applications from insurance companies on behalf of insured individuals. With a flat credit amount, however, insurance companies would know what individuals were eligible for and could act as intermediaries. We believe this type of system would have significant administrative advantages, not the least of which is that insurance companies would seek out those who were uninsured and had not yet claimed the credit.

The phaseout, moreover, is nothing more than another income tax—e.g., when each dollar of income reduces a credit by 20 cents, an effective income tax rate of 20 percent is created. The phaseout of various benefits already wreaks havoc with the tax structure. A strong case can be made that such phaseouts should be reflected more directly in the tax structure. Our current combined tax and transfer structure already imposes 70 and 100 percent tax rates on the additional income of many people who receive income assistance and Medicaid, including working families with wages up to three times the minimum wage.[20]

One type of phased-out credit was suggested by President George Bush late in his term. It would have imposed about a 55 percent "tax rate" on income in the phaseout range. When combined with normal income tax, Social Security tax, and earned income tax credit provisions, it would have forced almost every American to face a tax rate of close to 100 percent for that portion of earnings between 100 and 150 percent of the poverty level. For individuals with total income in this range, the rate would have applied to the last dollars earned as well. There would be limited gains from additional work or saving, not to mention very substantial marriage penalties.[21]

The case for making any income tax explicit is even stronger when a credit is close to universal. In this case, the tax is not on one category of recipients, but on most of the population. Then why not combine the health-based income tax with the regular tax structure? Transparency, after all, is considered a desirable attribute of tax systems. Some reformers advocate credits or vouchers because they would be more transparent than the existing exclusion, but they back up their proposals with a hidden tax so they can raise money to buy more insurance for more people.

We are not unsympathetic. Considering the extraordinary cost of health care today, advocates of universal care have been unable to come up with enough revenue to pay for the type of insurance they want for most low-income and middle-income individuals. They find it impossible to collect hundreds of billions more in taxes—a principal reason that some reformers tried to turn to direct cost controls in 1994. An all-or-nothing strategy, however, may be demanding too much. As noted, even a very modest credit would provide some insurance; additionally, it would tend toward creation of a system with more direct cost recognition.

Government can use a stick as well as a carrot to encourage the purchase of health care insurance. One stick would be a surtax on people with moderate or higher incomes who do not purchase health insurance—say, with some minimum characteristics over and above what might be available with a flat credit. For example, a 10 percent surtax might be imposed on existing tax liabilities, or personal exemptions might be denied. Many middle-income and upper-income taxpayers do not purchase insurance.[22] The stick would represent a fee for the risks imposed on others because, in an emergency or catastrophic health event, taxpayers and insured individuals may be forced to pay for the health care of the uninsured even when they could have bought insurance for themselves.

These three legs—cutting back on the value of the existing exclusion, providing a credit for health insurance, and penalizing those who do not purchase insurance—would serve as incentives for a significant number of individuals. Because these proposals would lead taxpayers to recognize the costs, they would put great pressure on the price of insurance and medical services. With costs increasing at a more moderate rate, people would find insurance more affordable.

These suggested changes are a significant departure from current law. For that reason alone, they should be implemented slowly and without exaggerated claims as to how many of our health care problems they would solve.

SOME OBJECTIONS

The type of reform offered here usually is met by three major objections. First, critics argue that it neither would extend comprehensive insurance to everyone nor would control costs completely. Second, it might forgo the advantages of using employers as intermediaries for employees. Finally, limiting the extent to which people can obtain tax-free income through employment health benefits could be difficult to administer.

Our answer to these objections is that, whatever their validity, this type of reform still would be a significant improvement.

- First, it would not do everything one would like, but it would increase coverage significantly while helping to lower costs.
- Second, we should take advantage of employers as intermediaries. There is no reason that a credit cannot be designed to do so.
- Third, there will be difficulties in moving to a system in which there is a more thorough accounting of health benefits provided to employees, but there are reasonable and manageable ways to get there, and a number of employers—in particular, the federal government—already have blazed the trail.

Doing Everything

There is a great deal that reforming the employer exclusion cannot do. At best, even if we could reallocate $70 billion or more in tax subsidies among the 60 million households[23] not receiving Medicare, Medicaid, or other direct public health benefits, we could provide only about $1,150 per household in subsidy. A compromise would be to concentrate on children.[24] This could be achieved either by offering a credit only for children or, to a lesser extent, by allocating credit amounts on a per capita basis. Because the health insurance costs of children are significantly below those of adults, much more of the cost of their insurance could be covered if money were provided on a per capita rather than per household basis. Wherever one starts, the credit can be increased later. Over time, other expenditure or tax changes would be considered, including gradual efforts to create greater parity between the elderly and nonelderly in health care subsidies. Growth in the economy would continue to provide government with more revenues, some of which might be spent on the credit. Even with some significant efforts at shifting expenditures and subsidies, however, it is highly unlikely that we would have enough to cover most of the cost of today's more comprehensive insurance policies. This has become the classic dilemma of health reform. The system has become so expensive—in part because of how inefficiently government spends all its health care subsidies—that to raise hundreds of billions more to fill gaps for the non-Medicare and non-Medicaid population would require much higher tax rates and would continue the conversion of the federal government into little other than a provider of health care and pensions. The costs to society from this trend are quite high: There are many pressing needs other than the medical care normally covered by insurance.

In fact, the existing exclusion also provides only partial relief, as well as much extra baggage. The trick is to try to set up the right structure first and then modify it as the subsidy competes honestly for money with other social needs. The need for a higher subsidy also will fall as the cost pressures from a more transparent and efficient credit structure compound and reduce the cost of a more comprehensive health policy relative to what it would have been.

We do not want to exaggerate our claims. Fixing the exclusion by itself will not answer all health care questions. Congress still will need to work on Medicare and Medicaid, and employers and employees will need to control costs further. What we will have achieved is the establishment of a viable structure within which the debate over the size of government health care subsidies can proceed honestly and transparently.

Maintaining the Employer Role

Employers should remain in the health market because they have several advantages. Larger employers, in particular, are efficient administrators and often can form the types of pools necessary for insurance more easily. Even when health insurance was in its infancy and tax rates and subsidies were quite modest, employers were major players in the health insurance market. For the same reasons, most would remain in the market under the plan suggested here. Nonetheless, some employers would be tempted to abandon their role in the absence of any subsidy. For this and other reasons, we would require them to offer plans on which any tax credit could be spent. In this way, the employer role in helping individuals to obtain insurance would expand, not contract. Of course, individuals would obtain a subsidy regardless of whether they used the employer pool for insurance. Thus, we avoid the problem of current law, which encourages employer involvement only by discouraging other groups from offering insurance.

Under current law, moreover, employer-based coverage is dropping, not increasing. The portion of the population covered by employer-based health insurance fell from 66.3 percent in 1980 to 58.5 percent in 1993.[25] If anything, those who oppose a credit-based system pose a greater threat to employer involvement than do those who are trying to design one that all employers might help administer. Today, many employers do not provide insurance either because they cannot afford the higher level of total worker compensation implied or because their workers are covered under Medicare or the plans of spouses. These employers could offer policies much more easily under a tax-credit system.

Assessing the Value of Employer-Provided Insurance

Some object that the attribution of insurance value is difficult because if we cap the amount of tax-free insurance, we will force employers to figure out more precisely the value to each employee. Admittedly, attribution could become quite complex, especially for those who tried to push the envelope of what is allowed under the law. Evaluation, moreover, is never precise because all individuals have unique characteristics that affect their risks and the value of their policies.

But this is not a new problem for insurance. When we buy life and car insurance, we pay market prices that do not reflect all or even most of our differences in risk. Although the pricing of those policies is not perfectly fair, we do not protest loudly or leave the market.

Moreover, there already is a model for attribution in a "capped" world: the health benefits provided to federal employees. Administratively, the system does not provide generous plans for employees and then attempt to value the excess. Instead, it achieves the same result by charging everyone who buys generous policies the difference between the price of the insurance and the maximum subsidy. If policies are offered at $300, $350, $400, and $450 a month, and if $350 is the maximum subsidy, then workers pay $50 for the $400 policy and $100 for the $450 policy.

Individuals effectively can pay in full for the excess over some basic policy, but the government does not need to collect any tax directly on this excess value. Why? Indirectly, if it already has collected the tax on the employee's entire cash wage, then when the employee buys extra insurance out of this after-tax income, there is no extra tax subsidy involved.[26] To put it another way, the employee effectively would pay for this extra insurance in the same way that other non-tax-preferred items are purchased. There have been almost no protests among government employees that this method discriminates against some of them, even though a full risk-adjusted assessment might determine price differently. Employees come to view this market just as they view any other insurance market in which they face a pricing structure with incomplete risk adjustment.

We submit that with a cap, employers and employees would copy this method of administration, which is straightforward and relatively easy to implement. Of course, a few employers or employee groups still might try to push the system to excess, leading to potentially difficult valuation problems; but the vast majority of employers would move to a government insurance type of structure, implement a basic subsidy in a reasonable manner under generally specified tax limits, and then charge employees if they bought additional insurance.

As noted, there are other ways to limit the tax benefits. One is through flat rate taxes. Under another method, some specific attributes of a plan—for example, catastrophic coverage in excess of $5,000 and an annual physical—are specified in law. Each employee could still be offered more health insurance but through a combination of plans: (1) a tax-favored plan carrying the specified attributes, covered out of before-tax income, or (2) an additional plan or plans that would be paid for by after-tax income. At the margin, individuals again would be paying for the full cost of additional insurance.

CONCLUSION

The bottom line is that government is in considerable trouble if it cannot begin to reform one of the largest open-ended tax subsidies or expenditures—especially one as unfair, regressive, and inefficient as the current exclusion for employer-provided benefits. Imagine how well the private sector would perform if it said that a $70 billion chunk of the economy—say the entire legal profession or hotel industry—could not be improved no matter how poorly they were serving the public who paid for them. When we clearly can do better, we should not allow improvement to be held hostage to some unattainable standard of perfection.

NOTES

[1] Much of this paper is taken from C. Eugene Steuerle's "Economic Perspective" columns from the February 26, March 4, and March 11, 1996, editions of *Tax Notes.*

[2] Based on data from unpublished Congressional Budget Office tables; the fiscal 1995 federal budget; Joint Committee on Taxation, *Estimates of Federal Tax Expenditures for Fiscal Years 1996–2000* (Washington, D.C.: U.S. Government Printing Office, 1995); and authors' assumptions. We use the conventional measure for tax expenditures, which measures the difference between tax liability under present law and the tax liability that would result from a recomputation of tax without the tax expenditure provision. The exclusion is worth almost $90 billion by the conventional measure if the Department of the Treasury's federal income tax expenditure estimates are used.

An alternative way to measure tax expenditures is to express their values in terms of "outlay equivalents." An outlay equivalent is the dollar size of a direct spending program that would provide taxpayers with the same net benefits as a tax expenditure. The principal difference is that if the value of the tax expenditure is nontaxable, as is the health exclusion, it is worth even more to the taxpayer.

[3] Robert E. Hall and Alvin Rabushka, *The Flat Tax,* 2nd ed. (Stanford, Cal.: Hoover Institution Press, 1995).

[4] The tax exclusion for employer-provided health insurance is the largest tax expenditure in the Department of the Treasury's estimates of tax expenditures and is likely to reach that status in future years under estimates from the Joint Committee on Taxation.

[5] See James Poterba, "Government Intervention in the Markets for Education and Health Care: How and Why?" in Victor Fuchs, ed., *Individual and Social Responsibility: Child Care, Education, Medical Care and Long-Term Care in America* (Chicago, Ill.: University of Chicago Press, 1996), for further discussion of why government might intervene in the markets for health care and Congressional Budget Office, *The Economic and Budget Outlook: An Update* (Washington, D.C.: U.S. Government Printing Office, 1995), for further discussion of public finance principles for evaluating subsidies.

[6] See Mancur Olson, ed., *A New Approach to the Economics of Health Care* (Washington, D.C.: American Enterprise Institute, 1982), for further discussion of how the free-rider problem may justify tax subsidies for health insurance.

[7] Where the pool is not stable, the redistribution is more likely to be confined to the period of coverage, as in the next period the healthy seek a cheaper pool that excludes those with higher expected health expenses from identified health problems.

[8] Not all government benefits and programs need to be progressive. Government does not exist merely to redistribute. For example, the benefits of highways very well may be regressive, but government should still provide them if social benefits are deemed to be in excess of social costs. As for progressivity, it is the overall benefit and tax system that is of concern, not each of its individual components.

[9] As we shall see, if in-kind benefits are to be provided, credits or vouchers may be superior to the provision of goods and services, which more narrowly restrict choices.

[10] Earlier discussions of the exclusion's failings can found in Alain C. Enthoven, "Recommended Low-Cost Changes to Existing Laws to Enhance Competition Among Health Care Financing and Delivery Plans," unpublished note, 1979, and C. Eugene Steuerle and Ronald Hoffman, "Tax Expenditures for Health Care," *National Tax Journal,* Vol. 32, No. 2 (June 1979), pp. 101–115.

[11] These results are similar to those found by Lewin/ICF for the Heritage Foundation and reported in Stuart M. Butler, "A Policy Maker's Guide to the Health Care Crisis, Part II: The Heritage Consumer Choice Health Plan," Heritage Foundation *Talking Points,* March 5, 1992.

[12] For a further discussion of the moral hazard that arises from the low cost of health care for insured individuals, see Mark V. Pauly, "The Economics of Moral Hazard: Comment," *American Economic Review,* Vol. 58, No. 3 (September 1968), pp. 531–537; Charles E. Phelps, "The Demand for Reimbursement Insurance," in Richard N. Rosett, ed., *The Role of Health Insurance in the Health Services Sector* (New York, N.Y.: National Bureau of Economic Research, 1976); and Henry J. Aaron, *Serious and Unstable Condition: Financing America's Health Care* (Washington, D.C.: Brookings Institution, 1991), pp. 10–13.

[13] See Congressional Budget Office, *The Tax Treatment of Employment-Based Health Insurance* (Washington, D.C.: U.S. Government Printing Office, 1994), p. 30.

[14] These figures are averages for all households, not just those receiving employer-provided health insurance.

[15] Cost containment mechanisms include encouraging employees to comparison shop among health plans and promoting efficient managed care plans. Only 22 percent of firms offering health insurance, however, currently offer a choice of plans. See Joel C. Cantor, Stephen H. Long, and M. Susan Marquis, "Private Employment-Based Health Insurance in Ten States," *Health Affairs,* Summer 1995, pp. 199–211.

[16] National health expenditures grew only 6 percent in 1994, the slowest rate in 30 years, and 7 percent in 1995. Whether the recent trends toward price competition will continue to moderate the growth of health spending is uncertain, as previous slowdowns in the mid-1980s and late 1970s proved temporary (CBO, *The Economic and Budget Outlook: An Update,* 1995). Even these rates of growth are faster than the economy—an unsustainable trend. Finally, these increases are taking place in a time of reprieve from many pressures: The upcoming retirement of the baby-boom generation will impose an enormous increase in demand for health care for the elderly.

[17] We treat a credit broadly to encompass options that make use of an expenditure credit, voucher, or tax credit. The primary economic issue in this choice is which can be administered most easily. From a budget standpoint, an expenditure is a superior means of accounting for the full budgetary cost of the proposal. Employers would not be required to pay for the insurance, and the credit would not have to be used on insurance purchased through an employer. See Stuart M. Butler, "Creating a National Health System Through Tax Reform," *Proceedings of the Eighty-Fifth Annual Conference of the National Tax Association–Tax Institute of America* (Columbus, Ohio: National Tax Association, 1993), and Mark V. Pauly, *Responsible National Health Insurance* (Washington, D.C.: AEI Press, 1992), for proposed health insurance tax credits.

[18] See C. Eugene Steuerle, "The Search for Adaptable Health Policy Through Finance-Based Reform," in Robert B. Helms, ed., *American Health Policy: Critical Issues for Reform* (Washington, D.C.: AEI Press, 1993); "Comments on the Proposal," in Stuart M. Butler, *Is Tax Reform the Key to Health Care Reform?* (Washington, D.C.: The Heritage Foundation, 1990), pp. 22–28; and *Mandating Employer Provision of Health Insurance* (Washington, D.C.: American Association of Retired Persons, 1990), pp. 38–40.

[19] Medicare, higher education, and highways actually are provided in greater amounts to those at higher income levels because they live longer, attain higher levels of education, and make more use of highways, both directly and through their higher consumption of transported goods.

[20] For a further discussion of the tax rates faced by welfare recipients, see Linda Giannarelli and C. Eugene Steuerle, "The True Tax Rates Faced by Welfare Recipients," National Tax Association Proceedings, Eighty-Eighth Annual Conference, 1995, pp. 123–129.

[21] See C. Eugene Steuerle, "Beyond Paralysis in Health Policy: A Proposal to Focus on Children," *National Tax Journal,* Vol. 45, Vo. 3 (September 1992), pp. 357–368.

[22] The ability of some to ride free on others' taxes and insurance is a problem at all income levels. Even at higher incomes, many people are not covered by insurance. Katherine Swartz in *The Medically Uninsured: Special Focus on Workers* (Washington, D.C.: Urban Institute Press, 1989), found that 22.9 percent of the uninsured have family incomes of three times the poverty level or more.

[23] Unpublished data from the Urban Institute's TRIM2 model.

[24] Steuerle, "Beyond Paralysis in Health Policy: A Proposal to Focus on Children," *op. cit.*

[25] See Congressional Budget Office, *The Tax Treatment of Employment-Based Health Insurance,* p. 7.

[26] In recent years there has been a significant expansion of other options for receiving tax-favorable treatment of employee contributions—such as Section 125 health care expense accounts. Generally speaking, these additional preferences would also be removed or subject to a combined cap. Our discussion here, however, focuses on a method of attribution that is administrable regardless of the level of tax preference on the attributable amount.

6

IMPROVING THE SYSTEM FOR DELIVERING SUBSIDIES: CAP OR SCRAP THE EXCLUSION?

John S. Hoff, Esq.

Excluding the value of employer-provided health insurance from the taxable income of employees has many drawbacks: open-ended tax expenditures, loss of individual sovereignty, lack of the economic discipline that results from individual purchasing, impediments to portability, and an untargeted federal subsidy for the purchase of insurance. This subsidy provides no benefit to the millions of Americans who do not have employer-based insurance and who are at the lower end of the income scale. Nevertheless, many believe that, although the exclusion is excessively open-ended and misdirected, it is valuable in making insurance widely available. They would retain the exclusion but limit and target it.

The exclusion is defended on essentially three grounds:

1. The subsidy facilitates the broad purchase of insurance;
2. Because it requires insurance to be purchased through employers, it gives employees the benefit of expert and aggregated purchasing; and
3. The employer group provides a form of risk pooling and de facto community rating that stabilizes the insurance market and makes it possible for high-risk individuals (who are

working or who are the dependents of a worker) to obtain insurance.

In discussing how the current system should be changed, therefore, the question is whether it is possible (and if so, whether it is sufficient) to reform the exclusion, or whether it should be replaced by a different subsidy mechanism.

CAN THE EXCLUSION BE FIXED BY CAPPING IT?

If the exclusion is to be retained, the main reform would be to cap it. Section 106 of the Internal Revenue Code, which excludes from taxation health benefits received by employees, would be amended to limit the amount of employer-provided insurance that could be excluded.

That change could cure the fiscal problem the exclusion poses. A cap imposed on a per-employee basis would end the current open-ended tax expenditure and—assuming the government could anticipate employee and employer behavior—permit the government to budget its subsidy cost.

But a cap presents a countervailing risk. An effort to save the exclusion by capping it might destroy its putative benefits. The lower the cap, the less subsidy it provides for the purchase of insurance, reducing the coverage purchased through employers and the supposedly attendant benefits of the employer-based system.

But let us assume the cap can be calibrated so that the government has budgetary certainty and the "appropriate" amount of insurance is subsidized (a balance that must be struck with any subsidy that is not open-ended). Would a cap cure the other problems posed by the exclusion?

Capping the exclusion automatically would require targeting of the subsidy. So long as the subsidy for health benefits is open-ended and subject only to the spending decisions of employers, the government does not consider how large it is or who gets it. The result is that a person living in an area with high medical costs receives a larger subsidy than one who lives where the same coverage can be purchased for less. A person who is covered by an expensive fee-for-service plan through his employer receives a larger subsidy than one who is enrolled in a tightly controlled managed care plan.

The discrepancy need not be addressed when no limit is set; the discrepancy is the result of individual actions, not government decision, and is not seen by the individuals involved or by the taxpaying public. Setting a limit, however, requires attention to how high the cap is and how the subsidy is distributed. Should the permitted level of exclusion vary by income? By geography? By age? By health status? How these questions are answered would determine how the subsidy is to be targeted.

Those issues must be resolved for any subsidy that is not open-ended; they are not unique to a capped exclusion. The cap, however, does pose a problem that is not presented by subsidies given directly to the individual. It would require downshifting an employer's gross expenditure into individual caps. With a cap on each taxpayer's exclusion, the tax man (or his agent, the employer) must allocate among each firm's employees the aggregate amount the firm spends for insurance. Although, as Glied points out, premiums currently are allocated among employees for purposes of calculating a departed employee's COBRA payment,[1] these amounts do not have to be dovetailed with an individually determined limit on the subsidy and do not determine the imposition of taxes.

Presumably, the allocation would not be difficult when the insurer quotes a premium for each employee. Nevertheless, there would have to be policing to ensure that an employer and an insurer did not adjust the individual premium quotes to take maximum advantage of the individual caps.

If, on the other hand, the insurer charges an employer an aggregate premium, it would have to be divided among the workers to determine whether employees' allocated premiums exceeded their individual caps. If the caps are adjusted to reflect employees' individual circumstances, the employer's premium should be allocated in the same way. Older workers would have higher caps and larger amounts imputed to them.

Either way, therefore, the employees will know their caps and then be told of their share of the employer's premium. The problem is that these might be entirely different. Employees would be forced to pay taxes on premiums allocated to them in excess of their caps and would have no control over the purchasing decision that led to the imposition of the tax. This could become politically untenable.

Even though a capped exclusion could be targeted on the basis of income, with a higher cap for those who need a greater subsidy, the targeting still would be circumscribed. The value of the exclusion would increase with income, as it does now, until the cap is reached. Most important, the exclusion would not channel any subsidy to those without employer-provided insurance. A cap would not correct the current anomaly by which subsidies go only to those who have such insurance and are denied to those who do not have employer-based insurance and who are at the lower end of the income scale.

Imposing a cap, of course, would retain the employer-based system. The reform would not introduce a market for individual purchasing, with its efficiencies and portability. Even when confronted with a cap, employees would not control their insurance dollars. The employer would still be making the decisions and providing the insurance. At most, when it began to bite, a cap would increase employees' sensitivity to the cost of insurance.

The question, then, is whether the employment-based system for delivering the subsidy, even if somewhat improved by a cap, warrants continuation.

WHY NOT SCRAP THE EXCLUSION?

With the notable exception of health insurance, Americans buy their own goods and services. Employers do not divert a portion of their workers' pay for the purchase of consumer products on their behalf. We do not buy homeowner's or car insurance through our employers. Nor are government subsidies for individuals conditioned on working for an employer who makes the purchases.

But that is how the health insurance system operates. The exclusion represents governmental promotion of corporate paternalism. It combines two different functions: employer purchases and government subsidies. This raises the basic question of whether the subsidy should be tied to employment.

CAN A SUBSIDY BE DELIVERED OTHERWISE THAN THROUGH EMPLOYERS?

The simplest solution to the problems presented by the exclusion would be to terminate it. People who do not benefit from the subsidy would be no worse off than they are now, and actually would benefit from the price restraint that would result from termination of the subsidy. Workers who receive the subsidy, however, would lose it, although part of this loss would be offset by the price restraint. But the government can deliver subsidies in other ways. The question is whether other delivery mechanisms would serve the country's policy goals better.

Government subsidies usually go to the people who need help. One would expect an insurance subsidy also to be based on need. This would bring health insurance in line with how other necessities, such as food and shelter, are subsidized. If we decide as a society to subsidize health insurance, we should ask why that subsidy should not be given directly to individuals and families according to need instead of being made contingent on employment. There are several ways this could be done.

Deduction for Insurance Premiums

A subsidy could be provided by letting individuals deduct the cost of insurance from taxable income. A deduction would be similar to the exclusion, but with several advantages. It would be available to all taxpayers, not just to those whose employers provide insurance. Because a deduction would be independent of employment, it would not skew the choice between wages and fringe benefits. Unlike the exclusion, it would promote a market responsive to individual choice.

A deduction, however, shares some of the exclusion's deficiencies. Like the exclusion, it makes the government a partner in the cost of the insurance: The more expensive the plan, the greater the government's cost. It also would have to be capped to impose budgetary control and to avoid subsidizing unnecessarily expensive insurance plans. A deduction does not target the subsidy on the basis of need. It gives the greatest subsidy to those with the highest taxable incomes. Like the exclusion, however, the cap on the deduction could be set higher for those with lower incomes.

A deduction does not equate the subsidy with the full cost of the insurance. The subsidy is only the percentage of the premium represented by an individual's tax bracket. This is true also of the exclusion; but because the exclusion applies only in cases in which the employer pays (or more accurately, appears to pay) for the insurance, the employee does not see the need for a further (government) subsidy to buy the insurance. The subsidy appears to be coming from the employer. Changing the subsidy to a deduction and removing it from the employment relationship would reveal both the amount a person must spend and the need for a subsidy; but a deduction, as normally structured, would not provide a subsidy equal to the cost of the insurance.

If the policy were to subsidize the full cost of the insurance, it would be necessary to make a technical change in how a deduction works: Low-income taxpayers would have to be permitted to multiply the premium by the factor necessary to make the tax value of the deduction equal to the cost of the insurance. That is not how deductions typically function, and such a change would not fit easily into the tax system.

Most important, however, the deduction does not provide a way to deliver a subsidy to people who do not file tax returns. A separate voucher system would be necessary for them.

A deduction, therefore, permits assistance to be given to more Americans than the exclusion does while also promoting an individual market. It is, however, a cumbersome and incomplete tool for providing assistance to the poor.

Tax Credit

A somewhat more effective way to deliver the subsidy would be through a tax credit. Like the deduction, a tax credit would support an individual market. At the same time, however, it would be a better mechanism for an income-related subsidy. The value of a stated amount of credit would not depend on the individual's income; a credit is worth the same to the low-income taxpayer as it is to the high. Thus, it would give the desired amount of assistance without the manipulations necessary with a deduction. At the same time, it could be adjusted to income. The credit, like the deduction, could be capped, and the cap could be lowered as income increases (subject to adjustments that may be necessary to meet other policy goals). The credit provides a better mechanism for assisting low-income taxpayers. If an individual's tax liability is less than the credit, it can be made refundable more easily than can a deduction and so provide the desired subsidy.

The credit, however, provides no benefit to those who do not file tax returns or who cannot afford to pay a premium that would be reimbursed later through a tax credit. A separate system, like a voucher, would be necessary to help those Americans buy insurance.

If the flat tax were introduced, a variant of the credit could be used to subsidize the purchase of insurance directly. On proof of purchase, the family allowance could be increased to equal the value of a tax credit. This approach, however, would be inconsistent with the principles of the flat tax. If the flat tax is adopted, it will be because the country decides the tax system should not be used to promote particular conduct. The premise of the flat tax is that the tax system should only raise revenues; any subsidies should be explicit. Treating health care differently would be a throwback to the discredited tax system.

Vouchers

A third course is to separate the subsidy from the tax code, regardless of whether the flat tax is adopted. Assistance could be provided directly to those who need it by means of vouchers, based on income, for health insurance. Vouchers would be issued to individuals in predetermined amounts. Eligibility would be independent not only of employment status (as would a credit or deduction), but of the tax system as well. Because the voucher would go directly to the individual, it would create an individual market and support families' ownership of their policies (and thus portable coverage).

Vouchers are the only way to reach all intended beneficiaries. They could be distributed on the basis of need, regardless of whether those who qualify for them file tax returns. Because vouchers would be universal and their value could be stated in explicit terms, they would be the best approach for administering an income-based subsidy. Unlike a subsidy delivered by a deduction or credit, a voucher would provide a unitary mechanism for people inside and outside the tax system.

IS THERE ANY REASON TO DELIVER THE SUBSIDY THROUGH EMPLOYERS?

Defenders of the exclusion believe the subsidy should be delivered through employer groups for the reasons discussed at the beginning of this chapter. The first is that the exclusion promotes the widespread purchase of insurance. As discussed, however, the exclusion is not necessary for that. On the contrary, vouchers would permit broader assistance through a seamless mechanism. They also would foster an individual and cost-conscious market and provide the most efficient method for targeting the subsidy.

This leaves two other grounds on which supporters principally justify retaining the exclusion: employer expertise in purchasing insurance and access to insurance for high-risk employees. Each of these warrants discussion.

Employer Expertise

Advocates of the exclusion are concerned that individuals lack sufficient information to buy their own insurance. The insurance market obviously is complex, but so are the markets for VCRs, personal computers, and cars. Moreover, even if one accepts the premise that health care is too complicated for individuals, it does not follow that the exclusion must continue.

It should be noted that, under the exclusion, the employer's role as purchaser is not totally benign. At the very least, it appears to involve a conflict of interest. Although (as the economists explain) employers use their employees' money to buy insurance, they—and more important, their employees—in most instances believe the employers are paying. Accordingly, workers typically think that any savings benefit their employers.

There is a basis for this belief. Employers who agree to provide health benefits have made a de facto commitment to provide a service without regard to cost. By providing a defined benefit rather than a defined contribution, they have taken on an open-ended obligation, and efforts to limit that obligation are seen merely as attempts to save money. Except perhaps in collective bargaining agreements, in which the tradeoffs are explicit and recognized, savings are not translated into wage increases, at least in the short term. Employers therefore have the incentive to purchase insurance more on the basis of price than on the basis of quality. More important, regardless of whether employers actually do this, employees believe they do. They are concerned that the purchasing decision was not made for their benefit. They may resent being placed in the plan their employer chose or having to select among limited options.

This dynamic affects employer–employee relations. It also is one of the challenges of managed care. Workers forced into managed care by their employer may bridle at its restraints. If, however, the exclusion ends and employees make their own decisions, their attitude will be different. People who choose managed care for themselves will react differently to its restraints: They are the ones who have invested, both financially and psychologically, in the plan and who stand to realize the benefits—including lower prices and better service—of that investment.

The expert assistance now provided by employers comes at a heavy price because it is tied to the employment-based subsidy distributed through the exclusion. But the exclusion is not necessary for employees to obtain assistance in purchasing insurance. Ending the exclusion and fostering an individual market would remove employers' conflict of interest while still permitting employers and others to help their workers buy insurance.

If individuals received vouchers, employers could research the insurance market and give advice. Employees could empower their employers to purchase insurance for them, aggregating their purchasing power. As agents, employers would be subject to fiduciary obligations that now are absent. They would be required to act solely in the best interest of their employees, who could terminate the arrangement if dissatisfied with their employer's decisions.

Employers even could make such an arrangement a condition of employment, regardless of whether employees saw any advantage in it, thus replicating the current system. But if employer-based purchasing really has advantages, employers would not have to impose it.

With an individual market, moreover, the sources of expert assistance would expand beyond the employer. Many people who were not tied to an employer would want advice. Brokers and experts would emerge to meet the demand. Affinity groups like churches and unions also would acquire information for their members. Employees would benefit from this enhanced competition by being able to obtain advice either from their employers or from independent sources.

Elimination of the exclusion, therefore, would not cost employees the expert assistance or pooled purchasing power now supplied by employers.

Access for High-Risk Individuals

The main argument against ending the exclusion, therefore, is that high-risk employees will have more difficulty buying insurance in an individual market than in a group market. Under the current system, firms purchase insurance as de facto community-rated risk pools. The employer seems to pay for the insurance, and the employee typically does not receive higher wages if he rejects it. Healthy employees, therefore, stay in the group. As a result, supporters of the exclusion point out, high-risk individuals are subsidized by their healthier coworkers.[2]

Advocates of the current system fear that giving assistance directly to individuals will segment the market: The healthy will choose not to buy insurance, and the cost of insurance for the sick will rise.

It is unclear, however, to what extent the employment-based system provides the benefits that justify this concern. The risk-spreading that is posited in defense of the system is only within a selected group. Those who are too sick to work do not receive the cross-subsidy. There may be community rating within the firm, but not between firms. Coal miners are likely to pay more than computer programmers, except in the unlikely event that differences in age and health are offset by dependents' risk experience. Low-risk individuals may avoid the assumed cost of cross-subsidizing higher-risk employees by working for a firm that does not provide insurance; high-risk individuals may stay with a firm out of fear of losing their insurance, resulting in its having a disproportionately high-risk profile.[3] Employers also may refuse to hire high-risk employees, leaving them unprotected.[4]

Even if viewed only in the context of the individual firm, however, and assuming that the cross-subsidy operates, it is not clear that the asserted benefits of risk-sharing warrant continuing a system that prevents the development of an individual market. Community rating is the rare exception, not the rule, in insurance. Economists explain that it is more efficient for people to pay the actual cost of the risk they present. Community rating affects the behavior of both the insurer and the insured. It increases the incentive for insurers to avoid bad risks, although this is not a factor with respect to members of a group that the insurer has committed to insure. Community rating even within the firm, however, reduces the insured's incentives to minimize risk (e.g., by avoiding smoking, losing weight, and staying out of hang gliders). High-risk employees do not see the financial effect of their conduct, and this increases their willingness to undertake risky behavior.

Community rating, despite these perverse incentives, is said to embody fairness. Its defenders believe that people should pay the same for care regardless of health. Because it is assumed that wages within a firm are not adjusted to reflect the relative cost of each employee's insurance, the current system imposes a hidden tax paid by the young and healthy (who are thought to be better able to pay) for the benefit of the old and sick (who are thought to be less able). But paying for insurance may not necessarily be easier for the young; older employees may have higher wages. Some sick people are quite able to pay for their insurance; some healthy ones cannot.

To the extent it exists, the cross-subsidy within a firm is hidden; in fact, this camouflage may be what proponents of the current system are defending. A social policy, sugar-coated by the government subsidy, is imposed on young and healthy workers without their knowledge. In effect, they pay a silent tax to help their older and sicker—but not necessarily poorer—coworkers obtain insurance.

Eliminating the exclusion and replacing it with a voucher would stimulate an individual market in which each worker knows what his insurance actually costs. Exposing hidden subsidies surely is good policy. The concern, however, is that the young and the healthy would not buy insurance voluntarily, at the same time making insurance more expensive for high-risk employees and leaving the young vulnerable to their own unexpected medical costs.[5]

The young and healthy are more likely to buy insurance if it is priced to reflect their own risk (which negates any cross-subsidy to the sick) and less likely to buy it if they are asked to cross-subsidize the higher risks (which reduces their own protection). If the goal is to encourage the young and healthy to purchase insurance for their own protection, it would be served by permitting insurers to charge on the basis of individual risk. If, on the other hand, the policy is to encourage low-risk individuals to purchase coverage in order to cross-subsidize the sick, premiums must be calculated on something more nearly approaching community rating. In a voluntary market, however, this would reduce the number of young and healthy who purchase insurance and consequently could be self-defeating.

The present system may be thought to have avoided this dilemma by ensuring that healthy workers are both protected for their own risk *and* required to subsidize coverage for high-risk people. It even may have achieved these two seemingly irreconcilable goals for one subset of the population (employees of firms that provide insurance). If it has, however, it is only by imposing a hidden tax on young and healthy workers. The exclusion for employer-provided insurance, therefore, can be defended as the appropriate way to subsidize insurance only if the goal is to require younger and healthier workers, without their knowledge or consent, to cross-subsidize their fellow employees.

Eliminating the exclusion would bring these issues to public attention. Insurers in a free individual market will charge according to individual risk rather than on the basis of a firm's aggregate experience. Those who believe the healthy should subsidize the sick could try to obtain mandatory and open community rating. But even if they were successful, they still might not achieve their goal: Many of the healthy would decide not to buy insurance.

This could lead to a requirement that the young and healthy buy insurance. A mandate that every American obtain insurance would be the most effective way to make certain that everyone bears the cost of his risk.[6] But that approach would be administratively complex and, some people believe, would infringe on personal freedom even if it was not accompanied by community rating. A mandate imposed with community rating would replicate the de facto mandate of the present employment-based system, with the difference that low-risk workers would see the cost of their insurance and better understand that they were subsidizing others. No mandate is politically feasible at this point; a mandate imposed in conjunction with community rating would encounter even less political acceptance.

There are more effective ways than community rating to help the sick (or, perhaps more precisely, the poor, whether sick or healthy) to purchase insurance without an explicit new mandate or the de facto mandate of the present system. A voucher could be tailored to the premium charged each person, for example, and adjusted further on the basis of income.

Linking vouchers so closely to premiums, however, would subsidize inefficient plans and reintroduce open-ended subsidies. It may be necessary, therefore, to have the voucher reflect the appropriate factors that presumably determine premiums, such as geography, age, and gender. The voucher could be based on what insurers in an area charge all the people in a particular matrix, adjusted for income.

The main variation in premiums would be based on health status. Vouchers that did not reflect this factor would be out of step with premiums. This discrepancy, while relatively unimportant in cases in which an individual (sick or not) is able to pay the difference between the voucher and the premium, would be most apparent in cases in which it was most significant: in the case of those who are sick and poor and unable to make up the difference.

So far, no satisfactory way to adjust for risk has been developed, and unless an accurate risk adjuster is developed in the future, the voucher might not reflect the premium accurately. This possibility, however, does not justify retaining the status quo. If the voucher varied too widely from the premium being charged, various other steps could be taken. For example, a supplemental subsidy could be provided, with the government making up a percentage, based on income, if the gap was greater than a certain amount. Alternatively, the individual could be eligible for a risk pool, with the gap made up by the taxpayers or insurance companies (and thus the insured). In either case, to avoid subsidizing an inefficient plan, the amount to be made up would have to be calculated on the basis of the average of a number of premiums quoted to the individual.

A risk pool could be abused. Government might fail to subsidize it sufficiently and then make up the shortfall by specifying how much pool members may be charged in premiums. Insurers then would avoid selling to the risk pool. Conversely, there is a danger that the pool could be a step toward government control. By expanding the entry criteria and increasing the subsidy, government could use the risk pool to socialize the cost of insurance, which would be likely to result in increased regulation of insurance and ultimately of the health care system.

A different route would be to require insurers to use the same risk adjustments in setting premiums that the government uses in determining the value of the voucher. Insurers would be free to quote their own standard rates, but they would have to vary them in parallel with the methodology used to adjust the voucher. This arrangement would shift the risk that the adjuster did not work from the insured to the insurer. No one plan would suffer competitively if the members for whom the risk adjustment did not predict costs accurately were distributed randomly. In effect, the plans would pool the unexpected risk equally among their members.

A problem could arise if one insurer received a disproportionate share of enrollees whose costs were higher than the risk adjuster assumed. Ironically, this is the same problem that can occur in cases in which community rating is required. The plan that received more high-risk members would be forced to raise premiums more rapidly than its competitors. This could result, it is said, in a "death spiral" caused by selection bias: Some of the sick stay in the plan because they want the benefits and are able to pay even though the voucher does not fully reflect their risk; the healthy exit to join a less expensive plan, leaving the fewer and sicker members to pay ever-higher premiums. In the end, the insurer exits the market or goes bankrupt.

It is not clear, however, that this would occur. If a plan attracted more than its share of unexpectedly high-cost members, it might be because its benefits were more attractive. It would be expected to bring them in line with other plans. If it were forced to raise its premium, some of the sick would leave because they could not afford to pay the gap between the voucher and the premium; they would join other plans, resulting in a better distribution of the high-risk people.

Moreover, even if a death spiral did kill one plan, it would not destroy the market. Members would join other plans and redistribute themselves. At worst, their provider relationships would be disrupted.

Another approach would be to require insurers to sell policies that were guaranteed renewable; that is, the premium could not be raised by more than a stated percentage over a period, regardless of change in risk, with no change in the voucher. Although this would lengthen the insurance policy, it would not protect the individual at the expiration of the renewal period.

The essential point is that the employment-based risk pools that result from the exclusion are not necessary to make insurance available to high-risk people. There are numerous ways to subsidize high-risk individuals who cannot afford insurance other than community rating within a firm. With the termination of the exclusion, these would be available to all Americans, not just those who work in certain firms. They would be financed more broadly and thus more equitably.

Ending the exclusion and the hidden mandate it supports will not necessarily reduce coverage. In fact, severing the link between subsidy and employment is likely to expand coverage. The subsidy would not be limited by the vagaries of the job market and could be targeted on the basis of need. If employees were given a voucher in place of the exclusion, many would purchase insurance (particularly catastrophic coverage, the most suitable for the healthy) without a mandate. Moreover, if insurers were permitted to deny coverage for preexisting conditions of first-time buyers, people would have an even stronger incentive to obtain insurance. The combination of a voucher to assist in the purchase of insurance and the threat of not being able to obtain insurance for a preexisting condition would result in widespread coverage—particularly among the young and healthy, many of whom are now working in jobs that do not provide insurance.

In any event, the effects of converting to an individual market can be monitored closely, and the government can take corrective action if the voucher is not high enough for individuals to purchase the amount of insurance deemed appropriate. No one knows exactly what will happen if the present system for delivering a subsidy for the purchase of health insurance is ended. But the inefficiencies and inequities of the present system and the likelihood that an individual voucher would fix those flaws make it difficult to explain the attraction of the status quo.

NOTES

[1] Sherry Glied, *Revising the Tax Treatment of Employer-Provided Health Insurance* (Washington, D.C.: AEI Press, 1994), pp. 29–30.

[2] Mark Pauly, however, suggests elsewhere in this book that high-risk employees to some extent actually may pay more for their insurance through wage offsets. To the extent this is true, the employment-based system is not providing the community rating that is said to be its advantage.

[3] See Glied, *Revising the Tax Treatment of Employer-Provided Health Insurance,* p. 7.

[4] *Ibid.*

[5] Another concern is not that low-risk individuals will refuse to buy insurance, but that they will delay doing so until they need care. Even if the insurer is not constrained by a community rating requirement, it will not have the same information as the individual who demands services without having adequately paid for his risk. Other members of the plan would make up the shortfall.

[6] See Mark V. Pauly, Patricia Danzon, Paul Feldstein, and John S. Hoff, *Responsible National Health Insurance* (Washington, D.C.: AEI Press, 1992), pp. 10–13.

7

TOWARD A UNIVERSAL MARKETPLACE FOR HEALTH CARE

David B. Kendall[1]

The U.S. health care system needs an alternative to employment-based health insurance. Although such insurance proved reliable for much of the period following World War II, runaway medical inflation has undermined it. During the past decade, the link between jobs and health insurance has been deteriorating.

Both the spread of coverage and the subsequent explosion of costs have been driven by a single government policy: the tax treatment of employment-based health insurance. Employers have a strong incentive to provide health care benefits because, unlike wages, these benefits are not taxed. Because this tax break is unlimited, workers have demanded, and employers have provided, the most costly health insurance.

Employers themselves have taken the first step away from the current system through their efforts to fight medical cost inflation. They no longer offer coverage with an unlimited choice of providers at no cost to workers; instead, they increasingly act as agents for workers and arrange a menu of health plan choices either directly or through a purchasing group. This approach empowers workers to decide for themselves whether they prefer the more expensive fee-for-service plan, a less costly health maintenance organization (HMO), or some other alternative. In effect, employers are transforming the character of the health insurance marketplace from wholesale to retail.

Reforming the tax treatment of health insurance offers the opportunity to buttress the fight against medical inflation, expand coverage to the uninsured, and broaden individual choice. A cap on the tax break would check the cost spiral simply by refusing to subsidize it. A tax credit for individuals would benefit those who lack job-based coverage or do not like the choices offered by their employers. The combination of a tax cap and tax credits would steel the employment-based system by creating a competitive alternative. Employers would have an even more compelling reason to meet the health coverage demands of their employees.

Both extremes of the political spectrum assert that the employment-based system is beyond repair, and would eliminate the tax break for job-based coverage altogether. In its place, liberals would establish a single-payer system, while conservatives would prefer an unregulated marketplace for individual insurance policies.

A "scorched earth" approach that needlessly threatens the existing coverage of millions of Americans is likely to produce the same ideological polarization and gridlock that has frustrated reform of the private marketplace and health care entitlements since 1993. It is important to remember that two-thirds of all workers and their families still get health insurance through a job.

Both the means and the opportunity to break the deadlock over reform are close at hand. A competitive alternative to the employment-based system would expand coverage to the uninsured without creating a vast new entitlement. The debate offers the opportunity to move toward a universal marketplace for health care based on the principle of securing progressive social goals through market means.

THE NEED FOR CHANGE

Federal tax policy regarding health insurance has not been altered significantly since the income tax was enacted in 1913. At first, the income tax did not apply to employee health benefits because they were offered only rarely. Benefits did not become widespread until World War II, when employers began to use them to attract workers whose wages were frozen by wartime price controls.

Like many other government policies that have escaped scrutiny, the tax treatment of health insurance is riddled with contradictions:

- It encourages people to seek coverage when they have a job but offers no help to workers who are laid off.
- It promotes personal responsibility by encouraging workers to rely on insurance rather than charity care, but it also encourages wasteful spending on "Cadillac" coverage because the tax break is unlimited.
- It puts small companies at a competitive disadvantage versus large companies, which can lower their administrative costs—and thus their labor costs—significantly by avoiding the underwriting and marketing expenses that are peculiar to the small-employer health insurance market.
- It achieves a measure of equality by pooling high-risk and low-risk employees but produces inequitable benefits for low-income workers because, like all tax deductions, it is worth more in higher tax brackets. Families with incomes less than $10,000 receive one-tenth the subsidy of families earning more than $100,000.

These contradictions are even more glaring in light of several recent trends: large layoffs due to corporate downsizing, the drive to restrain medical inflation, and the widening income gap between rich and poor. The time has come for an overhaul.

THE TAX REFORM THREAT

Tax reform would seem to provide the ideal opportunity to reform the treatment of health insurance. A top-to-bottom review of the tax system would have to include its deeply rooted connection with the health care system. At the moment, however, the tax reform debate is ignoring the issue and putting the health care system at risk.

Every major reform proposal would eliminate the tax break for employment-based health care coverage. The flat tax proposed by Representative Richard Armey (R–TX) and Steve Forbes would eliminate the deduction that businesses take for covering their workers. The consumption tax plans of Senator Pete Domenici of New Mexico and former Senator Sam Nunn of Georgia and of Representative Bill Archer (R–TX) and Senator Richard Lugar (R–IN), as well as the tax reform proposed by Representative Richard Gephardt (D–MO), would end the exclusion of employer-paid premiums from the income of employees.

Ordinarily, eliminating a government subsidy would be a welcome event because a subsidy can drive up the cost of a product by insulating consumers from the real price. In the case of health care markets, however, the tax subsidy plays an integral role. It encourages consumers to buy health insurance when they are healthy rather than take a "free ride" on charity care when they get sick. The result is lower insurance rates for everyone. In addition, health insurance secures better health outcomes when care is available in a timely fashion. The tax subsidy establishes health care as a key public expenditure.

Even though eliminating the tax break for health insurance would end the federal subsidizing of medical inflation, the cure would be worse than the disease. The Congressional Budget Office (CBO) estimates that the number of Americans with insurance would fall by 16 to 26 percent.[2] In addition, insurance premiums would skyrocket by 35 percent because young healthy individuals are likely to drop their coverage. Eliminating this tax break would disrupt a source of financing for health coverage that benefits 146 million Americans—more than twice the number covered by Medicare and Medicaid.

If tax reform were accompanied by a mandate that everyone had coverage, the free-rider problem would be minimized, but a mandate without subsidies for low-income workers is unlikely to be enforced or enacted.

The tax break for health insurance may be politically vulnerable because many Americans are not aware of it or of its value. Unlike itemized deductions, it requires no tax filings by individuals. Insurance premiums appear nowhere on any tax forms because they are exempt from all major taxes (federal and state income, payroll, and corporate taxes). Some employers do not even inform their employees of the value of their health care benefits. Perhaps the threat of tax reform will spur them to do so.

FROM THREAT TO OPPORTUNITY

A strategy to defend the tax subsidy for health insurance based on the status quo is likely to fail. To be sure, the prospect of a 35 percent insurance premium hike punctures the promise that eliminating tax breaks and lowering tax rates would save workers money. Tax reform poses three additional challenges on which the status quo falls short.

1. Forty million Americans would be better off with the lower rates from eliminating the tax subsidy because they lack coverage and do not benefit from the subsidy.
2. Second, those who do not like their job-based coverage might be better off because most employers would cash out their health care benefits in the form of higher wages, which workers could use to purchase their own coverage (even though it might cost them more money).
3. Third, medical inflation is likely to reignite if the tax subsidy remains open-ended.

The most straightforward response to these challenges is to expand insurance coverage and individual choice through tax credits and restrain medical inflation with a tax cap.

Tax Credits to Expand Access

A tax credit should be broadly available for individuals to apply toward the purchase of insurance through an employer, through a purchasing group, or directly in the marketplace. The tax credit would be refundable for those with no tax liability but would not be available to people covered by Medicare or Medicaid.

The amount of the tax credit would depend largely on the amount of revenue available to finance it. A $900-per-person tax credit used by half of the uninsured would cost $18 billion each year, which is roughly equal to the revenue raised by a tax cap.[3] State legislatures could provide additional credit by adopting a similar reform. Yet another source of revenue is a means test for Medicare benefits. Low-income workers, who often lack coverage and are raising families, should not be required to subsidize the coverage of wealthy retirees.

Tax credits are a well-established method for assisting lower-income workers. Like the earned income tax credit, a health care tax credit would avoid the stigma of welfare. The tough question is what size tax credit would induce most of the uninsured to purchase coverage. Since a $900 tax credit would cover roughly half the cost of basic coverage, a supplemental tax credit would be appropriate for the very poor who are not covered by Medicaid.

Tax Credits to Expand Choice

A $900 tax credit would enable about half of all families with job-based coverage to opt for individual coverage without paying higher taxes.[4] According to the CBO, the current tax break is worth $900 or less to families earning less than $40,000. Families with higher incomes who opt out might pay as much as $1,000 more in taxes, but they also have more resources with which to do so.

Workers still would face a penalty for giving up their job-based coverage if their employers did not make up the difference with extra wages, but requiring employers to cash out benefits on an individual basis would be an open invitation for insurance companies to "cherry-pick" healthy employees and leave behind the less healthy, more costly employees. It would be much better to let employers and employees make the decision to cash out as a group.

Giving workers a real choice to opt out of job-based coverage has the potential to diffuse the sentiment against managed care. Even though the claim that employers are forcing their employees into managed care plans has been exaggerated, the ability of employers to offer a wide range of high-quality choices varies widely, particularly among smaller businesses. Over 70 percent of large employers and 50 percent of medium-size companies continue to offer a fee-for-service plan.[5] Employers without a fee-for-service option usually offer a managed care / fee-for-service hybrid such as preferred provider organizations or point-of-service options. With the advent of these new products, the appeal of HMOs that restrict choice to a closed panel of providers is fading.

For smaller businesses, purchasing groups offer the expertise and purchasing power of large employers. Tax credits would accelerate the development of purchasing groups by empowering workers to press their employers for wider choices. Purchasing groups provide a menu that compares benefits, premiums, and quality for all types of health plans. They also enable workers to keep their health plan if they change jobs and their new company does not offer their plan as a choice. In short, purchasing groups offer the best hope for a competitive alternative to employment-based health care.

A Tax Cap to Restrain Medical Inflation

Although medical inflation has fallen to 30-year lows for employment-based coverage, most health care analysts expect higher rates in the near future. Such countervailing forces as new technology will drive up costs despite the success of cost-restraining competition among health plans. A tax cap would ensure that consumer decisions over added costs are not distorted by the tax subsidy, which causes consumers to place an inflated value on health care products. Enacting a tax cap now would be well-timed because it appears less threatening when inflation is moderate.

A tax cap also would provide the opportunity to resolve the dispute over Medical Savings Accounts (MSAs). MSA supporters argue that the tax code has promoted too much health care spending through insurance coverage and too little from out-of-pocket sources. MSAs would encourage the purchase of high-deductible plans by giving out-of-pocket expenses the same generous tax treatment as employer-provided insurance.

Economist Mark Pauly has asked the appropriate question: "Do Two Wrongs Make a Right?"[6] Creating an expensive new subsidy for out-of-pocket costs only adds to the current problem and diverts limited federal resources away from covering the uninsured. The tax cap avoids this dilemma by setting an overarching limit on the tax break, allowing employers and employees to sort out their preferred mix of insurance and subsidies for out-of-pocket expenses.

There are, of course, many additional issues that would need to be resolved to implement a tax cap/tax credit reform. For example, the rules governing insurance rates that prevent discrimination against the sick should be the same in all segments of the marketplace: employment-based coverage, purchasing groups, and individual coverage. Additional reforms are necessary to respond to concerns about the quality of care in the current marketplace, such as unequal access to innovative medical technology.

In sum, creating a competitive alternative to the employment-based system will give it the best chance to survive tax reform and into the period beyond reform.

HEALTH CARE REFORM IN 1996

A system of tax credits and a tax cap would pick up where recent legislation falls short. In 1996, Senators Nancy Kassebaum (R–Kan.) and Edward Kennedy (D–Mass.) successfully sponsored legislation that guarantees access to insurance coverage, regardless of preexisting conditions, as long as an individual maintains continuous coverage. Although this new law poses little problem for employers, it probably will drive up insurance premiums for individual coverage because it lacks a tax break to encourage healthy individuals to maintain continuous coverage. Tax credits would make portability reform in the individual marketplace much less likely to drive up premiums.

A strategy based on tax credits and a tax cap also provides an alternative to the expansion of MSAs, which were enacted on a trial basis as a part of the Kassebaum–Kennedy legislation. As currently structured, MSAs would expand the regressive, inflationary, and outdated employment-based tax subsidy system.

Regardless of the outcome of the current health reform debate, the key concern for the future is whether the extremes will continue to dominate or a strong center will emerge. Advocates from the left and right may believe that neglecting the immediate problems of the employment-based health system will work to their advantage in the long run, but such an approach is more likely to hurt everyone by increasing cynicism and weakening the country's capacity for self-governance. Progressive forces should seize this opportunity to move the United States toward a universal marketplace for health care.

NOTES

[1] The views expressed in this paper are the author's and do not necessarily reflect the views of the Progressive Policy Institute.

[2] Congressional Budget Office, *The Tax Treatment of Employment-Based Health Insurance* (Washington, D.C.: U.S. Government Printing Office, March 1994), p. 48.

[3] Part of the overall cost of a tax credit stems from the choice by some low-income workers to use the credit rather than the income exclusion for employer-paid coverage because the tax credit could be

worth more than the exclusion for many workers in lower tax brackets. A $900 tax credit would tempt roughly 30 percent of families with employment-based coverage to "trade up" from the tax exclusion to the tax credit. See Congressional Budget Office, *The Tax Treatment of Employment-Based Health Insurance,* pp. 30, 58.

[4] *Ibid.,* p. 30.

[5] Foster Higgins, "National Survey of Employer-Sponsored Health Plans," Philadelphia, Pa., 1995.

[6] Mark V. Pauly, "An Analysis of Medical Savings Accounts: Do Two Wrongs Make a Right?" American Enterprise Institute, Washington, D.C., 1994.

8

HEALTH CARE REFORM: WHY NOT TRY REAL INSURANCE?

Norman B. Ture, Ph.D., and Stephen J. Entin

Several so-called insurance reforms are being pushed on us as a result of the perception that the private insurance market has failed to serve the needs of the public. Among these reforms are community-rated premiums, guaranteed issue or renewal of policies to all comers (portability), prohibition of exclusions for existing conditions, and forced national insurance schemes. But charges that the free market has been tried and has failed are false. In fact, the free market in health insurance has been so thoroughly distorted by government regulation that it cannot be said to have been tried.

Federal intervention is defensible if market failure creates inefficiencies and if regulation can improve things. If, however, federal regulation created the inefficiencies in the first place, then the appropriate policy is to remove the offending regulation, not to pile on more.

The failures of the health care market are primarily the results of mistaken government policies, reflected on both the spending and revenue sides of the federal budget. On the spending side are enormous subsidies for health care consumption, principally those provided by Medicare and Medicaid. Both these programs allow their respective constituencies to purchase health care at a fraction of its real cost. The obvious result is that the subsidized individuals demand more health care than they would if they had to pay the full costs themselves.

A case can certainly be made for subsidizing health care for the very poor, although it is debatable whether Medicaid, with its huge bureaucratic overhead, is the most efficient way to do so. It is much more difficult to make a case for Medicare, particularly considering the existence of Medicaid. The mere fact that one reaches 65 is no excuse for being allowed to pay only a fraction of the cost of one's health care. Neither does it call for *requiring* one to participate in the subsidy.

On the revenue side, the existing tax treatment of health insurance encourages employer-based insurance that effectively masks the true costs of health care from the large number of people participating in employer-provided plans. Unlike most other compensation, individuals are not required to include the value of "employer-paid" health insurance premiums in their taxable income. In contrast, those who purchase their own insurance receive either no tax break for premiums or, in the case of the self-employed, only a partial deduction. The exclusion from tax makes employer-provided health insurance appear both less costly than insurance obtained from other sources and less expensive than other goods and services. Furthermore, many individuals are unaware of the amount of wages and other compensation they forgo in favor of that insurance. Consequently, they favor generous policies that require them to dig into their pockets for only the first few dollars of health care and, thereafter, usually for only 20 cents per dollar of care. Masking the costs necessarily throws off their economizing calculus.

Furthermore, by encouraging people to obtain health insurance at their place of work, tax policy creates problems related to the loss and change of jobs: namely, lack of portability and exclusion of, or higher premiums for, preexisting conditions. The majority of working people and their families have health coverage through employer-based plans. That leaves few people to seek individual-based insurance, reducing the size of individual-based pools and making it more likely that those people will be subject to hefty increases in premiums in the event of illness.

Because government programs and policies account for many of the alleged shortcomings in the health care market, it would seem obvious that the best solution would be for the government to stop doing what it has been doing. Medical care for the very poor should be discontinued as stand-alone programs and integrated into an overall welfare system. For those who are 65 years of age and older and who do not require public assistance, Medicare should be phased out and replaced by private insurance as rapidly as feasible. The Medicare subsidy for the very poor who are 65 and over also should be transferred into the welfare system.

The tax provisions pertaining to health insurance should be revised to transfer the tax favor to the individual. There are many ways to shelter people's health care and insurance costs from taxes without hiding those costs from them. To encourage people to economize, the opportunity cost—what they must give up to obtain health care—has to be obvious. Tax-deductible medical savings accounts would be highly effective if they did not restrict the use of accumulated savings, above amounts needed for the annual deductible and copayments under the individual's chosen health plan, to the purchase of medical care. Each dollar withdrawn to purchase health care would be one fewer dollar available for other purchases or saving, putting all other uses of the income in the accounts on the same tax footing and eliminating the incentive to over-consume health care.

Proposals for health insurance reform, from the Clintons' plan to the most recent offerings, fail to address some or all of the policy errors that have muddled the market. With some exceptions, they tend to treat only the symptoms, and those, badly. They leave direct subsidies in place for the elderly regardless of income, continue to focus the tax subsidy to employer-based insurance, and fail to bring people face to face with the cost of their health care.

There has been considerable concern over the fact that health care spending is 14 percent of the country's gross domestic product or that the unit price of health care rises more rapidly than other items in the consumer price index. These observations should impel policy initiatives only if they are symptoms of the health care market's malfunction; by itself, neither should raise a congressman's or senator's eyebrow. If the market were found to be reasonably efficient, the amount or share of our incomes we devote to health care should be nobody's business but our own.

Current policy errors, however, artificially inflate the use of health care, driving up unit costs, average premiums, and aggregate outlays. This has led to the two concerns that have driven the health care debate: the rising cost of Medicare and Medicaid and rising health insurance costs, which constitute a large portion of the labor compensation package.

Rather than deal with the policy errors, however, government and business have blamed rising costs on "cost-shifting" by the uninsured, and many have concluded that the solution is universal coverage. The basis for the focus on cost-shifting is the fact that when uninsured individuals obtain health care for which they do not pay, the costs borne by other people—including people covered by employer-provided insurance—presumably are raised. The result is higher insurance premiums. The nonpaying uninsured thus shift the cost of their health care to others. Considering that health insurance is a significant part of a worker's pay, cost-shifting significantly raises labor costs. Business leaders understandably, albeit unwisely, welcomed (at least initially) the government's enlarged intrusion into the health care market, assuming that it would reduce if not entirely eliminate the problem.

Roughly parallel is the policymaker's concern that cost-shifting, by elevating the unit price of health care, raises the costs that Medicare and Medicaid must cover. The result is exacerbation of the difficulties in constraining increases in federal and state spending on these programs, a major source of the persistent and rising federal entitlement spending. Ostensibly, eliminating cost-shifting by requiring that everyone be insured would address that problem.

The principal economic objective of the health care reform plan proposed by President Bill Clinton, therefore, was to reduce spending on health care to relieve the pressure on the federal budget. (President Clinton asserted in February 1993 that adoption of his yet-to-be-formulated reform plan would result in reduced federal spending of $313 billion over fiscal years 1995–2000.)

For two reasons, blaming "cost-shifting" was nonsense, as was the call for universal health insurance coverage. First, one might well ask how extending insurance to a significantly large number of people can reduce outlays for health care or depress its unit prices. Presumably, the greater the number of people who have insurance, the greater will be the demand for health care. The greater the demand, the greater will be the total amount spent and the higher will be its unit price. Our own calculation is that mandated universal coverage initially would add $55 billion to $60 billion to the health care bill. Averting that would require rigorous rationing of health care and severe price controls.

Second, most of the cost-shifting involves medical services for people too poor to buy health insurance. By definition, then, if the poor are to obtain health insurance, someone else must pay for it—which means that some form of cost-shifting is inevitable.

In effect, business wanted the government to pick up the tab for the poor, which was not the objective of the government's budgeteers. In any event, nearly all federal actions eventually involve federal taxes or unfunded federal mandates. Consequently, the Clintons' plan proposed to tax business, among others, to pay for the health insurance of the poor or to force the poor into insurance pools in which their care would be cross-subsidized by other policyholders. That was not the objective of the business community.

Mandating universal coverage is a mistaken solution to the problem. It would not eliminate cost-shifting; it would merely change the identity of those to whom the cost is shifted. Costs would be shifted to one or another group of taxpayers and to young and healthy policyholders. Employers would not find their labor costs reduced; what they might save in health insurance premiums they would pay in additional taxes, wages, or other compensation.

This conundrum reinforces a point made earlier. The lack of health insurance for the poor is a welfare problem, not an insurance problem. We can, and should, deal with it as we should deal with any poverty issue: with cash assistance or vouchers explicitly financed by general tax revenue. These would empower the poor to obtain insurance or health care in the same market as other citizens without distorting the price structure through price controls or such cross-subsidies as community rating or other devices.

Universal coverage was not to be restricted to the poor. There are individuals who can afford health insurance but who place a higher priority on other uses of their incomes. Some employees prefer other forms of compensation to health insurance. Some of these uninsured people might incur health care costs that they could not themselves defray, resulting in the cost-shifting that reformers see as anathema.

The same mindset that leads policymakers to believe that everyone must have health insurance also makes them insist on specifying the benefits for which health insurance must pay. Without this specification, some people would choose to purchase, on their own or through their employers, inexpensive, bare-bones policies with limited benefits, high deductibles, and high copayments. Some of those people would incur medical expenses that were not covered by their policies and that they could not afford. The result would be the cost-shifting reformers seek to eliminate. Here, too, reformers would mandate a result contrary to the wishes of consumers and employers and at odds with the requirements of a free market.

There is another reason sometimes offered for insistence on universal coverage. Without mandated coverage, many younger and healthier people would forgo coverage in favor of more valuable (to them) uses of their incomes. Their opting out would leave only older and less healthy people seeking insurance, supposedly boosting their premiums. Their premiums would rise because the insurance pool would consist only of people with higher-than-average health care costs.

This presumed increase in premiums, however, is a fallacy. Increases in the averages would represent real increases for those who remain insured only if those forgoing coverage otherwise would have borne part of the cost of the insurance and health care of those remaining. In an efficient market, the price of insurance for older and less healthy persons would closely reflect their higher cost and would not be shared by the young and healthy even if they were to buy policies for themselves at premiums reflecting their healthier status. The results of free choice, including opting out and its consequences for the level of health insurance premiums, are not undesirable if one is seeking improvement in the health care market. One would oppose self-selection only if one's goal were cross-subsidization of those with higher premiums and costs.

Indeed, cross-subsidies do seem to be the goal of most reformers. Virtually all plans call for community rating, permitting premium differentials only with respect to age, gender, and geography at most, and only within strict limits. The objective sought by broadly based community rating is to assure "affordability" of health insurance coverage lest some people choose to go uncovered and impose cost-shifting on others. Such community rating provides much lower premiums for people whose age, health, or other relevant attributes would call for substantially higher premiums. It entails, however, much higher premiums for the young and healthy than otherwise, making insurance a bad deal for them and making it necessary to force them to buy it. Thus, community rating also shifts costs, but its advocates somehow believe that this type of cost-shifting is acceptable. In any event, community rating would deny insurers the right to adjust premiums to reflect objectively determined risk differentials. This not-very-subtle form of price control obviously violates the free market.

These two objectives of universal coverage and affordability also lead to prohibiting insurers from denying coverage or charging higher premiums to people with medical problems. Clearly, if universal coverage is to achieved, no one can be denied insurance merely because the benefits he is likely to claim are much greater than the likely claims of healthy people. Most reform plans include such prohibitions, which belie the "free-market" label.

Many plans would prohibit insurers from denying renewals or charging higher renewal premiums for people who have developed medical conditions likely to lead to above-average claims. Those constraints obviously are required by the objectives of universal coverage and affordability, but they would transform insurers into quasi-government agencies guided by government dictates rather than by judgments of how best to meet the demands of people seeking health insurance.

The irony is that all these distortions of the free market seek to protect taxpayers or people with insurance from one type of *potential* cost-shifting by adopting a pricing structure that *guarantees* another type of cost-shifting. A young healthy person, who may be just out of school and earning a low beginner's wage, must pay a greater-than-actuarially-fair premium to hold down the premium for an older individual who may have a salary or other income five times as large and also may be perfectly capable of paying the higher premium his age or chronic condition otherwise might require. The cross-subsidies generated by these violations of the free market are not means-tested and are in no way tied to economic hardship. It would make far more sense to rely on free-market pricing and provide assistance only to those for whom the resulting premiums constitute a real hardship.

Grandiose plans to impose national health insurance and universal, mandated coverage fell of their own excesses. Nonetheless, most of the more modest reform proposals seek to address the preexisting-condition exclusion, price hikes in the event of illness, nonrenewability, and nonportability. These plans are far from efficient free-market proposals. They address the symptoms of current federal policy errors without addressing the policy errors themselves.

The essence of a free market is voluntary exchange between buyer and seller on terms freely negotiated. If the buyer is required to buy or the seller is required to sell, the most essential attribute of a free market is absent. If something other than the producer's perception of what best satisfies buyers' demands dictates the design of the product or service, the market is not free. If the price is determined in any way other than by unconstrained offers to purchase and to sell, there is no free market.

TESTS FOR REAL INSURANCE

Applying these tests, the policymaker should ask whether a health care proposal *requires* people to have insurance. By its very nature, any such mandate, no matter how it is to be implemented, is at odds with the free-market requirement of voluntary purchase.

- Does a plan specify the benefits the policy must provide? If so, the insurer would not be free to design the policy to meet the demands of different buyers, and customers would not be free to purchase the kind of policy they—not the government—believe would best meet their needs. In view of the enormous variety of the relevant circumstances of the people to be insured, no single "one-size-fits-all" policy can satisfy everybody. Such a plan constitutes government command and control, not a free market.
- Does a plan specify the terms of sale for coverage? Would the insurer be free to charge differing premiums for any given coverage based on actuarial assessments of the health risks of the differing groups to be insured? A health insurance plan that insists on broadly based community rating, and hence only very limited premium differentials, would severely constrain both insurers' freedom in marketing their policies and customers' freedom in choosing policies suited to their needs. It would impose higher premiums on younger, healthier members of the pool than are needed to cover the expected costs, making the insurance a bad buy and discouraging them from obtaining coverage.
- Does a plan either prohibit health insurers from denying coverage for any significant period of time to people with preexisting conditions or preclude the insurer's charging such

people a higher premium? Excluding existing conditions in determining whether insurance is to be offered is most assuredly inconsistent with a free market. It is particularly unworkable in small pools in which the inclusion of such people would involve a significant increase in the premiums of other policyholders.

- Does a plan insist on policy renewals with no increase in premium, regardless of any change in the person's health? In effect, this is equivalent to requiring insurers to offer—and customers to buy—lifetime policies at group rates. Imposing any such constraint on insurers violates their freedom to assess differences in cost conditions when designing and pricing their products. By requiring higher premiums than currently are being charged, it reduces affordability and discourages people from buying insurance.

Most of the health care reform proposals under consideration in Congress flunk one or more of these free-market tests.

Many concerns dealt with by these mandates are legitimate, but they arise in large part because of the regulatory constraints on small individual-based insurance pools and the siphoning off of participants into employer-based pools. The fixes proposed would fail in much the same way if applied to small pools. The concerns largely would disappear, however, if the employer-based system were phased out and individual-based pools were expanded to become the primary source of insurance.

Private individual health insurance can be strengthened and would be far more effective than the widely proposed nationalized or government-regulated health insurance. What would real insurance look like? How would it address those problems?

In a private individual insurance system, people would purchase policies in their own names. The policies would be portable rather than tied to their place of employment. (People still could purchase individual policies through groups at work or through religious, social, or professional organizations, both to cut down on the time spent shopping and to obtain quantity discounts.)

Any tax exclusion for insurance premiums and benefits would be extended to all individuals regardless of where they purchased their policies. Insurance would not have to be employment-based to receive tax relief. Ideally, the tax incentive would be designed to leave the full cost of using additional units of health care fully visible to the consumer.

Individuals would be risk-rated for many factors, including age, sex, geography, occupation, and existing conditions. Those with higher risks would be admitted to insurance pools with a higher premium (known as a "substandard load" in the industry).

Consumers would have to decide between purchasing a policy that guaranteed renewal without a premium adjustment in the event of protracted illness or "self-insuring" against that eventuality. Policies with guaranteed renewal would bear a higher premium than those that did not. Premiums would be lower for policies that require the individual to submit to re-rating and premium adjustments before renewal in order to reflect changes in health status. Insurance companies would offer the choice of such plans in a large free market if people demanded it.

Once an individual purchased a guaranteed-renewal policy with an appropriate rate differential, his future rate increases would match those of the pool. If individuals are rated correctly as to probability of illness when joining the pool, the insurance company should be able to accommodate the costs of those who get sick within the expected costs of the pool. There would be no need for a specific hike in the individual's future premium, provided the pools are large enough. That such policies are not widely used today may be due to several causes: There may be insufficient interest in the guarantee; there may be reluctance to pay the higher costs associated with the small size of individual pools, considering the prevalence of employment-based coverage; or state regulation may be preempting the ability of insurers to offer a variety of innovative policies.

Under a system favoring individual-based policies, pools would be far larger than is possible under the current system, in which the tax preference for employer-based plans siphons off the bulk of the population. Large individual-based pools would make it possible for private insurers to handle people with higher risk factors than at present. The pools would contain enough such people to make their claims conform closely to the national average for people with those risk characteristics and would enable the company to charge an actuarially fair risk premium without fear of exposure to an extraordinary level of claims. Consequently, some people currently classified as uninsurable would be insurable in a broader risk pool.

During the transition to a new system, there would be concerns about preexisting conditions. Some customers might prefer to forgo coverage of an existing condition in order to avoid a higher premium. Insurance companies currently sell policies that contain a denial of benefits for treatment of an existing condition, permitting a lower premium for coverage of all other conditions. Such choices would be possible because competition would force companies to offer a variety of plans tailored to the needs of their customers. In fact, plans offering various types of coverage—differential premiums, exclusions of existing conditions—are available now to meet a variety of needs. Once individual-based pools are the norm, people would be able to enter them from the start of their insured lives, either at birth or upon leaving home, and conditions therefore would not be preexisting. The problem of how to deal with people leaving employer-based pools to enter small individual pools would be rendered moot.

Actuarial science can handle risk-rating with sufficient accuracy to ensure the stability of large pools. The chief difficulty in accurately pricing risk today comes from restrictions laid down by regulators, especially in states that recently have "reformed" health care.

Any system would operate with more certainty and stability if reinsurance mechanisms or state-run risk pools existed for very high-risk or chronically ill individuals. State risk pools are appropriate mechanisms for dealing with people whose medical needs create financial hardship. Whether individuals or families need help because their incomes are too low to buy health insurance or because expensive medical conditions have raised premiums beyond their ability to pay, government should treat the problem as a welfare issue and provide means-tested financial assistance. State risk pools currently running into trouble are holding premiums below cost for all high-risk people of whatever income instead of assisting the poor to pay premiums that cover their risk factors.

Insurance is based on the assessment of risk, and different people have different risks. Those are facts of life that policymakers cannot repeal and can ignore only at our peril. A free-market approach to financing health care, therefore, would result in premium differentials. But premium differentials are not bad. They make insurance a fairly priced value to all consumers. By contrast, community rating—one premium fits all—overcharges people with low risk, such as the young, and causes them to prefer to go uncovered. Community rating cannot survive in a voluntary setting. All plans calling for it also impose—or are likely to lead to—mandated coverage, requiring individuals to buy policies regardless of whether they wish to do so. Even modified community rating may fail to work in a voluntary setting. In no way can one describe coercive mandates and price restrictions as "free-market."

A real free market in health insurance is possible. With sensible reforms of federal tax law, a free market could provide the vast majority of the people with affordable insurance, vested in the individual, portable from one job to the next, and with acceptable provisions regarding existing conditions. Congress should let the country try a free-market approach rather than rush to enact any of the socialized health care financing schemes currently being offered.

9

RESTRUCTURING THE CURRENT HEALTH INSURANCE TAX SUBSIDY TO COVER THE UNINSURED

Kevin Vigilante, M.D., M.P.H., Christopher D'Arcy, M.D., and Tammy Reina

INTRODUCTION

Although the uninsured figured prominently in the 1992 presidential debate, they since have been obscured by other issues. Nonetheless, they are still with us, and their numbers are likely to increase over the next decade. We will discuss the composition of this group, the forces likely to influence their numbers, and a practical proposal to provide them with coverage while enhancing the efficiency and equity of the current system.

WHO ARE THE UNINSURED?

The most recent comprehensive data on the uninsured population are drawn from the March 1996 Current Population Survey (CPS). The CPS estimates that 40.3 million people, or 17.4 percent of the nonelderly population, were uninsured during 1995.[1] Although approximately half the uninsured population are employed, the uninsured tend to be clustered in certain kinds of jobs and industries. These tend to be low-wage, low-skill jobs, and the uninsured workers filling them tend to have lower levels of education.[2] Low educational and income status are also associated with higher rates of disease, disability, and death.[3] It is an unfortunate paradox of our system that some of those who are most likely to need insurance also are the least likely to have it. The employed uninsured are more likely to work part-time or to be engaged in transitory or seasonal work, making it particularly difficult for them to acquire employment-based insurance.[4] Most uninsured workers work for small firms that often—although not always—are unable to offer insurance coverage.[5]

The difficulty small firms face may arise, on the one hand, from their limited profitability and, on the other, from the relatively higher costs they face when purchasing insurance. These higher costs may reflect the expenses insurance companies incur when marketing, underwriting, and administering to smaller companies. They are also related to the inability of small firms to diffuse risk over large numbers of insured, and to the greater health risks that may be inherent in the population working in the transient, low-wage jobs more often found in smaller firms.[6] Furthermore, small, unincorporated owner-run firms are not eligible for the same tax break that larger firms receive when purchasing insurance.[7] When you include their families and dependents, the working uninsured account for approximately three-quarters of the entire uninsured population.[8] In absolute numbers, most of the uninsured are white and between the ages of 25 and 44.[9]

Examining absolute numbers, however, does not reveal who is at greatest risk of being uninsured. Although most uninsured Americans are employed, those at greatest risk are the nonelderly unemployed who are most likely to lack insurance on a chronic basis.[10] Others at disproportionate risk are the unmarried, the poor, young adults, and minorities, particularly Hispanics.[11]

THE CHRONICALLY UNINSURED

Some people try to minimize the problem of the uninsured by stating that most are without insurance for six months or less,[12] but that means a substantial number of people are uninsured for more than six months. While the estimates of the chronically uninsured vary according to study and methodology used, the figures are not trivial. Swartz estimated that 36 percent of those who claimed to be uninsured were uninsured for an entire year. Applying this estimate to 1992 data, she calculated the number of chronically uninsured in 1992 to be 21 million.[13] As one might expect, being employed and having a higher income and educational level were associated with shorter uninsured spells.[14] Indeed, among the chronically uninsured, 45 percent were poor, 20 percent were near poor, 15.5 percent were unemployed, and 37.2 percent were not in the labor force.[15]

Downsizing and corporate layoffs have become so common that they have been prominent in the media and were an issue in the 1992 presidential election.[16] While the unemployment rate had fallen from 7.8 percent in 1992 to 5.5 percent in 1995, the rate for those unemployed for longer than one year had grown from 5.6 percent in 1990 to 12.2 percent in 1995.[17] Thus, estimates based on data from the 1980s are likely to understate the number of chronically uninsured today. While brief periods without insurance may be anxiety-provoking at best, longer periods at worst may have a deleterious effect on health.

THE HEALTH OF THE UNINSURED AND THE UNDERINSURED

Does underinsurance or the lack of insurance diminish access to care? And if so, does lack of access harm one's health? The answer to the first question is yes. Lack of insurance and underinsurance diminish access to care. A number of studies support this assertion, but a recent one by the Medicaid Access Study Group is most convincing.[18] Researchers called 995 clinics, private doctors, and walk-in centers and requested an examination for a sore throat, back pain, or painful urination within two days. When asked for insurance information, they claimed to have Medicaid. Only 26 percent got appointments. When they called back three weeks later and claimed to have private insurance, 60 percent got appointments within two days.

Does lack of health insurance harm health? That is more difficult to establish. Some studies have found that the uninsured have lower rates of hospital admission, shorter stays, and fewer procedures than insured patients, suggesting that the uninsured are getting substandard care.[19] But it also is possible the insured patients were staying too long or getting procedures they did not truly need. It is clear, however, that those without health insurance are less healthy,[20] although it remains difficult to sort out whether this is a causal relationship or the lack of insurance is merely a marker for other factors that contribute to poor health. Franks et al. followed 4,694 individuals enrolled in the National Health and Nutrition Examination study from enrollment, 1971 through 1975, until 1987. They controlled for a multitude of factors, such as age, race, social habits, income, education, employment, health, and disease status, and found that lack of insurance was independently associated with higher mortality.[21] We can say that lack of insurance is associated with poorer health and that there is evidence to support our intuition that lacking health insurance may be causally related to certain poor health outcomes.

FUTURE TRENDS IN THE UNINSURED POPULATION

From 1988 to 1995, the percentage of Americans without health insurance increased from 15.2 percent to 17.4 percent. In addition to the performance of the economy, at least three other major variables will affect the number of uninsured over the next decade. The first is the Reconciliation Act of 1995, establishing Medicaid and Medicare funding for seven years. The second is the role of managed care for Medicaid patients. The third is the revenue available for cost-shifting in order to subsidize Medicaid patients and the uninsured.

Sheils and Claxton of Lewin–VHI estimate that the number of uninsured in 2002 will be 45.9 million. Under the Reconciliation Bill, they expect that number to rise to 53.7 million.[22] To arrive at this figure, they make assumptions about states' spending behavior, efficiencies to be gleaned from managed care, and the degree of cost-shifting. The accuracy of their predictions depends on the validity of their assumptions as well as the performance of the economy.

It is difficult to predict what savings will be gleaned by imposing managed care on Medicaid. Bograd found that costs of care for previously uninsured enrolled in a health maintenance organization (HMO) were somewhat more than for an age- and sex-matched control group with commercial insurance.[23] Another study of 25 plans suggests 5 to15 percent savings in Medicaid managed care initiatives.[24] It is too early to tell, however, whether the promise of enhanced service at lower cost will be achieved consistently. The preliminary data are sparse and conflicting, although the experience in Arizona after 13 years is encouraging. After an initial increase in costs, it appears the Arizona Health Care Cost Containment System will yield savings of about 7 percent over traditional Medicaid delivery systems (more than $100 million between 1983 and 1991).[25] If managed care can deliver more comprehensive services with significant savings, a greater number of clients may be served and the growth in the uninsured population may not be as dramatic as predicted by Lewin.

The third factor, cost-shifting, is the practice of charging private payers more in order to offset the lower reimbursement rates of public payers. Cost-shifting is controversial; only a few good studies of it exist, and almost none are recent.[26] Some people argue that hospitals, like other industries, often charge different rates to different payers, but that as long as the marginal costs of care are covered by the rates negotiated, no dynamic cost-shifting occurs.[27] But hospitals do respond by limiting services.[28] Furthermore, interesting aggregate data compiled by ProPAC suggest a close relationship between reductions in public reimbursements and increases in revenues from private payers.[29]

Despite the technical debate about cost-shifting, it is clear that a hospital's ability to render uncompensated care to uninsured patients is enhanced by its profitability or surplus revenue. Its ability to charge selectively higher rates is determined by its degree of market dominance and the degree to which it competes on things other than price.[30] While in the past it was uncommon for hospitals to compete on price, a recent change in behavior has been fostered by the proliferation of managed care. Selective contracting, intrinsic to managed care, has produced genuine price competition among hospitals operating in that milieu.[31] Although this may manifest itself in increased efficiency, the continuing downward pressure on price in both the public and private sectors also may decrease the surplus revenue that previously was available for the uninsured. When viewed from this perspective, it seems that managed care may contribute to increases in the uninsured population.

THE ANGST OF THE UNINSURED

Managed care will create conflicting forces, some of which will tend to increase and some of which will tend to decrease the number of uninsured. The net effect is difficult to predict, but the uninsured population will persist, and probably will grow. The uninsured will suffer higher risks of disease and death, while other Americans will live with the angst that they are merely a pink slip away from losing their insurance. Indeed, 21 percent of those polled said that even though they had insurance, the fear of losing it was a significant worry.[32] Moreover, those who were secure with their own health insurance felt uneasy about the insecurity their countrymen must endure. The importance of this national uneasiness should not be underestimated. It had a significant influence on the 1992 presidential election. This is demonstrated by polling data that revealed consistently that, even though 70 to 95 percent of Americans were satisfied with the quality of their own care, 70 to 75 percent believe the system needed fundamental change. Two-thirds of those interviewed worried that others did not receive the care that they themselves enjoyed. It appears that empathy for and solidarity with the uninsured is a significant factor driving the desire for fundamental change in the American health care system.[33]

POLICY IMPLICATIONS

Although obscured by debate over the federal budget, Medicare, and taxes, the uninsured and the underinsured are still with us, and their numbers are growing. It is only a matter of time before they come into focus again. Several policy options address their plight. Among them are (1) a single-payer system; (2) an employer mandate with or without a "play-or-pay" provision; and (3) tax reform that subsidizes the purchase of insurance. I will comment briefly on the first two options and discuss the last in detail.

A single-payer system has pros and cons but is unlikely to receive serious consideration in the near future, both for cultural and for political reasons. Americans seem to reject a radical overhaul in favor of incremental change.

Employer mandates would help the uninsured population, but those in greatest need—the chronically uninsured, many of whom are outside the labor force—would not be reached.[34] Furthermore, under many employer-mandate plans, the smallest firms, whose employees are most in need, would be exempt. Others suggest that imposing mandates would increase business failures and dampen profitability, resulting in greater unemployment.

COVERING THE UNINSURED

Most Americans obtain health insurance at their place of employment.[35] Those who purchase insurance through their employer have the advantage of having its value excluded from taxable income.[36] The aggregate value of this exclusion (revenue forgone by federal and state governments) is estimated to be approximately $100 billion.[37] Unfortunately, much of this subsidy goes to those who need it least: those in the higher income brackets. In 1993, over 30 percent of this revenue went to the wealthiest 13 percent of families.[38] It would be better to restructure this tax benefit so that it favors those in greater need of a subsidy. This could be done by converting the exclusion to a tax credit or voucher. The subsidy then could be adjusted so that it is inversely proportional to income, making it a progressive benefit. All Americans in need, regardless of their employment status, would be eligible for the subsidy and could use it to select the coverage of their choice, including approved managed care plans, approved traditional indemnity insurance, or approved medical savings accounts. To be approved, these plans would have to meet quality and benefit standards established by law.

This approach would have a number of advantages. As noted, those in greatest need would receive the most assistance. The redistribution of revenue should be structured so that the middle class retains the same monetary benefit it now gleans from the tax exclusion, but in the more liquid form of a credit. Revenue would be redistributed from the upper- to the lower-income brackets to help fund coverage for the uninsured. The net cost of covering the uninsured is estimated at $20 billion to $50 billion.[39] If $20 billion to $30 billion of the subsidy that now goes to upper-income individuals were redirected to the lower-income groups, significant progress could be made toward covering the uninsured.

Moreover, health insurance would become portable because policies purchased with this tax credit would belong to individuals, not employers. Both the tax credit and the policy would follow an individual through job changes and spells of unemployment. This is very important in a volatile labor market. Gone would be the fear of losing coverage when voluntarily changing jobs—a fear that often locks people in jobs they have outgrown. Ending "job lock" would be good for the labor market and also could enhance productivity.

Finally, the credit creates an opportunity for choice. Currently, workers must choose among insurance plans presented by employers. An employer's principal concern is profit, and the managed care options he presents may emphasize price over quality. With a portable tax credit, employees could purchase insurance through other groups, such as unions or community associations, if they perceived their employers' options failed to meet their specific needs.

As Medicaid moves people into managed care, they will be limited to options presented by the state. They run the risk of being consigned to plans purely on the basis of cost rather than quality. The choice permitted by vouchers not only would give recipients autonomy, empowerment, and greater dignity, but also would give them additional protection against unscrupulous, unresponsive, or substandard providers of managed care. Chronically uninsured poor people have no choice at the moment. Providing them with tax credits or vouchers would enable them to choose from the same spectrum of providers available to everyone else in their community.

SOME OBJECTIONS

Some think that the Medicaid population and the uninsured who are poor will have difficulty making prudent choices. The ill-fated attempt to move California's Medicaid population into managed care during the 1980s left many public officials reluctant to again expose vulnerable people to the marketing ploys of fly-by-night providers.[40] Other choice-based initiatives for the underserved, like those in Arizona and Tennessee, suffered from implementation inefficiencies.[41] But the managed care market has matured and now serves a large portion of a very demanding American middle class. There is a good roster of reputable firms in most communities. The chaos that characterized the startup of Tenn-Care in Tennessee was not evident in Rhode Island, and the problems that accompanied the Arizona experiment 13 years ago did not reflect the steady condition it achieved several years later.[42] In Rhode Island, after an extensive, creative, and culturally sensitive information campaign, 88 percent of Medicaid recipients voluntarily chose a managed care plan. Only 12 percent were assigned by the state. At the end of the year, only 4 percent switched plans. It is encouraging that emergency room visits are down by 35 percent and primary care visits are up by 53 percent. The number of women on Medicaid receiving adequate prenatal care increased from 55 to 65 percent, and the infant mortality is the lowest it has ever been in Rhode Island. Over 95 percent of subscribers were satisfied or very satisfied with their care.[43]

Furthermore, abuses can be minimized by creating standards for providers that wish to compete for Medicaid patients and the uninsured who are poor. Another approach would be to mainstream this population into firms that have a significant middle-class base. Still another idea would be to use enrollment brokers to help disseminate information prior to enrollment. A broker is a private third party without a financial interest in how a client enrolls.

Although it is true that the poor are vulnerable in many ways, the argument that they cannot make prudent medical decisions for themselves is demeaning and excessively paternalistic. Coauthor Vigilante's experience as a physician suggests that, even though most patients in every socioeconomic group lack medical knowledge, virtually everyone knows when he or she is being treated with respect and compassion. Such important but intangible qualities are used frequently as markers for technical excellence, and they are reasonably good markers. The uninsured who are poor are every bit as able to discern disrespect and neglect as are the rich and well-insured. The problem is that there is little they can do about it right now.

CONCLUSION

Tax reform provides a practical and incremental approach to covering the uninsured. Although this reform is difficult to sum up in a sound bite, its political strength derives from its ability to address the equity concerns of the left and efficiency concerns of the right. In this proposal, the uninsured are the nexus in which equity and efficiency, liberal and conservative, come together most closely. It is notable that the Consensus Group, which represents a broad spectrum of prominent think tanks, has rallied around this single issue and that the Jackson Hole Group has incorporated it into its latest plan for national health care reform.[44] There remains a moral and medical imperative to address the predicament of the uninsured. Surprisingly, a mere technical modification of the tax code will help us to fulfill our obligation to this part of the population while enhancing the efficiency and equity of the entire system.

NOTES

[1] "Sources of Health Insurance and Characteristics of the Uninsured: Analysis of the March 1996 Current Population Survey," EBRI *Issue Brief* No. 179, November 1996, pp. 1–16.

[2] Alan C. Monheit, "Uninsured Americans: A Review," *Annual Review of Public Health,* Vol. 15 (1994), pp. 461–485.

[3] J. S. House, R. S. Kessler, and A. R. Herzog, "Age, Socioeconomic Status, and Health," *Millbank Quarterly,* Vol. 68 (1990), pp. 383–411.

[4] K. Swartz et al., "Personal Characteristics and Spells Without Insurance," *Inquiry,* Vol. 30 (Spring 1993), pp. 64–76.

[5] J. N. Edwards et al., "Small Business and the National Health Care Reform Debate," *Health Affairs*, Spring 1992, pp. 164–173.

[6] Monheit, "Uninsured Americans: A Review," pp. 461–485.

[7] S. M. Marquis and J. Buchanan, "How Will Changes in Health Insurance, Tax Policy and Employer Health Plan Contributions Affect Access to Health Care and Health Care Costs," *Journal of the American Medical Association,* Vol. 271, No.12 (March 23/30, 1994), pp. 939–944.

[8] "Sources of Health Insurance and Characteristics of the Uninsured: Analysis of the March 1995 Current Population Survey," pp. 1–28.

[9] H. E. Freeman et al., "Uninsured Working Age Adults: Characteristic and Consequences," *Health Services Research,* Vol. 24 (February 1990), p. 6.

[10] Swartz et al., "Personal Characteristics and Spells Without Insurance," pp. 64–76.

[11] Freeman et al., "Uninsured Working Age Adults," pp. 811–823.

[12] "Medical Reform Simplified," *Wall Street Journal,* October 18, 1993, p. A16.

[13] K. Swartz, "Dynamics of People Without Health Insurance—Don't Let the Numbers Fool You," *Journal of the American Medical Association,* Vol. 271 (January 5, 1994), p. 1.

[14] Swartz et al., "Personal Characteristics and Spells Without Insurance," pp. 64–76.

[15] Monheit, "Uninsured Americans: A Review," pp. 461–485.

[16] "On the Battlefields of Business, Millions of Casualties," *New York Times,* March 3, 1996, p. 1.

[17] "The Hopeless Jobless," *Economist,* December 2, 1995, p. 24.

[18] A. L. Kellerman and the Medicaid Access Study Group, "Access of Medicaid Recipient to Outpatient Care," *New England Journal of Medicine,* Vol. 330 (May 19, 1994), p. 20.

[19] J. Hadley et al., "Comparison of Uninsured and Privately Insured Hospital Patients," *Journal of the American Medical Association,* Vol. 265 (January 16, 1991), p. 3.

[20] P. Franks et al., "Health Insurance and Mortality. Evidence from a National Cohort," *Journal of the American Medical Association,* Vol. 270 (August 11, 1993), p. 6.

[21] *Ibid.,* pp. 739–741.

[22] J. F. Sheils and G. J. Claxton, "Potential Cost Shifting Under Proposed Funding Reductions from Medicare and Medicaid: The Budget Reconciliation Act of 1995" (Washington, D.C.: Lewin VHI Inc., December 6, 1995), pp. i–vii, 1–24.

[23] H. Bograd, "Extending Health Maintenance Organization Insurance to the Uninsured," *Journal of the American Medical Association,* Vol. 277, No. 13 (April 2, 1997), pp. 1067–1072.

[24] D. Freund and R. Hurley, "Medicaid Managed Care; Contribution to Issues for Health Reform," *Annual Review of Public Health,* Vol. 16 (1995), pp. 473–495.

[25] N. McCall et al., "Managed Medicaid Cost Savings: The Arizona Experience," *Health Affairs,* Vol.13, No. 2 (Spring 1994), pp. 234–245.

[26] M. A. Morrisey, *Cost Shifting in Health Care* (Washington, D.C.: AEI Press, 1994), pp. 46–59.

[27] *Ibid.*, pp. 11–22.

[28] J. Holahan, "The Impact of Alternative Hospital Payment Systems on Medicaid Costs," *Inquiry,* Vol. 25 (Winter 1988), pp. 517–532.

[29] "Medicare and the American Health Care System," Report to the Congress, Prospective Payment Assessment Commission, June 1995, p. 22.

[30] Morrissey, *Cost Shifting in Health Care,* pp. 46–59.

[31] R. Feldman et al., "Effects of HMOs on the Creation of Competitive Markets for Hospital Services," *Journal of Health Economics,* Vol. 9 (September 1990), pp. 207–222.

[32] R. J. Blendon et al., "Paying Medical Bills in the U.S.: Why Health Insurance Isn't Enough," *Journal of the American Medical Association,* Vol. 271 (March 23/30, 1994), pp. 949–951.

[33] L. R. Jacobs and R. Shapiro, "The Duality of Public Opinion: Personal Interests and the National Interest in Health Care Reform," *Domestic Affairs,* Winter 1993–1994, pp. 245–260.

[34] Swartz et al., "Personal Characteristics and Spells Without Insurance," p. 74.

[35] "Sources of Health Insurance and Characteristics of the Uninsured: Analysis of the March 1995 Current Population Survey," pp. 1–28.

[36] Marquis and Buchanan, "How Will Changes in Health Insurance, Tax Policy and Employer Health Plan Contributions Affect Access to Health Care and Health Care Costs?" pp. 939–944.

[37] M. V. Pauly and J. Goodman, "Tax Credits for Health Insurance and Medical Savings Accounts," *Health Affairs,* Vol.14, No.1 (Spring 1995), pp. 126–139.

[38] S. Glied, *Revising the Tax Treatment of Employer-Provided Health Insurance* (Washington, D.C.: AEI Press, 1994), p. 22.

[39] S. H. Long and M. S. Marquis, "The Uninsured Access Group and the Cost of Universal Coverage," *Health Affairs,* Vol. 13, No. 2 (Spring, 1994), pp. 211–220, and J. A. Meyer et al., "Universal Access to Health Care: A Comprehensive Tax Based Approach," *Archives of Internal Medicine,* Vol. 151 (May 1991), pp. 917–922.

[40] J. K. Inglehart, "Medicaid and Managed Care," *New England Journal of Medicine,* Vol. 332 (June 22, 1995), p. 25.

[41] McCall et al., "Managed Medicaid Cost Savings: The Arizona Experience," pp. 234–245, and Inglehart, "Medicaid and Managed Care," pp. 1727–1731.

[42] McCall et al., "Managed Medicaid Cost Savings: The Arizona Experience," pp. 234–245; Inglehart, "Medicaid and Managed Care," pp. 1727–1731; and T. Leddy, "The RITE Care Program, Effect on Use of Emergency Rooms: Presentation to National Health Policy Forum," Rhode Island Department of Human Services, February 9, 1996.

[43] "The RITE Care Program," *Program Results and Executive Summary: Rhode Island Department of Human Services,* 1997, pp. 1–6.

[44] P. Ellwood and A. Enthoven, "Responsible Choices: The Jackson Hole Group Plan for Health Reform," *Health Affairs*, Vol. 14 (Summer 1995), pp. 24–39.

10

MEDICAL SAVINGS ACCOUNTS: AN IDEA WHOSE TIME HAS COME

John C. Goodman, Ph.D.

Medical savings accounts (MSAs) give people the opportunity to move from a conventional low-deductible health insurance plan to a catastrophic plan with a high deductible and to put the premium savings in a personal account.[1] These accounts are used to pay for routine and preventive medical care while the high-deductible policy pays for major expenses. Employees and their families pay all medical bills up to the deductible from their MSAs and out-of-pocket funds. Their catastrophic insurance pays all expenses above the deductible. Money left over in the MSA at the end of the year can be withdrawn or rolled over to grow with interest.

For example, under the plan illustrated in Figure 1, $2,000 is deposited each year in an employee's MSA, and the employee faces a deductible of $3,000. Thus, the first $2,000 of medical expenses is paid from the MSA, the next $1,000 is paid out of pocket, and the plan pays all expenses above $3,000. If expenses are less than $2,000, the employee can spend the balance on nonmedical goods and services or save it.

In 1995, Congress passed legislation that would have extended the tax treatment given third-party insurance premiums to MSA deposits. Congress also passed an MSA option for Medicare beneficiaries. President Bill Clinton vetoed the measures as part of the overall

Figure 1

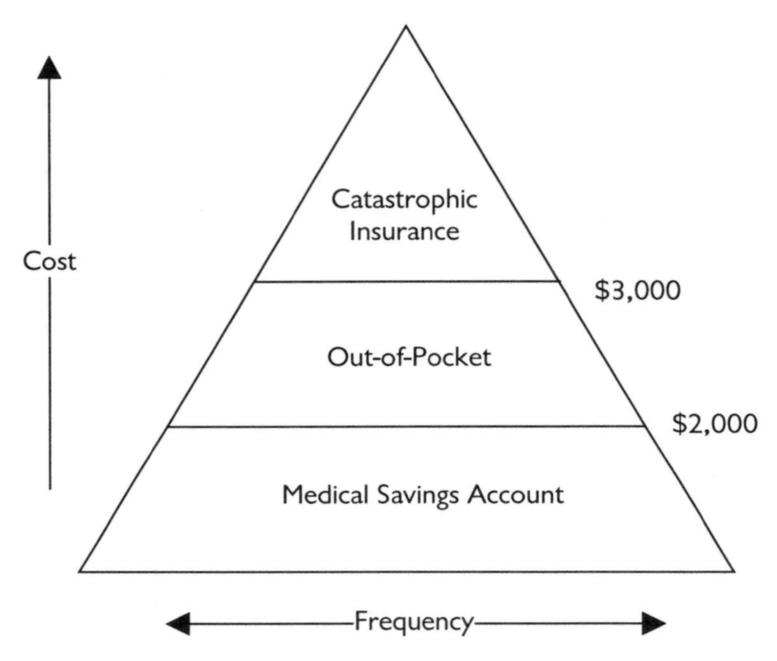

budget impasse. Under two pilot programs, however, tax-free MSAs are now available to 750,000 small employers and the self-employed as part of the Health Insurance Portability and Accountability Act of 1996 and to 390,000 Medicare beneficiaries as part of the Balanced Budget Act of 1997.

THE INCREASING POPULARITY OF MEDICAL SAVINGS ACCOUNTS

MSAs have been an attractive option, even without the provision of tax-favored treatment. According to one estimate, as many as 2,000 businesses had adopted some form of MSA plans by the end of 1995. The apparently universal experience is that MSA plans reduce employers' health insurance expenditures over time and benefit employees financially by helping them manage their health care dollars wisely.

MSAs are also popular among the states, many of which have passed state tax-free MSA legislation. They also are being proposed for Medicaid, and many would like to expand their role in Medicare. The city-state of Singapore has been using MSAs for longer than a decade. China has a pilot program for MSAs. And MSAs compete against other forms of insurance in South Africa.

Employer Plans[2]

More than a decade ago, the Rand Corporation found that, when people spend their own money on health care, they spend 30 percent less—with no adverse effects on their health. Some employers are putting this principle to work:

- In 1993, the United Mine Workers had a health plan with first-dollar coverage for most medical services. The following year, the union accepted a plan with a $1,000 deductible. In return, employees received $1,000 each at the beginning of the year and kept what they did not spend. The mine workers still have first-dollar coverage, but now the first $1,000 they spend is their own.
- In 1982, Quaker Oats established a high-deductible policy and paid $300 a year into the personal health accounts of each employee, who got to keep any unspent balance. As a result, over the next decade, the company's health-care costs grew an average of 6.3 percent per year while premiums for the rest of the country grew at double-digit rates.
- *Forbes* pays employees $2 each for every $1 of medical claims they do not submit, up to a maximum of $1,000. The magazine's health costs *fell* 17 percent in 1992 and 12 percent in 1993.
- Dominion Resources, a utility holding company, deposits $1,620 a year into a bank account for the 80 percent of employees who choose a $3,000 deductible rather than a lower deductible. The company experienced no premium increase for several years, while other employers faced annual increases of 13 percent.
- Golden Rule Insurance Company deposits $2,000 a year into MSAs for employees who choose a $3,000 family deductible. In

Figure 2

Medical Savings Accounts in the states

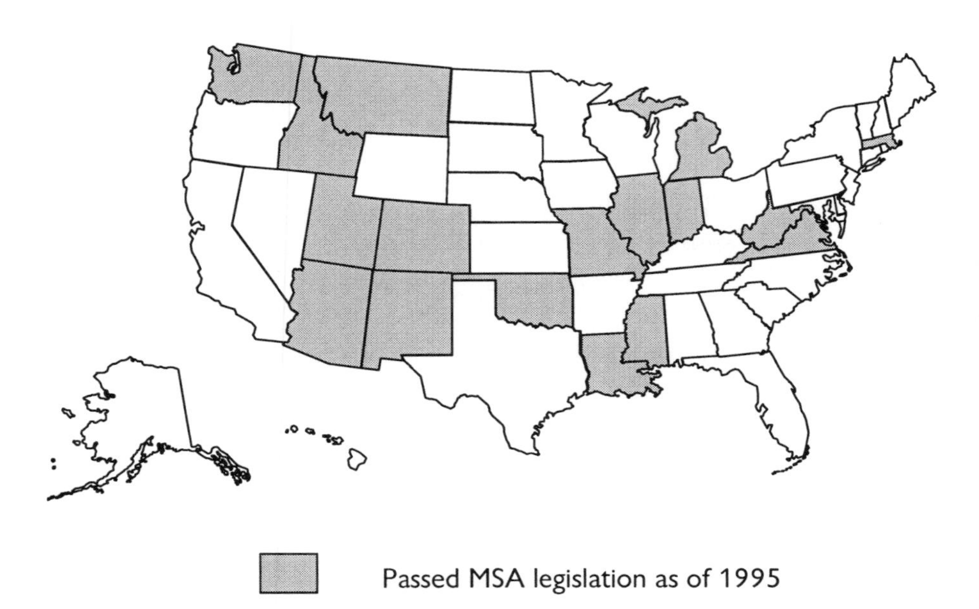

> 1993, the first year of the plan, the company found its health costs were 40 percent lower than they otherwise would have been.

These plans allow employees (1) to save money in an amount directly related to their own efforts; (2) to seek medical care without considering traditional out-of-pocket deductibles; (3) to use their medical savings to buy services not covered by the employer's plan; and (4) usually to consult any doctor they choose.

Medical Savings Accounts in the States

Although MSA legislation at the federal level became stalled in the 1995 budget impasse, a majority of the states introduced or enacted legislation providing for MSAs. Overall, MSA legislation was the single most popular state health care initiative in 1995 (see Figure 2). Specifically:[3]

- As of 1995, 17 states had approved MSAs and 11 had called on the U.S. Congress to pass MSA legislation.

Figure 3

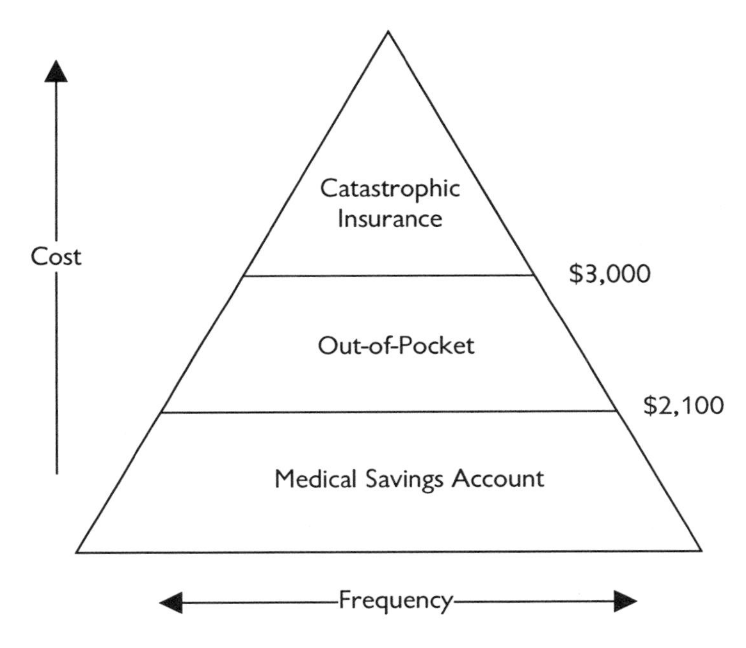

- Eleven additional states considered MSA laws in 1996.

Legislation at the state level exempts MSA deposits from state income taxes. All but four states provide a tax break for everyone who purchases health insurance individually, including the self-employed and employees who do not receive insurance from their employers.

Medical Savings Accounts for Medicare[4]

The Republican Medicare reform proposal of 1995 would allow the elderly to choose a catastrophic health insurance policy coupled with an MSA rather than remain in the traditional fee-for-service Medicare system. A study for the National Center for Policy Analysis by the actuarial firm Milliman & Robertson analyzed the options seniors would have under a plan similar to the one Congress passed that showed private plans could provide them with a high-deductible policy that would pay all expenses above $3,000 and could deposit as much as $2,100 in MSAs to pay for expenses below the deductible (see Figure 3).

This plan would provide better benefits than the current Medicare program for several reasons:

- The MSA plan would provide catastrophic coverage for all expenses over $3,000, while traditional Medicare coverage runs out after various caps and limitations are reached.
- The MSA plan would provide a maximum cap of $900 per year on out-of-pocket expenses for the elderly (the difference between the $3,000 deductible and the $2,100 in the MSA), while Medicare has no cap on out-of-pocket expenses.
- Because of gaps in Medicare coverage, 70 percent of the elderly have private insurance to supplement Medicare, which costs an average of $1,200 per year; with the MSA plan, the elderly could keep the $1,200 in a bank account and no longer would need supplemental (Medigap) insurance.
- The funds in the MSA could be used for any health expense, including eyeglasses, prescription drugs, and other items not covered by Medicare.
- Seniors would have a broader choice of doctors and services with MSAs than with Medicare because they would be able to pay market prices instead of having to rely on Medicare's low rates, which already are causing limited access to doctors and hospitals and some health care rationing.
- By returning health care money—and therefore decision-making power—to seniors, MSAs would restore the doctor–patient relationship, allowing doctors to become agents of their patients instead of agents of the Medicare bureaucracy.

The Milliman & Robertson study estimated that, under a reform plan similar to the one passed by Congress, 50 percent of retirees would choose the private option in the first year, with the number increasing to 80 percent by the seventh year.[5] Medicare spending, according to the study, would decrease by almost $200 billion over the next seven years.

Medical Savings Accounts for Medicaid[6]

Several states have introduced or are considering MSA Medicaid legislation:

- A 1994 Indiana proposal, which passed the state Senate but not the House, would have given each member of a family on

Medicaid an annual voucher of $100 for health care. In addition, the state would have returned to the family a percentage of the amount they saved in health care services that beneficiaries could spend on other in-kind services such as daycare and job training. Those spending more than $3,250 for health care would have had their medical bills covered by the state but would have received nothing at year's end.

- Legislation that would create MSAs for the "working poor and individuals who are eligible to receive medical assistance services" passed unopposed in committee in both chambers of the Virginia legislature.

Medical Savings Accounts in Singapore[7]

Singapore has had MSAs for 12 years—and they work. Singaporeans must put money into personal accounts, which they then use to pay medical bills and buy health insurance. Because they are spending their own money, they have a personal incentive to control health care costs. For example, the length of hospital stays in Singapore is about the same as the length of hospital stays for enrollees in health maintenance organizations (HMOs) in the United States and well below that of U.S. residents who have other health care policies.

MSAs are part of a larger system that requires Singaporeans to save for their own retirement and for other needs. They can use their savings to buy a home, health insurance, medical care, or college educations for their children. The program, in effect since 1955, has enabled Singaporeans to pay for goods and services that often are provided by governments in other countries. As a result:

- Singapore's savings rate (48 percent of gross domestic product vs. about 12 percent in the United States) is the highest in the world;
- Singapore's rate of home ownership (85 percent) also is the highest in the world; and
- In Singapore, 40 percent of an employee's wages (20 percent each from the worker and the employer) must be deposited with the Central Provident Fund (CPF), the publicly managed administrator of the private accounts. Of this amount, 6 percent goes into a Medisave account (an MSA).

Figure 4

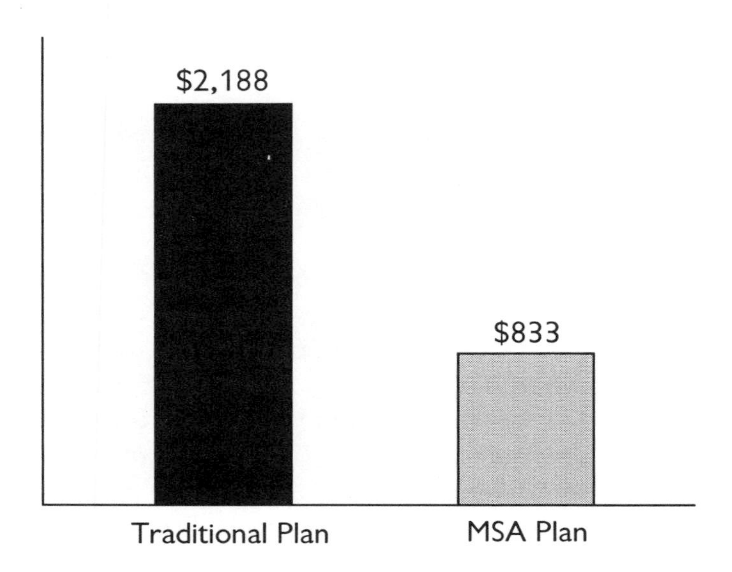

Note: Traditional plan includes an average deductible of $744 and a maximum copayment of $1,444. MSA plan includes a $2,000 deductible less the average employer contribution of $1,167.

ANSWERING THE CRITICS

MSAs have been the target of a number of criticisms. For example, John Burry, chairman of Blue Cross & Blue Shield of Ohio, has argued that MSAs would be a windfall for the healthy while undermining the financial stability of the health insurance industry.[8] Similarly, the American Academy of Actuaries has argued that the money saved when switching from a low-deductible to a high-deductible policy is so modest that only the healthiest people would benefit financially from an MSA.[9] As a result, these critics contend, very few people would choose MSA plans if they were widely offered.

The concern that only healthy people would choose MSAs leads to another criticism: that they would result in adverse selection, with

Figure 5

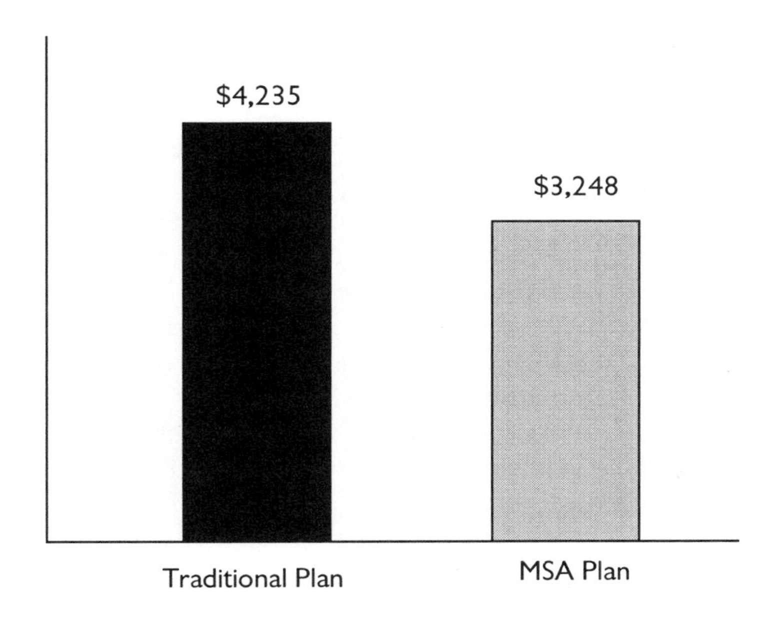

Note: Cost of traditional plan = premium. Cost of MSA plan = premium plus MSA deposit.

healthy people choosing one insurance pool and sick people choosing another, making the premiums in the pool with a disproportionate number of sick people unaffordably high.

Finally, some critics argue that employees would misuse their MSA money. For example, in recent testimony before Congress, John N. Sturdivant, president of the American Federation of Government Employees, AFL–CIO, which represents 700,000 federal and District of Columbia employees, declared that "Under MSAs...consumers would delay treatment until it was absolutely necessary."[10]

Despite these assertions, evidence reveals (1) that MSAs are saving employers about as much as managed care plans and could save them much more; (2) that few if any adverse selection problems are occurring; and (3) that no instances of employees inappropriately delaying treatment are being reported.

Do Medical Savings Accounts Lower Costs?

Because MSAs are relatively new, few scholars have evaluated the existing plans, but a study by Professor Michael T. Bond and others at Cleveland State University reports on 27 Ohio companies with such plans and compares them with fee-for-service insurance alternatives.[11]

With the traditional health-insurance plans:

- There was an average deductible of $300 per person ($744 per family) and a maximum average copayment of $660 for individual coverage ($1,444 per family).
- Thus, the average annual out-of-pocket exposure was $960 ($300 plus $660) for the individual plan and $2,188 ($744 plus $1,444) for a family plan (see Figure 4).
- Under the MSA plans, employees faced an average deductible of $1,500 for single coverage and $2,000 for family coverage.
- The average employer contribution to the MSA was $857 for single coverage and $1,167 for family coverage.
- As a result, the potential out-of-pocket exposure was $643 ($1,500 deductible minus a $857 MSA deposit) for those with single coverage and $833 ($2,000 deductible minus a $1,167 MSA deposit) for family coverage.

Thus, potential out-of-pocket costs decreased $317 ($960 minus $643) for the employee with single coverage and $1,355 ($2,188 minus $833) under a family plan.

Not only did an MSA result in financial savings for the employee, but it also enabled employers to lower their overall health care expenditures. MSA coverage for an individual cost employers an average of $359 more per year than a traditional plan. But coverage for a family averaged $987 less (see Figure 5), so employers realized a net saving overall.

When the individual and family MSA plans were considered together, employers' health care costs were about 12 percent lower than with a traditional plan. The savings are comparable to those from a switch to managed care from traditional health insurance. Under the MSA plan, however, employees have more freedom to make choices about their health care. In addition, the employee can withdraw unspent MSA money at the end of the year or roll it over and allow it to grow for future health care expenses.

Figure 6

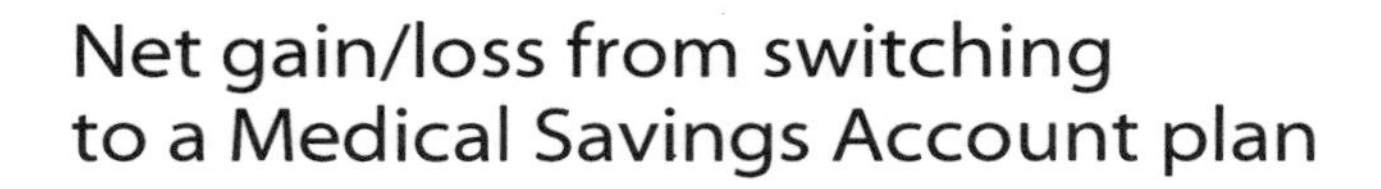

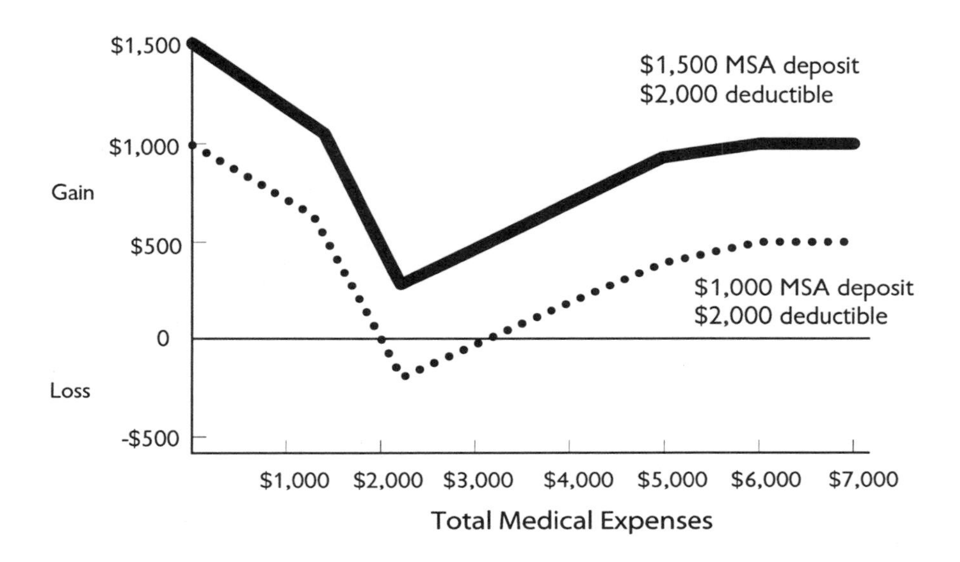

Note: Assumes a switch from a conventional health plan with a $500 deductible and a 20 percent copayment up to a maximum out-of-pocket limit of $1,500. The net gain is the difference between the MSA end-of-year refund (or out-of-pocket expenses under the MSA plan) and out-of-pocket expenses under conventional insurance.

Do Medical Savings Accounts Create Adverse Selection?

The Ohio companies surveyed did not appear to have experienced problems with adverse selection. A probable reason is that an MSA plan lowers the potential out-of-pocket cost for all employees, making it attractive to both the healthy and the sick.

Moreover, as Bond et al. point out, lowering employer contributions to the MSA so that the potential out-of-pocket costs for the traditional plan and the MSA plan were equal would eliminate even the threat of adverse selection. According to the authors, if employers made that adjustment, they would spend about 34 percent less for the MSA plan than for traditional insurance.

Adverse selection also is unlikely in other settings because MSA plans differ from traditional insurance in three important ways.

First, instead of making out-of-pocket expenses (to reach a deductible) the first tier of a health plan, MSA plans give the insured access to cash up front. Thus, a single mother living from paycheck to paycheck will not neglect her child's health because she cannot pay the doctor's fee. Yet she has an incentive to spend her MSA funds wisely because at the end of the year she can withdraw any money remaining in the account.

Second, rather than have a copayment that applies to small as well as large bills, MSA plans concentrate out-of-pocket spending on the gap between the MSA deposit and the catastrophic deductible. For example, with a $1,500 MSA deposit and a $2,000 deductible, patients spend the first $1,500 from the MSA and the next $500 out of pocket, and then rely on catastrophic insurance to pay all expenses above $2,000. Many MSA plans rely on managed care, or at least a preferred provider network of physicians, to control costs above the deductible.

Third, because MSA plans create more efficient (and more appropriate) incentives for patients, they almost always offer enrollees lower total out-of-pocket exposure than traditional plans. While the latter leave people exposed for several thousand dollars of medical bills, MSA plans usually limit this exposure to $1,000 or less. In the above example, total out-of-pocket exposure is only $500.

Experience shows, therefore, that MSAs do not create adverse selection and, in fact, can benefit those who critics claim would be most disadvantaged by them.

To determine whether someone would be better off or worse off with an MSA plan, we must consider all contingencies, including the possibility that a person will have small as well as large bills.[12]

As Figure 6 shows, healthy people clearly are better off with MSAs. Continuing with the above example, a person with no medical expenses would be able to withdraw the annual $1,500 MSA deposit at the end of the year and spend the money on nonmedical goods and services.

But sick people also do well under such a plan. Someone with $10,000 in medical expenses would pay only $500 out of pocket. Under a conventional insurance plan, that person would have paid $1,500, of which $500 would be the deductible and $1,000 would be a 20 percent copayment on the next $5,000 of expenses.

The person with moderate expenses does least well. This is because in the corridor between the MSA deposit and the catastrophic deductible, the patient is paying an out-of-pocket dollar for each dollar of medical care. By contrast, a person with conventional insurance would be paying only 20 cents on the dollar.

In general, someone with $2,000 to $5,000 of medical expenses is experiencing a brief medical episode from which recovery will be relatively quick, is on the way to a serious illness with large future medical bills, or is suffering from a chronic condition that lingers from year to year (e.g., diabetes). For the reasons given above, people in the first two categories would be better off over time with MSAs. By contrast, Figure 6 shows that people with chronic conditions that are moderately expensive to treat might experience little financial gain by choosing an MSA plan over traditional insurance.

Nevertheless, they are likely to prefer MSA plans for two reasons.

First, the cost of treating chronic conditions varies considerably. Given proper incentives, patients and their doctors can lower the cost of care—thus leaving the patient with a greater end-of-year refund. Second, even under traditional insurance, the chronically ill are hassled increasingly by bureaucrats. Many chronic patients believe that by managing their own health care dollars, they could get not only better care, but also less expensive care.

DO MEDICAL SAVINGS ACCOUNTS ENCOURAGE INAPPROPRIATE DELAYS IN MEDICAL CARE?

MSAs do not encourage people to defer needed health care. In fact, people with MSAs are more likely to get the preventive care they need. Under conventional health insurance, people receive no reimbursement until they have met the deductible, which can be a major out-of-pocket expense for low-income individuals. MSAs, by contrast, provide first-dollar coverage so that people with limited funds can pay medical expenses. A survey of Golden Rule employees who opted for MSAs found that one of every five used the MSA for a medical service he or she would not have purchased under the traditional insurance plan.

IDEAL DESIGN OF MEDICAL SAVINGS ACCOUNTS

A single deductible covering all types of health expenditures is a crude approach to designing a health plan. In all existing MSA plans with

Table 1

General rules

Individual Choice	Collective Choice
1. No risky medical event.	1. Risky medical event.
2. Price of third-party insurance is high.	2. Price of third-party insurance is low.
3. Failure to insure creates no externalities.	3. Failure to insure creates risk for others.

which I am familiar, there is a specific separation of financial responsibility between the insured and insurer. Expenses below a set deductible (say $2,000 or $3,000) are the responsibility of the insured; those above are the responsibility of the insurer. This design not only is ubiquitous in private-sector plans, but also is incorporated in congressional legislation creating tax-free MSA deposits for the general population and MSA options for Medicare recipients.

Although simplicity of design is laudable, it also is likely that enterprising people can improve on the current design. The tax system should be flexible enough to encourage such improvements.

Individual vs. Group Decision-Making

Participation in an insurance pool almost always results in some loss of autonomy. In deciding what benefits to cover and how to reimburse costs, insurers design the plan that will succeed best in the insurance marketplace. But such a plan is unlikely to match the preferences of any single individual exactly. To induce individuals to give up autonomy, the plan must offer some offsetting gain, such as a reduction of risk.

The willingness of individuals to concede some autonomy to achieve other goals will vary, yet some general rules are likely to apply. As Table 1 shows, individual choice is likely to produce better results in cases in which:

Figure 7

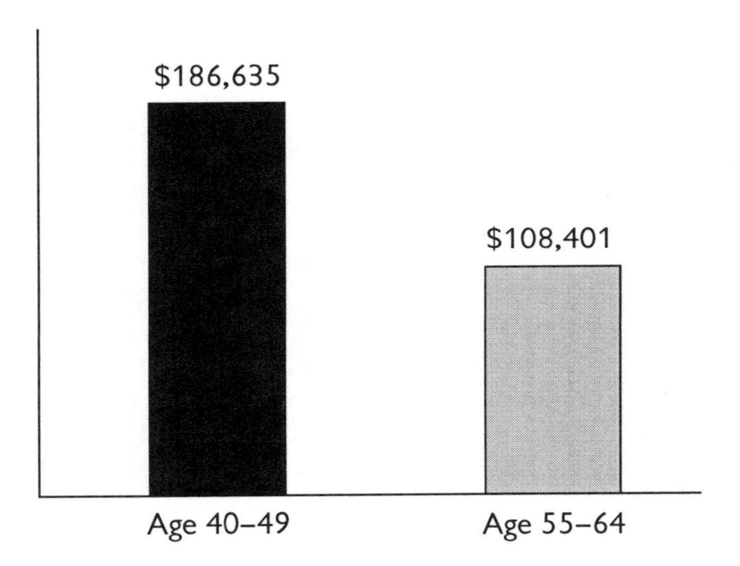

Source: Harvard Risk Assessment Project.

- No risky medical event prompts the need for the medical service and patients' use of a service is the result of their own preferences;
- The price of transferring exposure for payment for the service to an insurance pool is high (e.g., to accept a dollar's worth of exposure, an insurer might insist on 50 cents or more of additional premium); and
- Failure to purchase insurance coverage for the service creates no external benefits or costs for others, so that individuals (from a financial perspective) are indifferent as to whether others acquire service.

One service that fits these criteria is the "super" checkup offered by the renowned Cooper Clinic in Dallas. For $1,200, the clinic performs a series of tests, including a treadmill test and possibly a CAT scan. Customers include magnate Ross Perot and talk-show host Larry King.

No one claims that the Cooper Clinic checkup "pays for itself" through early detection and treatment of medical problems; it surely does not. Nor does anyone argue that everyone should get this service; if everyone did, the country's total health care bill would increase by more than 25 percent. And no one expects insurers to pay; if forced to cover the service, they probably would charge an additional $1,200 in premiums—about $1 of premium for each $1 of exposure.

Nevertheless, the Cooper Clinic checkup is ideal for those who place a very high value on reducing risk and are willing to spend the required time and money. Other services also may fall into the category of "appropriate for individual choice," and these choices easily could cost $2,000, $3,000, or more.

On the other hand, consider treatment for cancer. Victims have no direct control over the need for this service. The price of insuring for the treatment of cancer is low, and failure to insure creates risks for others since the cost of treatment could exhaust the average family's resources, causing them to rely on others. Even though the first few treatments may cost less than $2,000 or $3,000, the early treatment regime may well affect the success of later treatments. Thus, a case can be made for first-dollar cancer coverage by a managed care plan or third-party insurance.

Since this approach rejects conventional wisdom, a few examples may be helpful.

Case Study: Mammograms

The 1994 national debate over health care drew attention to a controversial decision made by the White House Task Force on Health Care Reform. On the implied standard that no more than about $100,000 should be spent to save one year of life, the Clinton plan proposed to cover regular mammograms for women in their 50s but not in their 40s (see Figure 7).

The mistake was not in the standard the task force used, which was in line with decisions people make about risk in other contexts.[13] The mistake was in believing that it is appropriate and desirable for the White House to make such a decision for all the women of the United States.

People differ in their attitudes toward risk and may be more averse to some risks than to others. With mammograms, this choice can be

Figure 8

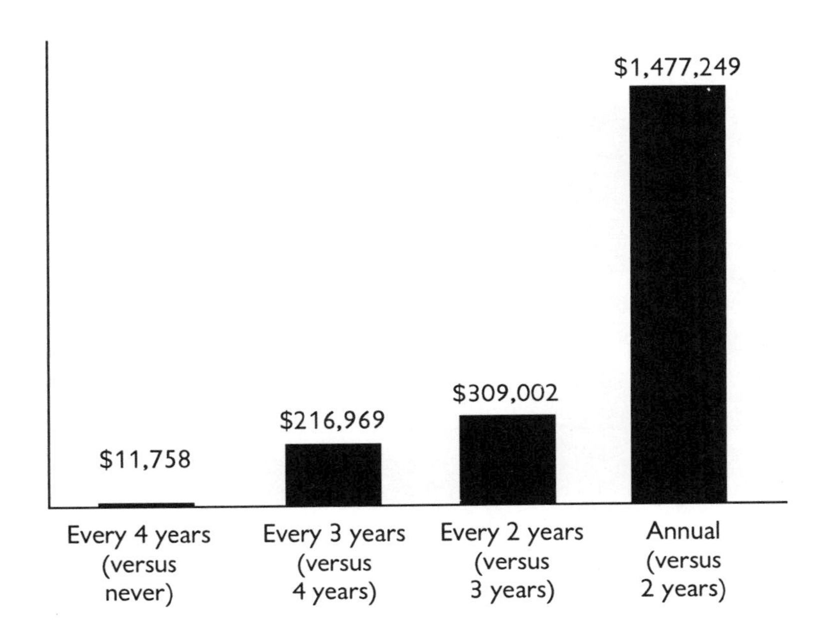

Source: Harvard Risk Assessment Project.

made by individuals. As Figure 7 shows, when all costs are considered, mammograms do not save health care dollars. So if one woman judges a mammogram to be worth the cost and another does not, other people have no financial reason to care about these decisions as long as the women are spending their own money.

Case Study: Pap Smears

Another controversial decision made by Hillary Clinton's task force was to cover cervical cancer tests every three years rather than every year, as recommended by many doctors. Presumably, the task force did not consider a pap smear every four years, which is a really good buy, costing less than $12,000 per year of life saved for the population as a whole. As Figure 8 shows, however, beginning with a test every four

Figure 9

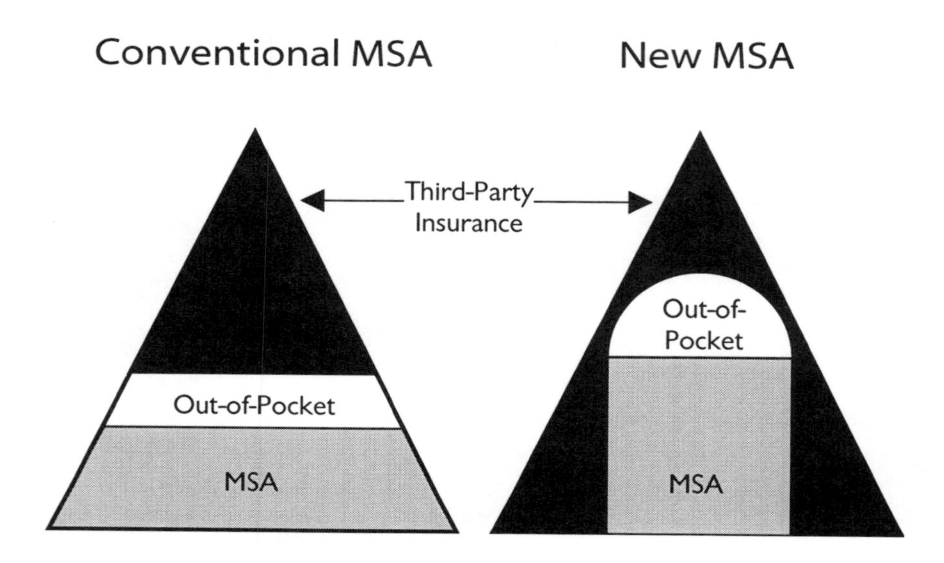

years, the cost per year of life saved rises steeply with more frequent testing. For example, the difference between an annual exam and a biennial exam is more than $1 million per year of life saved.

Again, the case for individual choice is strong. We would expect women who are extremely risk-averse with respect to cervical cancer to have the test annually. Other women will choose to be examined less frequently. Others have no reason to interfere with these choices if the women themselves are paying.

Implications for the Design of MSAs

Having identified the appropriate spheres for individual and collective decision-making, we need a mechanism to implement the funding. For individual decision-making, the appropriate mechanism is self-insurance through MSAs. For collective decision-making, it is third-party insurance. Thus, individuals would be solely responsible for most primary-care services, virtually all diagnostic tests, and perhaps such services as well-baby delivery. Third parties would be responsible for the treatment of serious illness, even paying the first dollar.

Figure 9 contrasts this ideal plan design with the conventional MSA plan.

MSAs AND MANAGED CARE

Employers are turning to MSAs for the same reason they turned to managed care: to control rising health care costs. Because employees keep any MSA money they do not spend, they have a financial incentive to shop prudently in the medical marketplace. In general, they will not spend a dollar on health care unless they receive a dollar's worth of value. Employer experiences with MSA plans show that, with this incentive, employees curtail health care spending significantly.

Even if they have MSAs, most employers or their insurance companies negotiate prices with doctors and hospitals and explore other ways to lower the cost of quality care. Some have gone further by combining MSAs with managed care.

Combining MSAs and Managed Care[14]

In 1995, the National Center for Policy Analysis adopted an MSA plan that limits employees' exposure and expands their control over their health care dollars. Employees of the National Center for Policy Analysis may use their MSA funds to see any doctor, enter any hospital, or pay any medical bill. Spending counts toward satisfying the deductible, however, only if the service or procedure is covered under the health plan. For example, employees can pay for dental care or eye glasses with their MSAs, but those expenses do not apply toward the deductible. Further, after they have exceeded the deductible, if they go outside the network of physicians and hospitals affiliated with the plan, only 75 percent of each "usual and customary" fee is reimbursed.

Over time, the buildup of MSA funds will give employees of the National Center for Policy Analysis important options with respect to expensive medical procedures. For example, the health plan will pay the full costs above the deductible only if the procedure is done by a network doctor in a network hospital, but employees will be able to use their MSA funds outside the network to pay that portion of the bill not covered by the insurance.

This example of "patient power" plus managed care is only the beginning. In the future, the two concepts are likely to be combined in even more interesting ways.

Managed Care in the Information Age

The traditional philosophy of HMOs was summed up by an HMO manager several years ago: "Patients do what their doctors tell them to do; therefore, if you can tell doctors how to practice medicine, you can cut costs." This approach assumes patients are compliant because they do not know what services they are not receiving. A model based on patient ignorance is unlikely to survive in the new Information Age.

Increasingly, patients will use the Internet and other computer services to tap into various medical libraries and databases, discuss ailments with other network users, and follow diagnostic decision trees. Thus, the best model for the future assumes that patients will know as much as their doctors, not about how to practice medicine, but about what medical practice offers.

One change that is almost certain to occur is full disclosure about how managed care organizations develop the protocols that doctors use to make important procedural decisions. Although managed care organizations insist their goal is cost-effective medicine, not one will discuss publicly the cost-benefit standards it uses in developing protocols. In the future, patients will be able to use their computers to discover for themselves what these standards are.

Being a Patient in the Information Age

The successful managed care clinic of the future will practice cost-effective medicine, using publicly announced protocols. Patients who agree with a clinic's general approach to the tradeoff between money and health risk will use that clinic for most procedures. Because of, say, a history of family illness, however, a patient may want to obtain a medical test even if it falls outside the clinic's protocols.

The services offered by these clinics need not be sold to employers as managed care usually is sold today. Instead, they might be sold to individuals who pay for them with MSAs. Considering that individuals have different needs and preferences, MSA payments seem preferable.

The model described here is not all that futuristic. Many managed care advocates say the Mayo Clinic practices cost-effective medicine, but most of the clinic's patients are fee-for-service customers.

Practicing Medicine in the Information Age

The doctor who makes decisions with no regard for cost will become obsolete. MSAs will seek doctors who are financial advisers as well as health advisers. Physicians will be aided by sophisticated computer programs. No large bureaucracy will be required. When all patients have ready access to information, doctors acting as their agents easily will outperform any bureaucracy.

CONSENSUS ON HEALTH REFORM: OPTIMAL PUBLIC POLICY TOWARD MSAs[15]

A consensus is emerging on the right way to reform our health care system. This consensus stems from the recognition that the tax system has shaped the health care system and fostered many of its problems. Health reform requires tax reform.

Problem: Encouraging Waste

Under current law, every dollar of health insurance premiums paid by an employer escapes, say, a 28 percent income tax; a 15.3 percent Social Security (FICA) tax; and a 4, 5, or 6 percent state and local income tax, depending on where the employee lives. The government, in effect, is paying half the premium—a generous subsidy that encourages employees to prefer health insurance to taxable wages even when the insurance is wasteful. For an employee in the 50 percent tax bracket, for example, $2 of nontaxed health insurance need be worth only slightly more than $1 to be preferable to $2 of taxable wages.

Problem: Encouraging Third-Party Payment

One reason health care spending is so difficult to control is that most of the time when we enter the medical marketplace as patients, we are spending someone else's money. Economic studies and common sense confirm that we are less likely to be prudent shoppers if someone else is paying the bill. The explosion in health care spending over the past three decades parallels the rapid expansion of third-party payment of medical bills. The patient's share of the bill has declined from 48 percent in 1960 to 21 percent today.[16]

The primary reason for the shift from out-of-pocket payment to third-party payment of medical bills is federal tax policy. Although employer payments for health insurance are excluded from taxable income, taxes take up to half of any amount employers give employees to pay their own small medical bills.

Problem: Penalizing the Purchase of Insurance by the Uninsured

The federal government currently "spends" about $70 billion a year in tax subsidies for employer-provided health insurance, and state and local governments spend another $10 billion. These subsidies arise because, as noted above, employer-paid health insurance is excluded from employees' taxable income.

At the same time, the self-employed, the unemployed, and employees of small companies that do not provide health insurance must pay taxes first and buy health insurance with what is left over. This can make the cost of health insurance twice as high for them as for those with employer-provided insurance. Small wonder that almost 90 percent of nonelderly people who have health insurance are insured through an employer and that 82 percent of uninsured workers are self-employed, unemployed, or working for small companies with fewer than 100 employees.[17]

THREE DIRECT SOLUTIONS

These three problems have three direct solutions.

Solution: Limit Tax Subsidies

The tax system should be changed so that it encourages people to obtain basic health insurance without encouraging them to overinsure. Beyond some minimum expenditure, people should not be able to lower their taxes by spending money on health insurance or medical care. One way to achieve this result is through fixed-sum tax credits, described below.

Solution: MSAs

Under traditional health insurance, people pay monthly premiums to an insurer such as Blue Cross, and the insurer pays medical bills as the subscriber submits them. With MSAs, insurance pays for expensive treatments that occur infrequently, while individuals use their MSA funds to pay small bills covering routine services. If MSAs receive the same tax treatment as health-insurance premiums, people can make unbiased choices between self-insurance and third-party insurance. Government should encourage health insurance while remaining neutral with respect to type.

Solution: Tax Fairness

Equity in taxation requires that all Americans receive the same tax encouragement to buy health insurance. Accordingly, a self-employed or unemployed individual, and anyone else who purchases health insurance on his own, should be entitled to a tax deduction or tax credit that is just as generous as the tax treatment he would have received if an employer had provided the policy.

IMPLEMENTING THE SOLUTIONS

The ideal way to implement these three solutions—a way that does not create new problems—is to adopt fixed-sum tax credits and back-ended MSAs.

Fixed-Sum Tax Credits

One way to achieve tax fairness and at the same time remove the distorting effect of tax subsidies is to give every taxpayer a tax break that (1) is conditional on the purchase of insurance but (2) does not increase if the taxpayer chooses more expensive coverage. Employers and their employees would make premium payments and MSA deposits with after-tax dollars, and employees would receive a tax credit for the purchase of insurance on their personal income tax returns.

Unlike a tax deduction, which benefits people more if they are in higher tax brackets, a tax credit can be structured to create more

Table 2

Equivalence of front-ended and back-ended MSAs

Front-ended MSA

Initial Sum	Taxes	MSA Deposit	MSA Withdrawal	Taxes	Final Sum
$1,000	0	$1,000	$2,000	$500	$1,500

Back-ended MSA

Initial Sum	Taxes	MSA Deposit	MSA Withdrawal	Taxes	Final Sum
$1,000	$250	$750	$1,500	0	$1,500

Assumptions: 1. Tax rate = 25%; 2. Tax-free growth double the initial deposit.

benefit for lower-income taxpayers. For those with very low incomes, the credit can be refundable, with government providing most of the funds for health insurance premiums through a system of vouchers.

Back-Ended MSAs

Under a front-ended MSA, deposits are made with pretax dollars, and the funds not spent on medical care are taxed upon withdrawal. Although these accounts are a substantial improvement over third-party payment of every medical bill, they retain some of the use-it-or-lose-it incentives that encourage overconsumption of medical care: Funds spent on medical care are tax-free, but funds withdrawn to purchase other goods are subject to taxes and (in some versions) penalties.

This problem is eliminated with a back-ended MSA, in which deposits are made with after-tax dollars and withdrawals are tax-free.

Figure 10

Ideal taxation of health insurance and Medical Savings Accounts

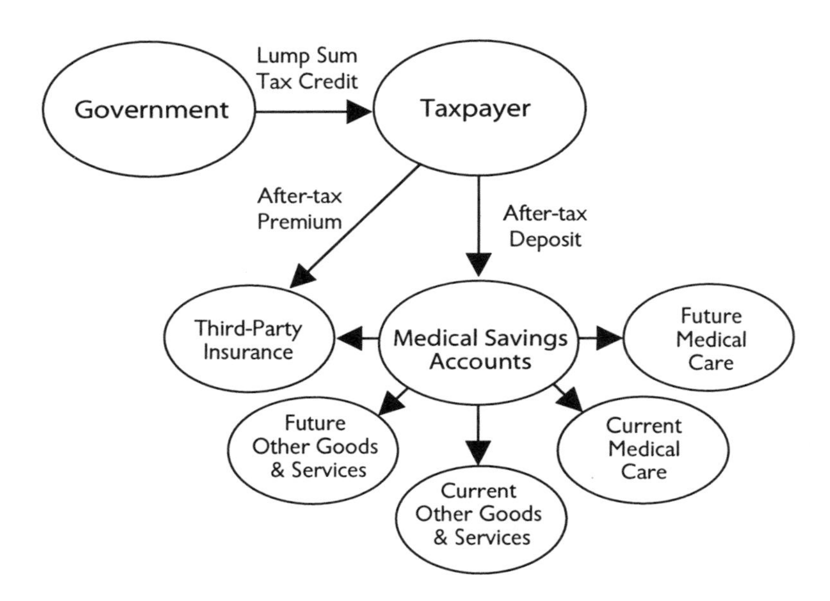

Note: The taxpayer receives a tax credit for acquiring health insurance: an HMO, a conventional indemnity plan, or catastrophic coverage combined with a medical savings account. Because the credit is fixed, people cannot lower their taxes by obtaining more expensive coverage. MSA deposits grow tax-free. But because MSA deposits are made with after-tax dollars, all withdrawals are tax-free. This makes tax policy neutral with respect to all uses of MSA funds.

For funds left in the account until the time of retirement, front-ended and back-ended accounts are equivalent (see Table 2). However, the incentives that affect withdrawal for health spending are different.

Interestingly, the Balanced Budget Act of 1997 may inadvertently have created an opportunity for senior citizens to use a new type of IRA (Roth IRAs) as a back-ended medical savings account. Roth IRAs require after-tax deposits and allow withdrawals to be tax-free, although earnings on the deposits can be withdrawn tax-free only if the account is held for five years. For those under 59½, there is a 10 percent penalty on withdrawals. However, for seniors who face no such penalty, these back-ended IRAs can serve as back-ended MSAs. Unlike a conventional IRA, taxpayers can deposit up to $2,000 per year in these accounts regardless of age. There is no requirement to start withdrawing at age 70½. Money in the account can be withdrawn to pay medical expenses, or for any other purpose, without penalty. Money not spent continues to grow tax-free.[18]

The back-ended approach is consistent with fixed-sum tax credits. Ideally, the taxpayer should be able to withdraw the funds at any time, and for any reason, without penalty. As Figure 10 shows, this would allow people to make unbiased choices between medical care and all other uses of money.

Consensus Solutions and Tax Reform

The reforms proposed here are consistent with the adoption of a flat tax, national sales tax, or value-added tax to replace the current income tax. All three alternatives are designed to tax consumption rather than savings.[19] Under each approach, savings would grow tax-free. This is consistent with a back-ended MSA approach.

NOTES

[1] See John C. Goodman and Gerald L. Musgrave, *Patient Power: Solving America's Health Care Crisis* (Washington, D.C.: Cato Institute, 1992); see also Mark V. Pauly and John C. Goodman, "Tax Credits for Health Insurance and Medical Savings Accounts," *Health Affairs,* Spring 1995, pp. 125–139.

[2] See "Medical Savings Accounts: The Private Sector Already Has Them," National Center for Policy Analysis *Brief Analysis* No. 105, April 20, 1994.

[3] Council for Affordable Health Insurance, "Full Coverage Special Report," February 16, 1996; see also Molly Hering Bordonaro, "Medical Savings Accounts and the States: Growth from the Grassroots," National Center for Policy Analysis *Brief Analysis* No. 170, August 3, 1995.

[4] See "Saving the Medicare System with Medical Savings Accounts," National Center for Policy Analysis *Policy Report* No. 199, September 1995.

[5] *Ibid.*

[6] Kristin Becker, "Medicaid as an MSA: A Solution for the States?" *Patient Power Report,* February 16, 1996; see also Brant S. Mittler and Merrill Matthews, Jr., "Can Managed Care Solve the Medicaid Crisis?" National Center for Policy Analysis *Brief Analysis* No. 155, April 10, 1995.

[7] See Mukul G. Asher, "Compulsory Savings in Singapore: An Alternative to the Welfare State," National Center for Policy Analysis *Policy Report* No. 198, September 1995; see also Peter J. Ferrara, John C. Goodman, and Merrill Matthews, Jr., "Private Alternatives to Social Security in Other Countries," National Center for Policy Analysis *Policy Report* No. 200, October 1995, and Thomas A. Massaro and Yu-Ning Wong, "Medical Savings Accounts: The Singaporean Experience," National Center for Policy Analysis *Policy Report* No. 203, April, 1996.

[8] John Burry, Jr., "A Windfall for the Healthy: How Medical Savings Accounts Will Hurt Americans and Hurt Business," Blue Cross & Blue Shield of Ohio, 1994.

[9] American Academy of Actuaries, "Medical Savings Accounts: An Analysis of the Family Medical Savings Account and Investment Act of 1995," October 1995.

[10] "Statement of John N. Sturdivant before the Civil Service Subcommittee of the Committee on Government Reform and Oversight on Adding a Medical Savings Accounts Option to FEHBP," December 13, 1995.

[11] Michael T. Bond, Brian P. Heshizer, and Mary W. Hrivnak, "Reducing Employee Health Expenses with Medical Savings Accounts," unpublished paper.

[12] See John C. Goodman, "Are Medical Savings Accounts Good for the Sick?" National Center for Policy Analysis *Brief Analysis* No. 182, October 17, 1995.

[13] John D. Graham, "Comparing Opportunities to Reduce Health Risk: Toxin Control, Medicine and Injury Prevention," National Center for Policy Analysis *Policy Report* No. 192, June 1995.

[14] John C. Goodman and Merrill Matthews, Jr., "Medical Savings Accounts and Managed Care," National Center for Policy Analysis *Brief Analysis* No. 157, May 5, 1995.

[15] See Pauly and Goodman, "Tax Credits for Health Insurance and Medical Savings Accounts," and John C. Goodman and Gerald L. Musgrave, "The Economic Case for Medical Savings Accounts," a paper presented at the American Enterprise Institute's Conference on "Restructuring Health Care," Washington, D.C., April 18, 1994.

[16] See Gary Robbins, Aldona Robbins, and John C. Goodman, "How Our Health Care System Works," National Center for Policy Analysis *Policy Report* No. 177, February 1993.

[17] Employee Benefit Research Institute, "Sources of Health Insurance and Characteristics of the Uninsured: Analysis of the March 1994 Current Population Survey," EBRI *Special Report* No. SR–28, February 1995.

[18] See John C. Goodman, "And the Death of Medicare's Monopoly," *The Wall Street Journal*, August 5, 1997.

[19] For an explanation of why the flat tax is a consumption tax, see Robert E. Hall and Alvin Rabushka, *The Flat Tax*, 2nd ed. (Stanford, Cal.: Hoover Institution Press, 1995); see also John C. Goodman, "Principles of the Flat Tax," National Center for Policy Analysis *Brief Analysis* No. 195, February 8, 1996.

11

PROMOTING A CONSUMER-DRIVEN HEALTH CARE SYSTEM

Senator Robert F. Bennett

Robert F. Bennett was elected by the citizens of Utah to represent their state in the United States Senate in 1992, a year in which health care reform had been an important campaign issue. When Senator Bennett arrived in Washington, he took a leadership role in the health care reform debate, winning praise from colleagues on both sides of the aisle for his willingness to consider all viewpoints.

As a successful businessman, he had concluded that the government-controlled health plan that had been crafted by the White House would be destructive to the health care system and to the economy, and he challenged the health policy community to focus on a viable market-based alternative. This challenge was instrumental in the formation of the Health Policy Consensus Group.

Senator Bennett delivered introductory remarks as the keynote speaker at the Galen Institute's conference on "A Fresh Approach to Health Care Reform," summarizing his views on problems and remedies for the health care financing system. We reprint here the text of a major speech he delivered on June 27, 1994, to his colleagues in the United States Senate, providing detailed insights into his views on the financing of health insurance. (In these remarks, he addresses the President Pro Tempore of the Senate.)

Mr. President, the issue of health care reform has been the top issue before the Congress. Indeed, as I listen to some of my more senior colleagues, they suggest it is perhaps the top issue to come before this Congress during their service and perhaps even—not to put too fine a point on it—in the history of the Nation, because we are talking about a bill that will create a social entitlement of a size unknown.

We spent a good part of last year in this body talking about entitlements and the impact of entitlements on the budget, and the possibility that entitlements could indeed break the budget and force the country on the verge of bankruptcy. It is perhaps not overstating the matter, therefore, to say that health care that would create a huge new entitlement is, indeed, one of the most serious social issues that we have ever debated within this body.

We are talking about regulating one-seventh of the total economy. Our transportation system is not that big. Our communications system is not that big. We do not have public utilities that are that big. Nothing approaching the size and complexity of this issue has ever come before us.

Given the importance of that, I have decided before I entered into a final vote on this matter that I had better do my homework, and I have tried to do that. I have talked to my constituents in town meetings all over my home State. I have talked to people outside of my home State. I have spent time with the various think tanks and study groups across the ideological spectrum, listening to their arguments—some of them in favor of a single-pay system, some of them in favor of alliances, some of them violently opposed to these things. I spent hours with the lobbyists who come to see us, presenting their points of view on this issue, including the lobbyists from the White House. Indeed, I have probably spent as much time with the White House lobbyist as I have with any individual lobbyist. And I have spent time with my colleagues. Senator Chafee, on the Republican side, has held breakfasts every week to discuss health care, and I have attended whenever possible. We have gone off on retreats and talked about it. I have spent time with my Democratic colleagues, talking about it, trying to understand the complexities of this issue.

Now that the time has come that we are nearing a vote, I think I need to rise and report what I have found and where I stand on this particular issue. This is what I have found.

PROBLEMS NEED FIXING

First, there is, indeed, a problem. Our system needs fixing. Those who say, "Oh, minor tune ups" are wrong, in my view. President Clinton deserves credit for forcing the Nation to confront this basic fact. Indeed, others have talked about it and have worked around the fringes of it, but President Clinton is the one who has looked the issue in the eye and forced us to confront the seriousness of this problem. Whatever passes, whatever ultimately happens will be a tribute to President Clinton's courage. And as a Republican Senator I want to add my personal tribute to his willingness to confront this particular challenge.

Second, a major reason why there is a problem in health care is the fact that market forces do not work in health care. In order to operate, a market requires informed and empowered consumers, and we do not have either one in the health care system. We are not informed as consumers because we do not have the proper medical training. When a doctor says, "You need a procedure," I cannot confront him and challenge him and say, "No, doctor, that is too expensive, I would prefer something else," the way I can challenge a used-car salesman. So the market does not work on the information side.

The market does not work on the empowered side. I am not empowered, as a consumer, to control my own destiny. Why is that? Because the coverage that I receive in the form of an insurance policy is determined by my employer. I do not get to decide what is in that policy. My employer decides.

Oh, you say, in the Government you have your choice. Yes, I have my choice of those plans that the employer—in this case the Federal Government—has decided would be good for me to make. When people say to me, we wish we could all have the health care plans that you in the Senate have, my response is, I wish I could have the plan I had before I came to the Senate, because I had a better plan prior to coming to the Senate. But because my current employer does not endorse that plan, I do not have that choice.

So as I say, market forces do not work because we do not have an informed consumer and we do not have an empowered consumer.

ATTEMPTS TO REPEAL LAW OF SUPPLY AND DEMAND

How did we get into this mess? You can go all the way back to the Second World War, and you will find that in one of its periodic attempts to repeal the law of supply and demand, the Government, in its wisdom, said we will enforce wage-and-price controls throughout the economy.

You have a booming economy. You are an employer, and I am your employee. Somebody offers me a job at a higher wage than you can pay and you cannot match it; the Government has forbade you from matching it. So you say to me: "Tell you what I'll do, Mr. Bennett. I'll keep you as my employee. Instead of giving you a wage raise, which is illegal, I'll buy an insurance plan for you, and that means I am increasing your compensation by the amount of the worth of that plan, but it will not be charged as a wage increase and this is the way I will get around wage controls."

So we started down the road of tying health coverage to the employer; we started down the road of giving the employer the right to determine what coverage the employee would have.

If I am right, the principal thing that is wrong with the system is that the market does not work. What is the solution? I have referred to the Second World War and how we got into our circumstance. If the Government caused the problem, the Government can solve the problem, and the solution is this: We must take the control of the payment system away from the employer and put the control in the hands of the individual consumer. Simply put, we must trust the American people.

RESTORE CONSUMER CONTROL

The Clinton plan does not do this. The plan that we have received from President Clinton, from his wife, and from Ira Magaziner, and the others who have worked with him, does not break the link between employer ownership of policies. On the contrary, it cements it and perpetuates it. Market forces will never appear under the Clinton plan, which is why the Clinton plan will never achieve the kinds of savings that politically are being advertised.

The Clinton people themselves know this. There has been a recent book published that is the buzz of Washington. It is called *The Agenda* by Robert Woodward. Everybody is all abuzz because it shows that the decisionmaking process in the White House is untidy. My reaction to that is the decisionmaking process in every White House is untidy. Why is this news?

But within the book, there is news. And the news is, with respect to health care, that the Clinton advisers realize that wage-and-price controls are necessary for them to be able to claim the kinds of savings they are talking about.

DEBATE OVER PRICE CONTROLS

If I may take you to page 122 of the Woodward book and quote, referring to Ira Magaziner, the principal author and architect of the Clinton plan. The book says:

> Magaziner said they had to consider some form of price controls on costs. He did not like explicit Government controls and knew all the arguments against them. He preferred to let competition in the marketplace set costs, but they needed savings, and for the Government to clamp on controls by fiat would be more certain to pull in savings in the near future. The administration could not continue to allow costs to skyrocket while they wrote their detailed plans.
>
> There was silence around the table. No one favored the controls, but no one seemed to want to speak up. Who was going to fall on the sword first? Alice Rivlin stepped forward and ripped the notion hard. "Nixon had tried price controls and they failed," she said. "An intricate system would require equally intricate price controls, a complicated task that would take weeks or months to figure out." Her remarks started an avalanche. Laura Tyson wondered how price controls might be put in place. "How would the Government gather the data? How would doctors and hospitals and others report? It probably would take a year to 18 months to implement even short-term price controls," she said, "and that would

> presumably be the point at which full reform would begin and price controls supposedly not be needed."
>
> Alan Blinder said that one of the first messages from the new Democratic administration should not be to put one-seventh of the American economy under the command and the control of the Federal Government. That would only reinforce the notion that Democrats didn't like free markets. Hillary was noncommittal.

Mr. President, Alice Rivlin was right. Laura Tyson was right. Alan Blinder was right. Price controls have never worked, do not work and will never work. Any bill that is founded on the forlorn hope that this time they just might work will produce dislocations in the economy that will be ruinous to us all.

Again, even the understanding of this began to dawn on some of President Clinton's people. Going back to the Woodward book, on page 120, it says:

> During the transition, a 16-member team had sent an 84-page reform memo to Clinton warning that reform would be expensive and its actual cost would hinge on the extent to which you employ short-term price controls. It listed four options for proceeding. Each one included an analysis of 1996 election politics and each forecast a dreary road ahead.

And then, a little later on the same page, referring to James Carville, the President's primary political consultant:

> This was serious, Carville realized. After the meeting, Carville told Magaziner, "I now see this as real. When I do a campaign and foul up, someone just loses. But if you foul up, you foul up the country." Magaziner just rolled his eyes.

I should note for the sake of historic accuracy, Mr. President, that in the book, Mr. Carville does not use the word "foul." He has another verb which I understand is improper for me to use on the Senate floor.

CONTROLS ARE "POISON"

The Clinton plan and its clone, the Kennedy plan, are, in my view, poison. They are based on the assumption that the only way they can work is through Government-imposed price controls. They must be defeated even at the cost of gridlock. Yes, filibuster if that is what it takes. This Senator is prepared to engage in that to see to it that neither of these plans comes to be law.

And to my friends on the Democratic side of the aisle who wish to lambaste us for talking about gridlock and filibuster, I say the American people are with us on this one. The latest poll shows that 70 percent of the American people are willing to wait until next year for reform if they are convinced that that is what it takes in order to get it right. It is more important that we do it right than that we do it now.

How did the Clintons go so far astray? They had a 500-person task force to go through all of the data and sift through all of this and give them guidance as to how this plan should be put together.

Once again, it is clear from the Woodward book that the task force was window dressing. The Clinton people already had their minds made up before the task force was convened. Quoting once again from *The Agenda:* On Friday, February 5, [1993], this is less than a month after Mr. Clinton's inauguration, before he has come to the Congress with his proposals.

> On Friday, February 5, Bob Rubin sent a short memo to the President saying that the economic team was going to meet over the weekend to discuss Hillary and Ira Magaziner's desire to incorporate reform into the economic plan.

Mr. President, we passed the economic plan in this body well over a year ago. We passed it under reconciliation, and one of the ideas that arose during that time was the possibility that it be included in reconciliation so that it not be subject to a filibuster. The 500-person task force was window dressing; it was giving lipservice to receive input from other places. On the 5th of February, they already knew what it was they were going to propose.

I said that the solution was to trust and, therefore, empower the American people on health care. How do we do that? As I said, the Government created the employer control of in the first place, back in the Second World War. The Government can uncreate it by changing the tax laws now.

PROVIDING TAX BREAKS TO INDIVIDUALS

Today, compensation for a worker comes in two forms: Taxable and untaxable—the wages that are reported on your W–2 form that are taxable, and the benefits that the employer deducts as part of his payroll costs that are untaxable. But make no mistake, both of these are compensation to the individual. It makes no difference to the employer whether the compensation is in one category or the other. There are costs he has to pay and costs he can deduct in either case. But the difference is to the employee because the employee currently has no control over how the nontaxable portion is spent.

Let us change that. Let us give the employee tax-free dollars deductible to the employer but not taxable to the employee as long as the employee spends them on a plan of his or her choice. Let the individual decide what to do with those nontaxable dollars.

The individual, therefore, controls and owns the policy and affordability in the issue goes away because the employee takes the policy with him or her wherever the job trail may lead. Cost control I believe would be automatic. Problems with preexisting conditions, of course, would go away along with affordability.

Why do I think cost control would be automatic? Because the individuals would now be measuring the cost to themselves. They would not be thinking they were spending other people's money as they do in the present circumstance. They could make the decision on their own: Do I want this kind of coverage or do I not? I believe very quickly we would see individuals beginning to create a gap between catastrophic coverage and everyday, routine aches and pains kinds of coverage.

HEALTH INSURANCE AND HOME INSURANCE

Let me give you an analogy which I realize is imperfect as all analogies are but which makes the point. Let me talk about homeowner's insurance. Now, in this country there is no Federal mandate that everyone have homeowner's insurance. The Government does not interfere and require this, and yet every homeowner has it because the market forces are so strong that it makes sense for everyone to have it. You have virtually universal coverage. What does your homeowner's insurance cover?

Well, in a time of catastrophe—my house burns down—it covers everything. My homeowner's insurance will not only replace the house; it will replace the carpet; it will replace the dishes and the shelves; it will replace the blankets on the beds; it will replace the pictures on the wall. I have absolute total coverage.

There is nothing, however, in my homeowner's policy that covers the cost of mowing the lawn or repainting the front door or replacing a broken window. Now, I suppose I could get a policy like that, but the premiums would be astronomically high. Therefore, I choose to take care of those things myself and save the premiums.

I have talked to insurance executives and said: What would happen if you provided only catastrophic? And they said: We could cover catastrophic insurance for everybody in the country for approximately 10 percent of the premiums now being paid.

CONSUMERS WOULD CONTROL COSTS

An individual American faced with that fact would be intelligent enough to make the right kind of choice as to how much catastrophic he needed, where to draw the line, and where to say this much I will cover. If the individuals knew what first dollar coverage costs, the individuals would immediately make wise choices as to the size of deductibles and copays and the level of insurance that makes sense for them.

Now, moving in this direction, uncoupling the control of insurance from the employer and passing it to the individual by changing the tax laws would be true structural and basic reform. It would require very careful study. It would require deliberate implementation over time because it is not a quick fix. But it is the right fix.

Now we come to the legislative situation. As I have said earlier, the Clinton bill and the Kennedy bill move entirely in the wrong direction in this matter, and I am prepared to fight them as firmly and totally as I know how. But it is becoming clear that neither the Clinton bill nor the Kennedy bill will be offered. The morning newspaper tells us of Senator Moynihan's desire to offer a bill, and Senator Chafee and some others are working to fashion a bill. Senator Dole has indicated his willingness to consider offering a bill.

ALLOWING MARKET FORCES TO WORK

So we come to the question: Should we pass one of these bills even as we reject the Clinton and Kennedy bills? I have not seen the details of them. I have not read them. But I ask this question of every bill that comes before us: What is the basic structural thrust of your proposal? Is it to perpetuate the notion that the American people cannot be trusted to decide their own future, that someone else—an employer, a Government agency, or a mandatory alliance—must do it?

If that is the thrust of your bill, I will not vote for it, and I would rather have no bill this year than that kind of a bill. However, I would say to a Senator offering a bill, if the basic thrust of your proposal is for a system that will move us toward the goal of allowing market forces to work their will, increasing the freedom of Americans to choose for themselves, then, yes, I would be willing to vote for a bill that goes in that direction.

In sum, Mr. President, the issue is tortuously complex and huge in its implications. The chances that we might produce enormously difficult and costly problems if we do it wrong are overwhelming. But complex as it is, it can be solved as other complex social challenges have been solved throughout our history. Trust Americans to make their own individual decisions. That is the key. If we do, we will wend our way through the thicket as we always have when we have made liberty our full star. This has been the sum and essence of our success as a people. It will not fail us here.

I yield the floor.

12

THE ROLE OF A UNIVERSAL HEALTH CREDIT IN WELFARE AND TAX REFORM

Representative Thomas E. Petri

I'd like to talk not only about changing health-care tax incentives but also about putting those changes in a broader context that includes welfare reform and general tax reform. If we look at all these related problems and focus on making all the pieces fit together, we can accomplish far more than we might have believed possible. If we take that kind of fresh approach, I am tremendously excited by the prospect of major improvements in all these areas—improvements vital for our country. But we need to engage the nation in this effort.

Now first there are some assumptions I won't talk about because I believe they are widely shared by advocates of reform.

I assume that the health-care cost increases we have witnessed are not inherent in the alignment of the stars or the nature of medical economics. They are caused by flawed government policies.

I assume that a lesser cause, because it affects only 60 million to 70 million people, is the growth of government health-care programs based on fee-for-service with third-party payment, in which neither doctor nor patient has much incentive to control costs.

I assume that the greatest of the flawed policies, now affecting roughly 150 million people, is the exclusion from individual taxable income of employer-paid health benefits. That creates a huge, open-ended, regressive subsidy for health-care spending. No wonder costs exploded. And if they are now being stabilized, at least in the corporate world, it is probably at too high a level.

Finally, therefore, I assume there can be no complete market-oriented health-care reform that fails to address this flawed tax incentive. For me, that's the starting point of the discussion we need to have.

Four alternatives are commonly suggested: capping the exclusion, eliminating it while lowering tax rates, converting it into a universal tax credit with the same cost, and augmenting it with Medical Savings Accounts (MSAs).

Capping it offers too little gain to be worth the pain. It's like combating smoking by limiting people to two packs a day. Why bother? At any politically acceptable cap, you would leave in place incentives to purchase more coverage for everyday expenses than would occur otherwise. On the other hand, the cap takes something away from the most powerful interests—those who have been able to win Cadillac benefits—without offering them anything in return.

Eliminating the exclusion would be accomplished by some flat-tax proposals, and in that broader context, it might be doable. But it is still a political stretch. It clearly offers substantial gain to go with its pain, but not as much as you might think. It does not provide any direct help to those without employer-paid benefits, for example. And it does not support the kind of Medicaid and welfare reforms we need. I'll explain what I mean by that in a minute.

I maintain that the approach with the most gain and least pain is the tax credit approach. We should count employer-paid benefits as taxable income to employees and give back all resulting revenue (as well as that from repealing the deductibility of medical expenses) as a universal tax credit. The higher this credit is, the more attractive the proposal. In the Petri bill, through a couple of scoring tricks, and by "strongly encouraging" the states with income taxes to do the same thing, we calculate the value of the credit for an average couple with children at about $2,000.

Taxpayers would use this credit in one of two ways. For those with employer-paid benefits (which the employers could still deduct as a business expense), the credit would offset other taxes, including those on their health benefits. Note that some taxpayers would have more credit than new tax. A taxpayer in the 15 percent bracket faces a total marginal tax rate of about 25 percent from federal and state income and Social Security taxes. His taxes on an average employer premium of $5,000 would be $1,250. But his new credit would be $2,000. He'd be $750 better off. Taxpayers in the 28 percent bracket with average benefits would be about as well off as before.

Taxpayers in higher brackets and those with Cadillac plans would face higher taxes, but they would benefit from the improved incentives and efficiencies in the entire health care system. In fact, with tax subsidies that are fixed and independent of the amount of coverage purchased, the people with Cadillac plans might decide they don't really need such expensive coverage after all and that they would rather have higher wages instead.

Those without employer-paid benefits would use their credits to purchase competitive health plans (hopefully under insurance market reforms). The only requirement for these plans would be that they include at least catastrophic coverage. Since the credit should be about enough to purchase such coverage, the bill would achieve universal catastrophic coverage at no increased taxpayer cost. Note also that this focuses the tax-subsidized dollars where they will do the least harm—on catastrophic coverage, which most conforms to a traditional insurance model and which everyone ought to have. People might well decide to purchase broader coverage, but tax policy would be neutral on those decisions.

This approach is completely egalitarian. The amount of tax subsidy is independent of both personal income and the receipt of employer-paid benefits. Those who might prefer the current regressive subsidy would be "for the rich."

Suppose organized labor threatened to oppose this reform. I'd say, "Make my day! You mean after all your years of rhetoric about standing up for the little guy, you would oppose a reform that's better for most of your members in favor of a subsidy that's greater the higher the tax bracket? You mean you're really for the rich after all? Thank you so much for clarifying that!"

Let's review the advantages of the tax credit approach to this point. Tax subsidies are:

- fixed rather than open-ended;
- egalitarian rather than regressive;
- focused where they will do the least harm—on catastrophic coverage; and

- universal, achieving universal catastrophic coverage at no increased cost.

Moreover, employers, who have negotiating leverage with providers, still can offer coverage.

This is just a small change in tax incentives, which can be accomplished in just a few pages of legislation.

There is one more advantage, which is of crucial importance. It is surely impossible to do welfare and Medicaid reform right without a universal health-care tax credit. Let me explain.

Part of the Republican vision for America is that welfare should be replaced by work, that we should all be able to improve our situations by earning more, and that we should have incentives (or at least not face crippling disincentives) for forming two parent families within marriage. Theoretically, the first of these goals is easiest—we can simply refuse to provide cash benefits without work, even government-provided work if necessary. In practice it is not so easy, but at least it is theoretically doable. However, providing people incentives to get ahead once they are working is actually more difficult because they face a crippling array of marginal tax rates that result from the phaseouts of public programs designed to help them.

Start with federal and state income and Social Security taxes adding up to 25 percent. Then add a 21 percent tax rate for the phaseout of the earned income tax credit (EITC) for families with two or more children. That is a total marginal tax rate of 46 percent. For four million families in public housing, rent is 30 percent of marginal income. The marginal tax is now up to 76 percent. And we haven't mentioned food stamps, school lunch, WIC (the Women, Infants, and Children program), Head Start, energy assistance, added child care expenses for working extra hours, and so on.

Now consider acute care under Medicaid. We need to change it from an open-ended fee-for-service model to something else. Most market-oriented health-reform proposals would convert it to a voucher for the purchase of competitive plans, with the voucher value phasing out as income rises. To me that seems clearly the way to go. But there is a big problem. To phase down such a voucher to zero requires a phaseout rate of about 30 percent. Add that to the 76 percent we already have from standard taxes, the EITC, and housing, without considering anything else, and you have a total marginal tax rate of 106 percent. That's crazy. You actually lose money by earning more. You are trapped at a low income. Even without public housing, you have a 76 percent marginal tax rate from the other three main sources, which is still ridiculous.

This is a crucial problem that simply must be addressed. First we need to get rid of the marginal tax rate effects from public housing and other welfare programs, which I believe can be done.

We cannot get rid of the EITC. In fact, we have to have an EITC as a vital adjunct of welfare reform, because our society does not deem a minimum wage income to be enough to support a family. We have to have a wage supplement for the lowest skilled workers with children, and that is the job of the EITC. Even with a flat tax, we'll have to have an EITC or something like it.

We can, however, get the EITC's phaseout rate down, and the drive for a $500 per child tax credit in the Contract With America provides a unique opportunity to do that. Separately, I have developed a proposal to integrate that credit with the EITC by doubling it to $1,000, eliminating the personal exemption for those children, making this new credit refundable, and substituting it for a major portion of the EITC. Since the $1,000 credit is universal and does not need to be phased out, that enables us to get the phaseout of the rest of the EITC down to a rate of 11 percent. By the way, the proposal, among other benefits, also drastically reduces marriage penalties in the EITC.

Now let's go back to Medicaid. If you have a universal health-care tax credit amounting to $2,000 for families with children, you only need to phase down a Medicaid voucher to that amount rather than to zero. That's crucial. It reduces the Medicaid phaseout rate to about 12 percent. That can only be accomplished with a universal health credit. You can't do it by capping the exclusion. You can't do it by eliminating the exclusion. And you can't do it with MSAs.

Now you can envision welfare reform in which the basic income of able-bodied low-skilled people with children comprises wages plus an EITC and a Medicaid voucher. If you got rid of all other program phaseouts, marginal taxes would combine standard taxes of 25 percent, an EITC phaseout of 11 percent, and a Medicaid voucher phaseout of 12 percent, for a total of 48 percent.

Despite all the innovative reform it takes to get there, however, clearly even that is not good enough. One final step is necessary: tax reform that pushes the income tax threshold up so that income taxes do not begin until the EITC and Medicaid phaseouts have ended. A flatter tax that retains the EITC and a refundable health credit would accomplish that.

With that final piece in place, total marginal tax rates for lower income families would be down to about 33 percent. That is what we have to achieve to provide economic opportunity to lower income Americans and get rid of the poverty trap. It is not all we have to do—I haven't mentioned education, crime, home ownership, and other topics. But it is a necessary part of what we need to do.

We have to accomplish every piece of this marginal tax-rate reduction. We have to get rid of the phaseouts in other programs. We have to get the EITC phaseout down. We have to get rid of the overlap of income taxes with the other two main phaseouts. And we have to get the Medicaid phaseout down. Anything less is just not good enough.

So, when you look at our problems in a broader context, a universal health credit is a vital component of the solution.

I'd like to close with a few thoughts about MSAs. A system in which a broad cross section of people has MSAs rather than third-party coverage would be an improvement over our current system. Unfortunately, it is not good enough and not conservative enough.

MSAs are still regressive because they are based on a tax exclusion or deduction. They don't help those without employer coverage unless they are extended at enormous additional cost. If it is difficult to take money out of the MSA for nonmedical purposes, the system retains a huge tax subsidy for spending on health care rather than other goods. And the more you spend, the more subsidy you get. On the other hand, if it is easy to take money out for other purposes, costs will explode because everyone will max out on an MSA to avoid taxes. Most important, if we spend our tax subsidy on MSAs, we simply cannot reform Medicaid and fix the terrible economic incentives facing lower income families.

Finally, MSAs are not as good as a credit from the point of view of most workers. Suppose you do not have employer-paid coverage, but you do have an option for either an MSA or a credit and you are satisfied with only catastrophic coverage. With the credit, your catastrophic plan is paid for up front, you don't need to lay out any cash until expenses arise, and then you can decide to spend your money on health or other goods as you see fit.

With an MSA you have to lay out $2,000 of your own cash for the catastrophic policy and sock away another $3,000 or more in the MSA in order to receive the $2,000 tax benefit you get in the 28 percent bracket. You're out $3,000 net, and you're restricted to spending that amount on medical care. It is not nearly as good a deal. If you would rather purchase broader coverage through an HMO or other plan, a credit easily facilitates that while an MSA option may not.

For workers with employer coverage, the analysis is similar. If all you want is catastrophic coverage, you are better off with that and wages than with that and an MSA. If we all agree that the purchase of at least catastrophic coverage should be a condition of the receipt of any tax subsidy for health care, it simply makes more sense to focus all the subsidy on the catastrophic coverage itself rather than spreading it out over that and additional medical spending.

In short, MSAs are an attractive concept that turns out to be an enormous red herring. It is distressing that it has thrown so many good conservative bloodhounds off the true health reform scent.

The hour is late, the trail is cold, and the forest is dense and difficult. Yet we must not give in to despair. We must press on and pursue these immensely difficult issues, if only because the prize is so great.

With hope in our hearts, a clear vision of the entire landscape guiding us, and all of us working together, we can achieve the comprehensive set of reforms our country so badly needs.

13

THE WORKERS' RIGHT TO CHOOSE

Edward Ryan Moffit

I am a teacher and a local union president, and I am proud to be both. I teach air-conditioning and refrigeration technology at the Bucks County Technical School in Bucks County, Pennsylvania, a suburb of Philadelphia. It is still a working-class area; and even today, although many representatives of management are fair and enlightened, every union member in Pennsylvania knows that there is no guarantee of justice for working people unless they have the right to organize and negotiate decent wages and benefits for themselves and their families. Pennsylvania union members and families have a keen sense of these rights, for they are the heirs of a long tradition of bitter struggles including the Coal Wars and the Molly Maguires of the past century.

In my capacity as president of the local union, my chief responsibility is to the welfare of the teachers and their families, the men and women who elected me to look after their best interests and to fight to maintain honorable working conditions. The burdens on teachers today are probably greater than ever before. Most Americans realize that the serious problems with young people today, many of whom come from broken families, eventually wind up in the classrooms. Being a teacher in the '90s is a tough job.

As the local union president, I have been engaged in protracted contract negotiations with the School Board of Bucks County since January 1995. During our negotiations, it became clear to us that the rising cost of health insurance was a major stumbling block to reaching a settlement. When I and my fellow negotiators for the union looked at the figures, we could not help but agree that management's concerns were legitimate. Monthly premiums for health insurance were skyrocketing.

In trying to address that issue and at the same time protect the quality of the health benefits for my members—the hard-working teachers I represent—I was impressed by an innovative new approach: the introduction of medical savings accounts (MSAs) for payment of routine medical services. This approach is used by a growing number of private companies and has been developed for public employees by Brett Schundler, mayor of Jersey City, New Jersey. Schundler's office kindly gave us an outline of the Jersey City plan.

I discussed the new approach with my members, and they were impressed. The MSA approach is innovative. It guarantees each employee a cash transfer into a private account for the payment of deductibles and routine medical expenses, plus a catastrophic insurance plan. If the employee exhausts the deductible in the account, the insurance company takes over and pays 100 percent of the coverage. Meanwhile, the insurance company is largely taken out of the cash flow of health care services, administrative costs are reduced, and the employee and his family are given direct control of health care spending.

On September 13, 1995, I unveiled the MSA option to management. Instead of rejoicing at the union leadership's offering them a genuinely market-based approach that promises to control costs in a serious way, the managers balked at the very idea. They thought it was absurd to offer employees some measure of direct control over what is, in fact, their own money.

That is the remarkable point. As economists know, the employer's contribution toward the employees' health care package is not the employer's money. It is the employees' money: compensation, just like wages. And working people know very well that getting the kind of health care benefits they have today generally has required sacrificing wage increases. Even though the MSA option offered by the union would protect members' families from catastrophic illness and at the same time enhance their control over their own health care dollars, it also would guarantee them an unfettered choice of their own doctors.

Management has made its own position clear: Choice, quality, and employee control over employee dollars is simply not an acceptable option. Their proposal is for the teachers to give up their current Blue Cross / Blue Shield plan and move into a managed care plan regardless of whether they like it.

The Bucks County debate has become even more interesting. In the course of these negotiations, the union has asked for health care census information. Initially, management refused to release such information and essentially blocked the union from processing competitive bids and quotes. It is our health care plan, but we are not supposed to know the financial details even if we are trying in good faith to negotiate a fair and just contract. This kind of management stonewalling is, of course, no surprise to union negotiators, especially those born and bred in Pennsylvania. But conservative politicians should take note: Don't depend on your friends in management to stand by the free market, especially if, for some mysterious reason, it is not politically or financially convenient.

The little struggle in Bucks County, Pennsylvania, is doubtless being replicated in labor–management disputes all over the United States. It is a tart foretaste of the next round of the national debate on health care reform. Employees have a right to know what they are getting and what they will be paying, and they should have the right to spend their own money on the medical services they need without being dictated to or restricted by management.

In Pennsylvania, thank God, we have solid working people who still have the brains and the guts to fight for their rights. There is a rock-solid labor tradition in Pennsylvania of confronting an unfair management. When they push down, we push up. When it comes to quality and choice of health care benefits, American workers should start pushing.

14

HEALING THE PHYSICIAN–PATIENT RELATIONSHIP

Sewell H. Dixon, M.D.

"If you don't know this, doctor, someday you'll kill somebody!" All of us in that sleepy freshman medical school class 35 years ago were jolted by the biochemistry professor's challenge as we struggled to understand the effects of insulin upon the cellular transport of sodium and potassium.

As junior medical students in a large charity hospital, we eagerly learned how to "break a diabetic out of control." We pushed insulin, administered large volumes of intravenous fluids, frequently checked the urine for glucose and acetone, and drew many blood samples, which we hurried to the lab for determinations of glucose and electrolytes.

As interns and residents, we became accomplished at concurrently managing large numbers of diabetic patients on the ward. We relied on routine daily lab tests and the results of the frequent urine analyses to guide the administration of various formulations and dosages of insulin. If any questions arose, we ordered a "stat blood sugar."

Later, as a cardiovascular surgeon, I would spend many hours in the operating room performing extensive revascularization operations on diabetic patients to salvage a jeopardized foot or even a toe. Special anesthetic techniques were required, and the operations were undertaken only after an extensive pre-operative evaluation, including detailed x-ray studies and angiograms performed by specialty radiologists.

These diabetic patients—representing about a third of all those requiring cardiovascular surgery—often were medically precarious, with a significant potential for attendant morbidity from cardiac, renal, and wound complications that could necessitate extended hospitalizations. Post-operative care in the intensive care unit with constant nursing attention, continuous intravenous insulin infusions, and frequent lab determinations was routine, and consultations from other specialists were obtained frequently.

And we never asked what anything cost.

Today, this seems a tale from Neanderthal times. When I entered medical school in 1960, total national health expenditures were $27 billion, or $143 per capita. When I started private practice 14 years later, total expenditures were $102 billion, or $464 per capita. By 1991, 30 years after I began medical school, these expenditures had risen to $752 billion and $2,868, respectively.[1]

This twentyfold increase in personal medical expenditure over three decades was accompanied by a fivefold increase in the consumer price index. During this same period, the gross domestic product increased from $513 billion to $5.723 trillion (in current dollars), representing an increase in national health care expenditure from approximately 5 to 13 percent of gross domestic product.

While personal medical expenses were increasing at a rate four times the rate of inflation, the number of doctors was increasing at a rate four times greater than that of the general population. In 1960, there were 260,484 doctors; by 1994, there were 684,414. This represented an increase from 142 doctors per 100,000 population to 263 per 100,000. In other words, in 1960, there was a physician for every 703 persons; by 1994, there was one doctor for every 380 Americans.

How could generations of American doctors be so unconcerned with the costs of medical care?

Thirty-five years ago, as medical students and residents, we were taught that the patient comes first, which translated as "do everything." Both my generation and subsequent generations of physicians were taught by precept and example that many tests, examinations, procedures, or even operations were not only justifiable, but mandated.

Once we were out in practice, these teachings were inculcated further by clinical experience and buttressed by private third-party and federal fee-for-service compensation. If questions of cost arose, the physician, patient, and family typically responded with "It's covered by insurance." When the elderly expressed concern about their savings, they usually were rebuffed with "But you have Medicare." In general, those patients who were not covered by insurance still were cared for with implicit cost-shifting, providing sufficient reimbursement for providers.

In 1960, 19.5 percent of health care expenditures went to physician services. Thirty years later, this declined slightly to 18.9 percent. However, the growth in expenditures—much greater than inflation—generated a net increase in physician incomes. Median net income for doctors rose from $82,000 in 1982 to $148,000 in 1992. This represented an annual growth rate of 6.1 percent, which (after controlling for inflation) translated to a 2.2 percent annual increase, or $102,000 in 1982 dollars. During this same period, median family income, adjusted for inflation, grew at 0.8 percent annually.

The distribution of physician income is not a bell-shaped curve. It has a long, rightward displacement so that the median exceeds the mean. According to data from the American Medical Association (AMA), the median income for all physicians in 1992 was $148,000 with a mean of $123,000; but the standard error of the mean was $174,400.

Distribution of income attributable to different specialties is also instructive. In 1992, the median income for specialists in internal medicine was $130,000. For general/family practice, the median income was $100,000; for surgery, $207,000. Clearly, medical practice has been financially rewarding to the individual practitioner, with proportionally greater compensation for those providing more complex services.

During the same three-decade period, hospitals and other ancillary providers functioned essentially on a "cost-plus" basis and competed with each other for clients by providing ever-increasing services, equipment, and convenience at ever-increasing costs.

MANAGED CARE: DECISION BY DEFAULT?

Although partially underwritten by federal money, the entire provider system was supported, stimulated, and facilitated by seemingly ubiquitous and inexhaustible employment-based health insurance and a tax policy that treats health insurance as a nontaxable fringe benefit for employees. Employees believed the money spent on their health insurance came from the company and covered most medical bills. Thus, users were separated from true costs. This promoted overutilization, lack of meaningful competition, and little incentive for cost control by either user or provider. The physician—whose decisions affected 80 percent of health care costs—usually practiced medicine with indifference to these costs (except for those in the few specialties whose services where not covered by insurance) and yet received high personal financial rewards. There was no educational, scientific, or economic incentive for providers of medical care to examine, discuss, or attempt to control their costs.

The basic disconnect between payer, consumer, and provider obscured economic reality except for those paying the bills: the insurance companies and their employer customers. As technological competition, defensive medicine, regulations, administrative and transaction expenses, cost-shifting, and even legitimate concerns for improvements in patient care continued to drive the cost of health care higher and higher, the payer—who seemed to be the only one concerned with cost—had to try to control expenditures. Because there was little interest in parsimony on the part of consumers, and none by providers, the payer had to save its business by saving the employer's bottom line. Enter managed care.

HOW PHYSICIANS DEALT THEMSELVES OUT OF THE HEALTH CARE DEBATE

As managed care organizations began—tentatively at first—to question physician decisions, we all reacted the same way: "But I am a physician; I know what is best for my patient." When health maintenance organizations (HMOs) entered the local scene talking about cost containment, utilization review, and market share, we each responded by saying, "But I am a physician. I am not some businessman. I know what is best."

When Medicare imposed the system of payment according to Diagnostic Related Group, its action was dismissed as typical government interference in the practice of medicine. Actually, it was—and it was just the beginning.

Of practicing physicians, 37 percent graduated from medical school in 1980 or later—the time span during which HMOs grew from 9 million enrollees to the 65 million estimated for 1996. Forty percent of today's doctors graduated prior to 1970, however, before federal regulations establishing HMOs were promulgated and enacted.

Generally, both by force of personality and because of their defining educational experiences, physicians tend toward a certain rigidity of response. In addition, traditional medical practice has strongly emphasized individual, not group, effort, as well as dogged adherence to scientifically based, often simplistic principles and endless repetition of tried and true experience-based techniques. The personal financial rewards for successful and repetitive practice also constitute an incentive system that is generally antithetical to community rather than personal concerns and to unscientific business ideas. Any concept that might require a significant concession of autonomy is seen as an absolute and maximal threat.

The incomes physicians have enjoyed are viewed by them as deserved and as appropriate to their education, long years of sacrifice, and life-and-death responsibilities. Ultimately, these incomes become not only a determinant of buying power, but also—and very importantly to them—a symbol of their special place in society: in other words, of their autonomy.

The most obvious threat to physician autonomy was the Clinton health care proposal, yet physicians were much more interested in the latest local HMO threat than in the federalization of medicine. During the debate over the Clinton plan, there was no identifiable united physician response. The American College of Surgeons endorsed a single payer system; several internal/family medicine groups—in line to be gatekeepers—strongly recommended the Clinton plan; and the AMA loftily vaunted its Patient Protection Act with its provision to prevent dismissal of doctors from HMOs, which was disparaged in Washington, D.C., as a "doctors' right to work act."

Although protesting publicly that "Doctors, not insurance companies, should make decisions about medical care" and that "We are not going to be dictated to," many doctors privately (and rapidly) cut the best deal they could with managed care organizations to preserve their autonomy—in reality, their income.

In my view, the lack of any meaningful and unified response by physicians to the Clinton initiative emboldened managed care organizations. Circumventing what they quickly found was an archaic Maginot line, these organizations were able to capture many confused doctors who turned out to be willing to respond to threats—real or imagined—to their autonomy / income by accepting the quickest truce with the best compensation.

THE FUTURE IS NOW

The relationship between payer, provider, and consumer has been seen traditionally as a three-dimensional equilateral triangle of roughly equivalent x, y, and z axes with a stable center of gravity. The length of the cost axis became excessive, however, and the construct became unstable; now it has crashed.

For the best of American medicine to survive and provide inclusive, scientific, and effective health care for the next century, an amalgamation must be forged between ethical and scientific medical practices and efficient and sustainable business practices. A circle must be developed to replace the now-destroyed triangle.

Doctors certainly had no incentive to learn to control costs over the past three decades. Perhaps they simply were not equipped to understand policy issues. Now, however, after the crash, perhaps they will shake themselves awake and learn the essential lessons in a healthy way.

This points to the need for changes in the underlying structure of the health care financing system that once again will put patients and doctors in charge. Individual ownership of health insurance, supported by reforms in tax policy, will weed out the excessive and unnecessarily expensive bureaucracy of an intrusive third-party payment system. Freed from the cost-containing whims of managed care bureaucracies, patients once again will be able to trust their doctors to provide them with the best advice on the treatments they need to protect and restore their health.

NOTE

1 Statistics in this paper are drawn from the following sources: *Statistical Abstract of the United States,* 1994; American Medical Association, *Socioeconomic Characteristics of Medical Practice,* 1994; American Medical Association, *Physician Characteristics and Distribution in the U.S.,* 1995 / 1996 ed.; and American College of Surgeons, *Socio-Economic Factbook for Surgery,* 1994.

Appendix A: ABOUT THE AUTHORS

GRACE-MARIE ARNETT

Grace-Marie Arnett is president of the Galen Institute, Inc., which promotes public education on tax and health policy issues. She speaks and writes extensively on health policy issues, focusing on tax policy and incentives to promote a better functioning market, and is a founding member of the Consensus Group, a group of health policy experts who advance ideas on a market-based approach to reform.

Ms. Arnett also has served as a vice president of the Heritage Foundation and as executive director of the National Commission on Economic Growth and Tax Reform. The 14-member commission was chaired by Jack Kemp and issued its recommendations for major tax reform in January 1996. Previously, she operated Arnett & Co., a policy analysis and communications firm, for 12 years.

SENATOR ROBERT F. BENNETT

Robert Bennett (R) was elected to the United States Senate from Utah in 1992. He serves on six committees: chairman of the new Senate Committee on Year 2000 Technology Problems; Appropriations; Banking, Housing, and Urban Affairs; Small Business; Environment and Public Works; and the Joint Economic Committee. In the 104th

Congress, Senator Bennett was appointed by then-Majority Leader Robert Dole to serve as chairman of the Republican Health Care Task Force.

Before his election to the Senate, Senator Bennett was the chief executive officer of Franklin Quest, one of the country's fastest-growing time management firms. When he joined Franklin Quest in 1984 as CEO, it had only four employees; when he resigned prior to his run for the Senate, the corporation employed over 700 people. Senator Bennett has had a distinguished career in business and public service and is a published author.

SEWELL H. DIXON, M.D.

Sewell Hinton Dixon, M.D., is president of Greenleaf Health Enhancement System of Greensboro, North Carolina, and president of the Dixon Group, Ltd., a health care consulting firm. He has advised on health care policy initiatives, has collaborated on publications and presentations to members of Congress, and has worked on health care policy development to provide effective market-based alternatives that enhance individual responsibility and control.

Dr. Dixon was in the private practice of cardiovascular and thoracic surgery in Greensboro, North Carolina, for 20 years and was president of his practice corporation—one of the largest practices of its type in the state—for 14 years. He also was an original national investigator for peripheral laser angioplasty and has authored more than 30 scientific articles. Dr. Dixon received his B.A. and M.D. degrees from Emory University and served as chief resident in surgery at Duke University Medical Center. He is a trustee of the Galen Institute, Inc.

STEPHEN J. ENTIN

Stephen J. Entin is executive director and chief economist of the Institute for Research on the Economics of Taxation, a pro–free market economic policy research organization in Washington, D.C. He was a key economic adviser to the National Commission on Economic Growth and Tax Reform, playing a major role in the drafting of its report and writing several of its support documents.

Mr. Entin joined the U.S. Department of the Treasury in 1981 under President Ronald Reagan, serving as deputy assistant secretary for economic policy. He participated in the preparation of economic forecasts for the president's budgets and in the development of the 1981 tax rate cuts and the provision for indexing the personal income tax for inflation. Before joining the Treasury Department, Mr. Entin was a staff economist with the Joint Economic Committee of the U.S. Congress, in which capacity he developed legislation for tax rate reduction and incentives to encourage saving.

JACK FARIS

Jack Faris is president and chief executive officer of the National Federation of Independent Business, the nation's largest small-business advocacy organization. NFIB was established in 1943 and has 600,000 members throughout the 50 states. He has led the NFIB since 1992, drawing on his experience both growing up in a family service-station business and owning his own small business.

Before joining the NFIB, Mr. Faris served in a variety of positions, from senior loan officer to vice president of marketing and public relations, in the banking industry in Nashville, Tennessee. He then worked with the international construction firm of Joe M. Rodgers and Associates, where he was responsible for marketing, personnel, and planning. For 12 years, he also owned his own marketing and management consulting firm, working primarily with small and independent businesses.

The NFIB, recently named the fourth most powerful lobby in Washington, D.C., by *Fortune* magazine, is currently leading a nationwide crusade to sunset the IRS tax code by December 31, 2001.

JOHN C. GOODMAN, Ph.D.

John Goodman is president of the National Center for Policy Analysis, a Dallas-based public policy research institute. Founded in 1983, the NCPA concentrates on health care, tax, and environmental issues and since its inception has been a leader in health care policy: It first proposed the idea of medical savings accounts in 1984. Its studies also have examined issues related to Social Security, education, crime, and privatization.

Dr. Goodman holds a Ph.D. in economics from Columbia University and has taught or done research at seven colleges and universities. He is the author of seven books and numerous articles published in professional journals. His most recent book, *Patient Power: Solving America's Health Care Crisis,* has sold more than 300,000 copies.

ROBERT B. HELMS, Ph.D.

Robert Helms is a resident scholar at the American Enterprise Institute, where he serves as director of health policy studies, and has written and lectured extensively on health policy, health economics, and pharmaceutical economic issues. He currently participates in the Consensus Group, an informal task force that is working to identify common principles for health care reform.

From 1981 to 1989, Dr. Helms served as assistant secretary for planning and evaluation and deputy assistant secretary for health policy in the U.S. Department of Health and Human Services. He holds a Ph.D. in economics from the University of California, Los Angeles.

JOHN S. HOFF, ESQ.

John Hoff graduated magna cum laude from Harvard University in 1962 and cum laude from Harvard Law School in 1965. He has been engaged in the practice of law in Washington, D.C., for 30 years, after service as law clerk to Judge Warren E. Burger, United States Court of Appeals for the District of Columbia Circuit.

Mr. Hoff specializes in health care law, representing hospitals, physicians, managed care companies, and others involved in the health care delivery system, and for a number of years has been a leader in the effort to develop market-based health care reform. He is a co-author, with three health care economists, of a monograph setting forth a plan for *Responsible National Health Insurance*, published by the American Enterprise Institute in 1992, and is the author of *Medicare Private Contracting: Paternalism or Autonomy,* published by AEI Press in 1998. He was a special employee of the National Bipartisan Commission on the Future of Medicare and served as project director for the Committee on Economic Development in connection with its study of the Economics of Legal Reform. He also has served as a member of the National Advisory Board on the Ethics of Reproduction and is a trustee of the Galen Institute.

DAVID B. KENDALL

David Kendall currently serves as the senior analyst for health policy at the Progressive Policy Institute (PPI). Before joining the PPI in 1994, he served for seven years on the staff of U.S. Representative Michael Andrews (D–Tex.), where he held several positions including legislative director and senior policy director.

In 1986, Mr. Kendall was a legislative assistant to Representative James R. Jones (D–Okla.), a former chairman of the House Budget Committee. Mr. Kendall worked extensively with the Jackson Hole Group and Representative Jim Cooper (D–Tenn.) on the Managed Competition Act. In 1993, he served on the President's Task Force on National Health Care Reform. He is the author of several reports and articles as well as a chapter on "Modernizing Medicare and Medicaid: The First Step Toward Universal Health Care" in *Building the Bridge: 10 Big Ideas to Transform America,* edited by Will Marshall and published by Rowman and Littlefield Publishers, Inc., in 1997.

GORDON B. T. MERMIN

Gordon Mermin was a research assistant until 1997 at the Urban Institute, specializing in public finance, health, and retirement issues. Among his other research, he co-authored a paper on the history of federal domestic spending. He graduated with distinction from Stanford University with a B.A. in economics in 1994 and is pursuing graduate studies at the University of Michigan.

EDWARD RYAN MOFFIT

Edward Ryan Moffit is on the faculty of the Bucks County Technical School in Bucks County, Pennsylvania, where he teaches air conditioning and refrigeration technology to high school students. Since 1980, he has been a teachers' union representative and has handled numerous contract settlements on behalf of the local union.

In June 1995, Mr. Moffit was elected president of the Bucks County Techincal School Education Associaton. During his tenure as president, in 1995 and 1996, he was involved in negotiating the teachers' contract with management representatives of the local school board. A main stumbling block to reaching a settlement was the issue of employee choice and the quality of the teachers' health care plan. Management proposed that the teachers be required to join a managed care network. Mr. Moffit, on behalf of the local union, made a counterproposal to allow teachers to keep the option of seeing the doctor of their choice through a medical savings account or maintaining the traditional indemnity plan. Management strongly opposed the union's MSA proposal and bitter contract negotiations ensued, along with a great deal of local media attention. After a job action and subsequent court intervention, the local union was forced to accept management's health plan. Contract negotiations reopen in 2000, and Mr. Moffit is pledged to renew the fight for employee choice in health care.

Edward Moffit lives with his wife, Rosemary, and their three children in Philadelphia, Pennsylvania.

ROBERT EMMET MOFFIT, Ph.D.

Robert Moffit is director of domestic policy studies at the Heritage Foundation in Washington, D.C. During the administration of President Ronald Reagan, he served as deputy assistant secretary for legislation at the U.S. Department of Health and Human Services, before which he served as an assistant director of the U.S. Office of Personnel Management.

A prominent Washington, D.C., health policy analyst, Dr. Moffit has published essays and articles in such journals as *Health Affairs*, *Health Systems Review*, *The Journal of Medicine and Philosophy*, and *The Wall Street Journal*. He also has appeared as a guest on The Jim Lehrer NewsHour, ABC News, NBC Nightly News, CNN, and CNBC.

Dr. Moffit holds three degrees in political science: a B.A. from La Salle University in Philadelphia and an M.A. and Ph.D. from the University of Arizona. He lives with his wife, Barbara, and their four children in Severna Park, Maryland.

MARK V. PAULY, Ph.D.

Mark Pauly currently holds the position of vice dean of Wharton doctoral programs and Bendheim Professor at the Wharton School. He is professor of health care systems, insurance and risk management, and public policy and management at the Wharton

School and professor of economics in the School of Arts and Sciences at the University of Pennsylvania.

One of the country's leading health economists, Dr. Pauly has made significant contributions to the field of medical economics and health insurance. He has published extensively, with over 100 journal articles and books in the fields of health economics, public finance, and health insurance.

Dr. Pauly is an active member of the Institute of Medicine, a former member of the Physician Payment Review Commission, and an adjunct scholar at the American Enterprise Institute. His most recent book is *Health Benefits at Work: An Economic and Political Analysis of Employment-Based Health Insurance,* published by the University of Michigan Press in 1997.

REPRESENTATIVE THOMAS E. PETRI

Thomas E. Petri (R) was elected to the U.S. House of Representatives from Wisconsin's Sixth Congressional District in 1979. He is a member of the House Transportation and Infrastructure Committee and chairman of its Surface Transportation Subcommittee, as well as the second most senior Republican on the Education and the Workforce Committee.

Termed a "notably independent, creative legislator" by *Washington Post* columnist David Broder, Representative Petri is known for his efforts to apply innovative solutions to entrenched problems, with a commitment to cost-effectiveness. Some of his initiatives include health care reform, student loan reform, federal highway spending allocations, tax and welfare reform, and banking reform. The *1992 Almanac of American Politics* stated that Mr. Petri "specializes in thoughtful, original proposals which cut across ideological and party lines." The National Federation of Independent Business has named him a Guardian of Small Business.

Representative Petri's administrative assistant, Joe Flader, served as a key policy adviser to, and worked closely with, members of the Consensus Group in planning the 1996 Galen Institute conference and in preparing Mr. Petri's presentation.

C. EUGENE STEUERLE, Ph.D.

Eugene Steuerle is a senior fellow at the Urban Institute and author of a weekly column, "Economic Perspective," for *Tax Notes* magazine. At the Urban Institute, he conducts extensive research on budget and tax policy, social security, health care, and welfare reform. He has published a number of articles on the financing of health care, the use of mandates, and the economic effect of tax subsidies.

Dr. Steuerle has served under four presidents in various positions in the U.S. Department of the Treasury, including deputy assistant secretary for tax analysis. Between 1984 and 1986, he served as economic coordinator and original organizer of the Treasury Department's tax reform effort. "During the past decade," a former Commissioner of Internal Revenue has written, "few people have had greater impact on major changes in the tax law and the principal improvements in tax compliance and administration."

Dr. Steuerle's publications include seven books, more than 100 reports and articles, 500 columns, and 45 congressional testimonies or reports. His latest book, *The Government We Deserve,* co-authored with Edward M. Gramlich, Demetra Nightingale, and Hugo Heclo and published by the Urban Institute Press in 1998, examines how fiscal, economic, and social policy must be made adaptable to the modern economy and allow for innovation and reform of social insurance in such areas as health care and retirement policy.

MICHAEL TANNER

Michael Tanner is director of health and welfare studies at the Cato Institute in Washington, D.C. He also is an adjunct scholar with the Mackinac Institute in Michigan and the Alabama Family Alliance.

Before joining Cato in 1993, Mr. Tanner served as director of research for the Georgia Public Policy Foundation in Atlanta. He also spent five years as legislative director with the American Legislative Exchange Council, where he specialized in health and welfare issues. He is the author of five books on health care reform.

NORMAN B. TURE, Ph.D.

The late Norman B. Ture was president of the Institute for Research on the Economics of Taxation (IRET) until his death in August 1997. IRET is a nonprofit, nonpartisan public policy research institute in Washington, D.C., which Dr. Ture founded in 1977.

Dr. Ture joined the Reagan administration early in 1981 as under secretary of the treasury for tax and economic affairs and resigned his Treasury post in June 1982. Among other previous positions, he was head of Norman B. Ture, Inc., an economic consulting firm; director of tax studies at the National Bureau of Economic Research; and a member of the staff of the Joint Economic Committee of the U.S. Congress. He had been a visiting professor of economics at George Washington University and a visiting lecturer at the Wharton School of Finance, among other academic positions.

Dr. Ture held an M.A. and Ph.D. in economics from the University of Chicago. He was a long-time advocate of the free market and favored fundamental tax reform to eliminate existing tax code biases against saving and investment to promote a strong and efficient economy.

KEVIN VIGILANTE, M.D., M.P.H.

Kevin Vigilante, a clinical associate professor of medicine at Brown University, is former director of emergency services at the Miriam Hospital in Providence, Rhode Island. He currently cares for HIV-positive women and is director of the Community Outreach Clinic, which provides medical care and social services to high-risk HIV-negative women after they are released from prison.

A congressional candidate in the 1994 elections, Dr. Vigilante was selected in 1995 by *Time* magazine as one of 50 outstanding leaders under age 40.

Appendix B: A VISION FOR CONSUMER-DRIVEN HEALTH CARE REFORM

Health Policy Consensus Group

OVERVIEW

The United States does not have a properly functioning market for health care, and the financing system needs to be reformed. The market is distorted by a tax policy that is mistargeted, miscalibrated, and open-ended. This tax policy provides generous benefits to those who have higher incomes and receive health insurance through the workplace. Yet it offers little or no assistance to those at the lower end of the income scale. Particularly at a disadvantage in the current system are those who fall through the cracks between this tax subsidy and Medicaid.

Reforming the tax treatment of health insurance is essential to creating a more efficient and equitable market for medical services and health insurance in the United States. Correcting the tax distortion would lower the costs of health insurance coverage in both the public and private sectors and thereby allow broader access to quality health care.

This paper describes the Consensus Group's vision for consumer-driven health care reform based upon tax reform. The health policy experts listed in this paper have developed these principles and recommendations, which are integral to each of their market-based proposals for health care reform. There is unanimous agreement on the nature of the problem, and consensus on directions indicated by the recommendations for reform.

THE HEALTH POLICY CONSENSUS GROUP

The Health Policy Consensus Group is a task force of leading health care economists and health policy analysts, including researchers at the major market-oriented think tanks. The Consensus Group is working to increase public awareness that the tax treatment of employment-based health insurance underlies many of the problems facing the private health sector in the United States.

The incentive-based reforms the group proposes are intended to strengthen and rationalize the health care market. The Consensus Group believes that the competitive marketplace is the most appropriate way to restrain costs and to give Americans more responsibility and opportunity to choose their health insurance and health care arrangements.

The group considers different approaches to reform and provides education on their benefits and disadvantages to help the public and policymakers understand the balances that must be struck in any reform effort. The group endorses basic principles but does not offer specific legislative proposals; its members have been working together to provide policy advice since 1993. The Galen Institute, a not-for-profit health and tax policy research organization, coordinates and facilitates the work of the Consensus Group.

The ideas in this document are based upon many meetings and exchanges of information by members of the Consensus Group, who are listed as signatories at the end. The views expressed in this document reflect those of the individual signers and not necessarily their organizations. Grace-Marie Arnett, president of the Galen Institute, and John S. Hoff, health care attorney and Galen Institute trustee, were the principal writers for this vision statement.

A Rich But Hidden Tax Subsidy: The History

Early in the 20th century, the link between health insurance and the workplace began to be established in the United States. During and after World War II, however, employment-based health insurance became more widespread, and the link became much stronger.

Factories were pushed to meet wartime production schedules. Competition for good workers was intense but was hampered by wartime wage controls. Employers found they could compete for scarce workers and boost compensation without running afoul of these controls by offering health insurance as a benefit in lieu of cash wages. In 1943, the Internal Revenue Service ruled that employers' contributions to group health insurance would not count as taxable income for employees.

That ruling, a later codification of it by Congress in 1954, rising tax rates on middle-class incomes, and the rising demand for health insurance all combined to create a strong incentive for health insurance to be obtained through employment-based groups.

The generous tax preference accorded job-based health insurance is a historical accident that has increased automatically over the decades without legislative authorization or appropriations. It has percolated through the economy for 50 years to become the foundation for a system that provides subsidies and therefore strong incentives for at least 140 million Americans to get their health insurance through their jobs. The subsidy for employment-based health insurance now is worth an estimated $100 billion a year in forgone federal and state taxes. However, tens of millions of Americans are locked out of this system and benefit little or not at all from this rich but hidden tax subsidy.

This paper provides guidelines to begin to restructure the system to provide greater equity and efficiency, leading to more affordable, accessible health insurance.

Problems and Distortions in the Health Sector

Employment-based health benefits are part of employee compensation. However, health benefits are not counted as part of an employee's taxable income. This policy distorts the health care marketplace in a number of ways:

- It undermines cost consciousness by hiding the true cost of insurance and medical care from employees.
- Because the full cost of health insurance is not visible to employees, it artificially supports increased demand for medical services and more costly insurance.
- As a result, inefficient health care delivery is subsidized at the expense of efficient delivery.
- Cash wages are suppressed.
- Many employees with job-based coverage are frustrated because they have little choice and control over their policies and their access to medical services.
- The self-employed, the unemployed, and those whose employers do not offer health insurance are discriminated against because they receive a much less generous subsidy, if any at all, when they purchase health insurance.
- The tax benefits are skewed to favor higher-income individuals and those who demand the most expensive health coverage and medical treatments.
- Those with equal incomes are taxed unequally.

The Tax Subsidy for Employment-Based Health Insurance: How It Works

The tax code offers an exclusion from taxable income to those who get their health insurance at work.

Employment-based health insurance is part of the compensation package many employers provide to their employees—a form of non-cash wage.

Employers can take a tax *deduction* for the cost of this health coverage, as they do for most other forms of employee compensation. They write the check for the premiums, and some pay medical bills directly if they self-insure. Businesses can deduct these costs from their earnings since they are part of the total compensation package paid to workers and must be deducted to measure net profits correctly.

What makes health insurance different from cash wage or salary compensation, however, is that workers do not pay taxes on the part of their compensation package they receive in the form of health benefits.

Section 106 of the Internal Revenue Code provides that the value of health benefits is not counted as part of the taxable income of employees—in tax terminology, it is *excluded* from their taxable income. However, workers may receive this tax-favored benefit *only if* health coverage is provided through an employer. The value of the health coverage, the tax benefit employees receive, and the costs in forgone wages are largely invisible to them.

Principles of Consumer-Driven Reform

The following are core principles to guide policymakers and the public in making key decisions about creating a true consumer-driven health care system.

Consumer choice: Individuals should have choices in the medical care and health coverage they obtain, whether they secure coverage as individuals or through their employers or other groups. Government policies should expand the opportunities for individual choice without dictating or distorting these choices.

Competition: Consumers of medical services will receive the best value when providers are competing to offer the best price, quality, and services. Therefore, the system should rely on market competition, not government regulation or price controls, to promote efficiency, quality, and value.

Responsible budgeting: Government incentives to help targeted populations obtain private health coverage should be explicit, on budget, and reviewable.

Fixed and limited incentive: Individuals and families with the same incomes should receive the same benefit when purchasing health insurance, regardless of their employment status or whether their employers offer health insurance. Individuals should not be able to increase their claim on taxpayer revenues by purchasing more health coverage.

Expanded access: In a market based upon consumer choice, a more attractive range of options for health coverage would be available to a wider range of people, including those currently without health insurance. Once the market is functioning more efficiently, it will be clearer whether further legislation is needed to enhance people's ability to secure health coverage.

Responsible insurance: Health coverage should provide, at a minimum, protection against catastrophic loss—namely, high-cost, low-probability medical events. The tax system has encouraged movement away from the basic principles of insurance; instead, health coverage has become a way to pre-pay routine medical bills. A first step toward reducing the number of Americans without health insurance is through insurance that provides access to medical care and protection against large expenses in the event of catastrophic medical events.

Public-sector choice: Given the rapidly rising costs in federal health care programs, especially Medicare and Medicaid, the federal government should make full use of private-sector competition to control costs by giving beneficiaries more options to participate in the private market.

Cost awareness: Programs that enhance individual purchasing power will be more efficient because costs will be more visible to consumers. Programs and plans that make payments directly to providers insulate consumers from costs, artificially increase demand, and distort the health care marketplace.

Full information: Employers who provide health insurance should periodically inform their employees about how much of their compensation is being spent on health benefits and that this spending has reduced their cash wages by a commensurate amount.

Community versatility: The strength, diversity, and vitality of private-sector community organizations are an important resource in the health sector. Communities should experiment with public–private partnerships and other solutions for providing health care to low-income citizens, utilizing local resources to solve unique community problems.

Group purchasing: Tax and regulatory barriers to creating competitive private health care purchasing groups should be eliminated. Barriers to the creation of innovative provider groups should also be eliminated.

Value: As a result of implementing these principles, consumers will obtain better value for their health care dollars. The price system will convey consumers' needs and demands. Competition will facilitate more efficient use of technology and continued innovation in products and service delivery, and will reduce waste and duplication.

Recommendations for Change

The following are policy recommendations of the Consensus Group. They are not intended to provide a complete blueprint for reform, and reasonable men and women may differ over the details of how they should be implemented. However, these recommendations and the principles upon which they are based can provide a powerful guide for the policymaking process in achieving important goals of health care reform.

Every American should be able to obtain needed medical care. Reforming the tax treatment of health insurance is central to achieving this goal.

Congress could begin by providing a new set of incentives for people who do not have health insurance. These incentives should be properly structured to create an opportunity for everyone to purchase his or her own health coverage in an open and competitive market. We provide guidelines on how that might be accomplished.

We believe that following these recommendations will lead to a system in which costs will be restrained, private insurance coverage will expand rather than continue to contract, and quality will be enhanced primarily through additional competition and better consumer incentives.

The Principled, Responsible Alternative

We recommend providing credits or other comparable fixed incentives, explicitly determined by legislation, to assist people in obtaining private health insurance.

The size of the incentive will depend on how much taxpayer money lawmakers deem to be available. It can be structured in different ways.

Options

- Credits or other fixed incentives could be used to purchase private group or individual health coverage, in combination with medical savings accounts for those who choose them.

- If tax credits are provided, they could be refundable, over and above the Earned Income Tax Credit.
- The size of the credit or alternate financial incentive could be adjusted to reflect risk or need, or it could be used to buy into a high-risk pool for the uninsurable. These adjustments should be made while minimizing their effect on marginal tax rates.
- To expand access to coverage, state mandated benefit laws could be preempted for insurance purchased with this federal assistance, thus allowing a broader range of more affordable insurance products.

Some Benefits of This Approach

- Millions of Americans not eligible for the current tax subsidy would receive help in purchasing health insurance.
- Assistance can be targeted to those who do not have health insurance.
- It can be targeted to those in specific age, income, or other categories which legislators deem most worthy of the assistance.
- It gives individuals more choice in where they obtain health insurance.
- It allows individuals the opportunity to select the kind of health coverage that best suits their needs.
- It helps to minimize distortions in the marketplace.
- It is more equitable across income groups.
- The subsidy does not expand when an individual purchases more expensive insurance.
- It is available whether an individual's insurance is organized through employment-based groups or elsewhere. The role of employers in assisting employees to obtain health insurance could be maintained by each employer, if they so desired.

Key Decisions

Some of the many questions that must be addressed:

- How much money should the federal government spend on the incentive?
- How much will it be worth to individuals and families?
- Who will be eligible?
- Does the amount vary with income?
- How will risk adjustments be structured to keep policies affordable?
- How does one define what level of coverage must be purchased to qualify for the assistance?
- How will compliance be monitored and enforced?

Guidelines for a More Efficient and Equitable System

The following guidelines will help lawmakers in making policy decisions about reforming the tax treatment of employment-based health insurance to promote a more efficient market in the health sector.

1. Incentives for purchasing health coverage or medical services should not be provided through open-ended tax preferences or defined in terms of covered services, but rather should be limited to a fixed dollar amount, which could be adjusted over time through legislation and also adjusted by an individual's income and risk factors.

2. Incentives for purchasing health insurance should be provided directly to individuals and families.

3. This assistance could be in the form of credits or other incentives to be used to purchase medical services or health coverage. Employer groups are efficient mechanisms for the pooling of risk, and some proposals would have employers

offer plans on which the individual credit could be spent. However, the money also could be used to obtain coverage in a variety of other ways, either individually or through participation in groups, such as health plans sponsored by unions, trade or fraternal organizations, schools, or churches.

4. To eliminate the distortions in the current system and to provide even broader access to coverage, policymakers should consider capping or eliminating the tax exclusion for employment-based health benefits. By simultaneously providing offsetting assistance to individuals, the changes we recommend need not result in an increase in the tax burden for the American people and could even reduce taxes.
5. In view of concerns about the complexity of the income tax system, it should be noted that there are alternative administrative options available and that there is no necessary conflict in theory or in practice between the provision of a health care incentive and simplification of the income tax. The incentive could take many forms: direct assistance which is administered through a stand-alone outlay program or as part of other incentive programs; in conjunction with the payroll tax; or, as now, via the income tax.
6. Health insurers and health plans should have the flexibility to offer rewards and incentives for healthy lifestyles.
7. Reform of the Medicare system should expand private-sector options for beneficiaries. Medicare benefits should be defined in terms of a risk-adjusted dollar amount, not in terms of an open entitlement to covered services.
8. Beneficiaries should be able to elect to participate in traditional Medicare or to privately purchase health coverage or medical services of their choice.
9. Medicaid beneficiaries should be incorporated into the private health care system envisioned by these principles. Beneficiaries also should be able to purchase health coverage through the private sector. Just as with Medicare, Medicaid benefits should be defined in terms of a dollar amount, not in terms of an open entitlement to covered services.

Signatories

Grace-Marie Arnett
Consensus Group Coordinator
Galen Institute

Bradley D. Belt
Center for Strategic and International Studies

Stephen J. Entin
Institute for Research on the Economics of Taxation

Robert B. Helms, Ph.D.
American Enterprise Institute

John S. Hoff, Esq.
Health Care Attorney
Galen Institute Trustee

John Goodman, Ph.D.
Merrill Matthews, Ph.D.
Jack Strayer
National Center for Policy Analysis

David Kendall
Progressive Policy Institute

Naomi Lopez
Pacific Research Institute

Marty McGeein
The McGeein Group

Robert E. Moffit, Ph.D.
Carrie J. Gavora
The Heritage Foundation

Mark V. Pauly, Ph.D.
The Wharton School, University of Pennsylvania

C. Eugene Steuerle, Ph.D.
The Urban Institute

Michael Tanner
Darcy Olsen
Cato Institute

Kevin Vigilante, M.D.
The Miriam Hospital

The views in this document reflect those of these individuals and not necessarily their organizations.

For more information, please contact:
Grace-Marie Arnett, Consensus Group Coordinator
President, Galen Institute
P.O. Box 19080, Alexandria, VA 22320–0080
Phone: (703) 299-8900
Fax: (703) 299-0721
E-mail: *arnettgm@ibm.net*

Appendix C: TAX REFORM: THE HEART OF HEALTH CARE REFORM

The following commentary article drew on months of work by members of the Consensus Group in articulating their views on the distortions caused by the tax treatment of health insurance. It was published on the editorial page of the Wall Street Journal *on March 29, 1994, and gave widespread attention to the group's vision for a market-driven health care system.*

IT'S TAXATION, STUPID
by Grace-Marie Arnett

With the Clinton plan on the ropes, the time has come to shift the health care debate to expose the underlying cause of much of what ails the health care system—the tax treatment of employer-provided health insurance.

The tax policy that ties health insurance to employment can be traced to wage and price controls during World War II. Employers competing for scarce labor offered health coverage as a substitute for pay to boost compensation packages without running afoul of wartime wage controls. The IRS later endorsed this practice, ruling that employer-provided health benefits—unlike virtually all other forms of compensation—could be excluded from the taxable income of employees.

The IRS decision has cascaded through the U.S. health care system for nearly half a century to dictate its structure and create many of its problems, demonstrating the awesome power of tax incentives.

The benefits that employees receive as health insurance lead many recipients to believe erroneously that the money spent on health insurance premiums is their company's and not their own. Most also believe health insurers finance most of patients' medical bills. These illusions obscure the truth about the real price employees pay in lost wages, inflated prices and insecurity.

No Raise

Take the example of a photographer whose salary is $30,000. Her company also offers health insurance, but the $4,000 cost of the policy covering her family is excluded from her taxable income.

Because she has been encouraged to believe that her premiums are paid by her employer and are therefore "free," she and her colleagues have negotiated a rich policy with low deductibles. But the bigger the checks her employer writes for health insurance, the smaller her wage increases have been. She may not see the connection, but she sees the result: She hasn't had a pay increase in three years, but she stays at her job because she has good health benefits. The fastest growing element of compensation is benefits, making up 39% of total employee compensation in 1992.

Health economists have been writing about the distorting and costly effects of the tax treatment of health benefits for more than 20 years, but politicians have been reluctant even to discuss it. Most, including the president, build on the current job-based system and would lock its flaws into law.

The primary problem is that users are separated from cost. Insured patients buy doctor and hospital services at a deep discount, usually paying less than 20 cents on the dollar out of pocket, giving them an incentive to overuse medical services. They have little reason to force providers to compete. Prices inevitably rise; this drives up the cost of insurance, fewer companies and individuals can afford coverage, and the number of uninsured rises, up to an estimated 38.5 million Americans at last report.

The current system also breeds insecurity. Consumers can get a tax break only if their employers buy their health insurance for them.

They don't own their policies themselves, and they are at the mercy of decisions by employers and insurance companies about premium costs and benefit structures. Worse, they may lose their health insurance or be forced to go for months without coverage if they lose or change jobs.

The rich tax subsidy for employer-provided health insurance is highly regressive. Those who purchase their own insurance receive no benefit from the exclusion, and those who have employer-provided insurance receive larger tax benefits the higher their income.

Reform could direct the tax benefits more fairly, but it means detaching health insurance from employment. In a more rational system, individuals and families would be able to directly claim the tax benefit for purchasing health insurance or health care. This prospect appears unsettling to some workers and politicians. But changing the tax code would add choices, not eliminate them.

Reforming the tax treatment of insurance would not change employers' incentives to continue providing insurance. However, it likely will cause workers to ask for this part of their compensation to be included in their take-home pay. The photographer still could get her health coverage at work. But if she doesn't like the HMO or the managed-care plan her employer offers, she would be able to shop for another plan that better suits her needs. She might join a group organized by her church, professional organization, union or employee association. Most important, she would own her own health insurance policy, just as she owns her auto and life insurance policies, and wouldn't lose it because she changed jobs.

Tax relief could come as tax credits or vouchers to be used to offset the costs of catastrophic health insurance, out-of-pocket expenses, or the opening of medical savings accounts, depending on personal choice and individual family circumstances. The impact on the market would be profound. Millions of consumers shopping for individual or newly formed group policies would suddenly wake up to the real cost of health insurance. In shopping for their own coverage and making medical purchases, they would reward the efficient and cost-effective medical providers and punish the inefficient and overpriced providers.

Every American should be able to obtain needed medical care, and reforming the financing mechanism for health insurance is the most realistic and efficient way to reach that goal. Tax reform would eliminate the primarily middle-class fear that losing a job means losing health insurance. The poor could obtain private health insurance with explicit federal subsidies.

A wider range of options for health insurance would be available in a market catering to individual rather than corporate choice. Health insurance would more likely be purchased as true insurance to protect against catastrophic loss, reducing paperwork to process hundreds of millions of small bills. Insurance would be more affordable and flexible, and many more people could afford coverage. These changes would increase the affordability of health care without triggering the job losses and wage reductions that would result from employer mandates.

Critics argue that health care decisions are too complex for the average consumer. But Americans somehow manage to buy houses, automobiles, computers, legal services, and other forms of insurance by educating themselves about their options. More than 90% of medical decisions are made in a noncrisis environment, and people have time to get answers and make choices.

Each of the three main market-oriented think tanks in Washington is pursuing its own politically bold but economically sound health care ideas. When attention is paid to them, discussion has focused more on their differences than their similarities, thus fueling confusion among conservatives about how to craft a viable market-based alternative to the now-troubled Clinton plan.

But after a group of conservative senators, including Pete Domenici of New Mexico and Robert Bennett of Utah, called upon the think tanks to focus on what they held in common, health policy experts Robert Helms of the American Enterprise Institute, Robert Moffit of the Heritage Foundation, and Michael Tanner of the Cato Institute took up the challenge. This Consensus Group quickly determined that tax reform was the center of each of their market-oriented approaches. Around this core idea they have developed a broader conceptual approach to health care reform.

Individual Power

Most Americans agree that government control is not the answer. The more government is involved in health care, the more it will increase costs and add regulation while reducing quality and choice. The Clinton plan and most of the liberal alternatives increase the power of the state while the Consensus Group's approach increases the power of the individual.

By forging this consensus, the three think tanks help clarify the policy choices to show that tax reform is at the heart of health care reform. Once others join this parade, there can be a real debate between those who advocate a government-run system and those who favor a system that allows the individual to unleash the full force of a competitive marketplace.

Ms. Arnett, [then] of Arnett & Co., health policy consulting in Washington, D.C., coordinates the work of the Consensus Group.

Appendix D: PETITION ON HEALTH POLICY REFORM

In late 1994, members of the Health Policy Consensus Group developed and signed a petition identifying the problems created by the current tax treatment of employment-based health insurance. They invited economists and others to join them in signing it.

The petition was circulated in late 1994 and early 1995 by Elizabeth Kern Terry and Consensus Group coordinator Grace-Marie Arnett, then president of Arnett & Co. health policy consultants. Accompanying the petition was a "Dear Colleague" letter explaining the rationale for the project. The "Dear Colleague" letter and Consensus Group petition follow, along with the names and affiliations of the signatories:

HEALTH POLICY CONSENSUS GROUP

November 30, 1994

Dear Colleague:

The health care reform debate over the past two years has not yet produced a clear national consensus on policy solutions to address the fundamental problems in the health sector. The debate will continue next year, and we believe that the economic community can give it direction by identifying a key distortion that leads to many problems—the tax treatment of employment-based health insurance.

A diverse group of economists and health policy analysts has developed a petition to present a diagnosis of this problem, and we ask you to join us in signing it. This petition has been developed as a volunteer effort.

We would appreciate your reviewing the petition accompanying this letter. If you agree with it, we would be pleased if you would join us in signing it. We will use this petition to demonstrate the support in the economic community for addressing the inefficiencies in the health sector created by current tax law. We plan to publicize the petition in the national media along with the signatures we gather.

Please return the petition, with your signature, address, and affiliation, to the fax number or address listed on the petition. We want as many economists and health policy specialists as possible to participate in this effort. If you believe any of your colleagues would wish to sign it as well, please share the petition with them. Thank you for considering this important national policy issue. We look forward to receiving your reply at your earliest convenience.

Stuart Butler
The Heritage Foundation

John C. Goodman
National Center
for Policy Analysis

Robert B. Helms
American Enterprise Institute

Debra Miller
Center for Strategic
and International Studies

William Niskanen
Cato Institute

Robert Shapiro
Progressive Policy Institute

CONSENSUS GROUP PETITION

Petition concerning the tax treatment of employment-based health insurance:

Health Policy Reform: Diagnosing the Problem

Reforming the tax treatment of health insurance is essential to creating a more efficient market for medical care and health insurance in the United States.

Employment-based health benefits are actually part of employee compensation. However, these health benefits are not counted as income for tax purposes. This tax policy distorts the health care marketplace. It undermines cost consciousness by disguising the true cost of insurance and medical care to employees. It artificially supports increased demand for medical services and more costly insurance. As a result, inefficient health care delivery is subsidized at the expense of efficient delivery, and cash wages are suppressed. Further, the current tax law discriminates against the self-employed, the unemployed, and those whose employers do not offer health insurance.

We support reforming the tax treatment of employment-based health insurance to promote a more efficient market in the health sector. We support restraining costs through competition and consumer incentives rather than through destructive methods such as price controls and limits on private spending set by government.

________________________ ____________________

Signature Please print name

____

Title and Affiliation

____

Address and Zip Code

Telephone number: ( )______________ Fax number: ( )__________

Please return to:
Petition Coordinator, Grace-Marie Arnett
[Current FAX (703) 299-0721] Telephone (703) 299-8900

Petition Signatories

The petition was developed and initially signed by Consensus Group members, including:

Arnett, Grace-Marie	Galen Institute
Ferrara, Peter	Formerly, National Center for Policy Analysis
Goodman, John C.	National Center for Policy Analysis
Helms, Robert B.	American Enterprise Institute
Hoff, John S.	Health policy attorney
Kendall, David	Progressive Policy Institute
McGeein, Marty	Formerly, National Council of Community Hospitals
Miller, Debra L.	Strengthening of America Commission, Center for Strategic and International Studies
Moffit, Robert E.	The Heritage Foundation
Pauly, Mark V.	Wharton School University of Pennsylvania
Tanner, Michael	Cato Institute

The following economists are among those who signed the Consensus Group Petition (as of March 1995):

Alexeev, Michael	Indiana University
Allen, John W.	Texas A&M University
Allen, William R.	University of California at Los Angeles
Allsbrook, Ogden O.	University of Georgia

Anderson, Annelise	Hoover Institution
Anderson, Terry L.	Montana State University
Anderton, Charles H.	Holy Cross College
Andreano, Ralph	University of Wisconsin–Madison
Antel, John	University of Houston
Aranson, Peter H.	Emory University
Arnould, Richard J.	University of Illinois
Austin, D. Andrew	University of Houston
Baden, John A.	University of Washington and Foundation for Research on Economics and the Environment
Baetjer, Howard, Jr.	George Mason University
Bailey, Martin J.	Emory University
Baird, Charles W.	California State University at Hayward
Baker, Samuel H.	College of William and Mary
Baker, Charles D., Sr.	Northeastern University
Balke, Nathan	Southern Methodist University
Ball, Ray	University of Rochester
Baltagi, Badi H.	Texas A&M University
Barnum, Howard N.	The World Bank
Baughaum, Marshal Alan	Federal Energy Regulatory Commission
Bays, Carson W.	East Carolina University

Bazzoli, Gloria J.	Hospital Research and Educational Trust
Bean, Richard N.	University of Houston
Benham, Lee	Washington University
Berger, Mark C.	University of Kentucky
Bittlingmayer, George	University of California at Davis
Black, Dan A.	University of Kentucky
Blomquist, Glenn C.	University of Kentucky
Bogan, Elizabeth C.	Princeton University
Bohanon, Cecil E.	Ball State University
Borts, George H.	Brown University
Boudreaux, Donald J.	Clemson University
Bradford, David F.	Princeton University
Breeden, Charles H.	Marquette University
Brennen, Dennis	Harper College
Bronfenbrenner, Martin	Duke University
Brown, Douglas M.	Georgetown University
Browne, Mark J.	University of Wisconsin–Madison
Browning, Edgar K.	Texas A&M University
Buchanan, James	George Mason University
Burke, Thomas R.	The LaSalle Group

Burstein, Philip L.	Workers' Compensation Research Institute
Butler, Henry N.	University of Kansas
Butler, Stuart M.	The Heritage Foundation
Cagan, Phillip	Columbia University
Caldwell, Bruce	University of North Carolina at Greensboro
Calfee, John E.	American Enterprise Institute
Cameron, Rondo	Emory University
Chaloupka, Frank J., IV	University of Illinois at Chicago
Chapman, Kenneth S.	California State University, Northridge
Chappell, Henry W., Jr.	University of South Carolina
Cheng, Wen-Yu	Marietta College
Chiswick, Barry R.	University of Illinois at Chicago
Chiswick, Carmel U.	University of Illinois at Chicago
Clark, William M.	University of Oklahoma
Clarkson, Kenneth W.	University of Miami
Coats, R. Morris	Nicholls State University
Coelho, Philip R. P.	Ball State University
Cogan, John F.	Stanford University
Conant, John	Indiana State University
Coomes, Paul A.	University of Louisville

Cosimano, Thomas F.	University of Notre Dame
Craig, Steven G.	University of Houston
Curran, Christopher	Emory University
Daniel, Kermit	The Wharton School, University of Pennsylvania
Danielsen, Albert L.	University of Georgia
Danzon, Patricia	University of Pennsylvania
Dauterive, Jerry W.	Loyola University
Davidson, Audrey B.	University of Louisville
Davis, Michael L.	Southern Methodist University
DeAlessi, Louis	University of Miami
Decker, Sandra	New York University
Delemeester, Gregory	Marietta College
Derrick, Frederick W.	Loyola College (Maryland)
DeVany, Arthur	University of California at Irvine
Dobitz, Cliff P.	North Dakota State University
Dowd, Bryan E.	University of Minnesota
Dranove, David	Northwestern University
Dunkelberg, William C.	School of Business and Management, Temple University
Dvorak, Eldon J.	California State University at Long Beach
Dwyer, Gerald P., Jr.	Clemson University

Edwards, Franklin	Columbia University
Elliot, Evel	University of Texas at Dallas
Ellis, John M.	University of California at Santa Cruz
Ellwood, Paul M.	Jackson Hole Group
Enthoven, Alain	Stanford University
Entin, Stephen J.	Institute for Research on the Economics of Taxation
Erickson, Edward W.	North Carolina State University
Evans, Paul	The Ohio State University
Famulari, Melissa	University of Texas
Fand, David I.	George Mason University
Feigenbaum, Susan	University of Missouri at St. Louis
Feldman, Roger	University of Minnesota
Feldstein, Paul J.	University of California at Irvine
Finkler, Merton D.	Lawrence University
Fishback, Price V.	University of Arizona–Tucson
Frech, H. E., III	University of California at Santa Barbara
Freund, Deborah	Indiana University
Friedman, Milton	Hoover Institution
Froeb, Luke	Vanderbilt University
Gallaway, Lowell	Ohio University

Galles, Gary M.	Pepperdine University
Gardner, B. Delworth	Brigham Young University
Garratt, Rod	University of California, Santa Barbara
Gay, David E. R.	University of Arkansas
Gaynor, Martin S.	Johns Hopkins University
Geddes, R. Richard	Fordham University
Getzen, Thomas E.	Temple University
Giacalone, Joseph A.	St. John's University
Gifford, Adam, Jr.	California State University, Northridge
Gisser, Micha	University of New Mexico
Glied, Sherry	Columbia University
Goddeeris, John H.	Michigan State University
Gohmana, Stephan F.	University of Louisville
Goho, Thomas	Wake Forest University
Goldhammer, Mark L.	Rutgers University
Goldsmith, Scott	University of Alaska at Anchorage
Goodman, Allen C.	Wayne State University
Goodman, John C.	National Center for Policy Analysis
Grabowski, Henry	Duke University
Greene, Kenneth V.	Binghamton University
Gresik, Thomas A.	The Pennsylvania State University

Griffin, James M.	Texas A&M University
Grossman, Herschel	Brown University
Gwartney, James	Florida State University
Haberler, Gottfried	American Enterprise Institute
Hahn, Robert	American Enterprise Institute
Hamermesh, Daniel S.	University of Texas
Hanke, Steve H.	The Johns Hopkins University
Hansen, Robert G.	The Tuck School, Dartmouth College
Hanson, John R., II	Texas A&M University
Harsh, Michael D.	Randolph-Macon College
Hegji, Charles E.	Auburn University at Montgomery
Helms, Robert B.	American Enterprise Institute
Henderson, David R.	Washington University
Henderson, James W.	Baylor University, Henry W. Block School of Business and Public Administration
Herren, Robert Stanley	North Dakota State University
Hicks, Donald A.	University of Texas at Dallas
Higgs, Robert	The Independent Institute
Hill, P. J.	Wheaton College
Hirshleifer, Jack	University of California at Los Angeles
Hobbs, Bradley K.	Bellarmine College

Hoffmeyer, Ullrich	National Economic Research Associates
Hogan, Andrew J.	Michigan State University
Holcombe, Randall G.	Florida State University
Holt, Charles	University of Virginia
Horowitz, John B.	Ball State University
Horvath, Janos	Butler University
Horwich, George	Purdue University
Houston, Douglas	University of Kansas
Hughes-Cromwick, Paul	Center for Research on Health Care at the University of Pittsburgh
Hunter, William J.	Marquette University
Ihnen, Loren A.	North Carolina State University
Ireland, Thomas R.	University of Missouri, St. Louis
Jansen, Dennis W.	Texas A&M University
Jensen, Gail A.	Wayne State University
Johnson, Dennis A.	University of South Dakota
Johnson, Ronald N.	Montana State University
Johnson, Thomas	North Carolina State University
Kamlet, Mark S.	Carnegie Mellon University
Kaserman, David L.	Auburn University
Kassouf, Sheen T.	University of California at Irvine
Kauf, Teresa L.	University of California at Berkeley

Kelley, Allen C.	Duke University
Kenny, Lawrence W.	University of Florida
Khorassani, Jacqueline	Marietta College
Klein, Daniel B.	University of California at Irvine
Kosters, Marvin	American Enterprise Institute
Krol, Robert	California State University, Northridge
Krouse, Clement G.	University of California at Santa Barbara Leadership Center
Kushman, John E.	University of Delaware
Lambrinos, James	Union College
Lee, Bartholomew	Golden Gate University
Lee, Dwight R.	University of Georgia
Lee, Sang H.	Nicholls State University
Leeds, Michael A.	Temple University
Leyden, Dennis Patrick	University of North Carolina at Greensboro
Libecap, Gary D.	University of Arizona
Lindsay, C. M.	Clemson University
Lipford, Jody W.	Presbyterian College
Little, Mark	SAS Institute
Liu, Gordon	University of Southern California
Logue, Dennis E.	Dartmouth College

Long, James E.	Auburn University
Lott, John R.	University of Chicago and the University of Pennsylvania
Lowenberg, Anton D.	California State University, Northridge
Luwish, Hadassah Balsam	City University of New York
Lyman, R. Ashley	University of Idaho
Lynch, Michael	Pacific Research Institute
Macaulay, Hugh	Clemson University
Macey, Jonathan R.	Cornell University
MacLeod, Gordon K., M.D.	University of Pittsburgh
Makin, John H.	American Enterprise Institute
Maltsev, Yuri N.	Carthage College
Manning, Richard L.	Brigham Young University
Margolis, Stephen E.	North Carolina State University
Masten, Scott E.	University of Michigan
Mathys, John	De Paul University
Mayor, Thomas H.	University of Houston
McCarthy, Thomas R.	National Economic Research Associates, Inc.
McCloskey, Donald	University of Iowa
McCombs, Jeffrey S.	University of Southern California
McCormick, Robert E.	Clemson University

McCracken, Paul W.	University of Michigan
McGreevey, William	The World Bank
McGuire, Martin C.	University of California at Irvine
McLure, Charles E., Jr.	Hoover Institution
Medwig, Thomas M.	St. Clair Hospital
Meltzer, Allan H.	Carnegie Mellon University in Pittsburgh
Mennemeyer, Stephen T.	University of Alabama at Birmingham
Mercer, Lloyd J.	University of California at Santa Barbara
Michalak, Stanley J.	Franklin and Marshall College, Milken Institute for Job and Capital Formation
Miller, Debra L.	Strengthening of America Commission, Center for Strategic and International Studies
Miller, Mertom H.	University of Chicago
Miller, Oscar	University of Illinois at Chicago
Moberly, H. Dean	Auburn University at Montgomery
Moore, Thomas G.	Hoover Institution
Moore, William J.	Louisiana State University
Moroney, John R.	Texas A&M University
Morrisey, Michael A.	University of Alabama at Birmingham
Morse, Jennifer Roback	George Mason University

Mueller, Curt D.	Project HOPE
Mullahy, John	Trinity College
Muth, Richard F.	Emory University
Newman, Robert	Louisiana State University
Niskanen, William	The Cato Institute
Noether, Monica	Abt Associates, Inc.
Nunn, Geoffrey E.	San Jose State University
Nyman, John	University of Minnesota
O'Hara, David J.	Metropolitan State University
Ohsfeldt, Robert	University of Alabama at Birmingham
Olasky, Marvin	University of Texas at Austin
Parkman, Allen M.	University of New Mexico
Parsley, David C.	Vanderbilt University
Pasour, E. C., Jr.	North Carolina State University
Patton, Judd W.	Bellevue University
Pauly, Mark V.	The Wharton School, University of Pennsylvania
Peden, Edgar A.	Health Care Financing Administration
Peirce, William S.	Case Western Reserve University
Peltzman, Sam	University of Chicago
Peppers, Larry C.	Washington and Lee University
Perfect, Steven B.	Florida State University

Phillips, Kerk L.	Brigham Young University
Pieper, Paul	University of Illinois at Chicago
Pipes, Sally C.	Pacific Research Institute
Porter, Philip	University of South Florida
Poulson, Barry W.	University of Colorado
Provenzano, George	University of Maryland, School of Medicine
Raisian, John	Hoover Institution
Ramsey, James B.	New York University
Rasmusen, Eric	Indiana University
Raza, M. Ali	California State University at Sacramento
Reed, Robert	University of Oklahoma
Reinhardt, Uwe	Princeton University
Reynolds, Morgan O.	Texas A&M University
Ricardo-Campbell, Rita	Hoover Institution
Rieber, Michael	University of Arizona
Roberts, Russell	Director of the Management Center, Washington University
Rohacek, Jerry K.	University of Alaska at Anchorage
Rose, David C.	University of Missouri, St. Louis
Rosegger, Gerhard	Case Western Reserve University
Rosko, Michael D.	Widener University

Roth, Timothy P.	University of Texas at El Paso
Rowen, Henry S.	Hoover Institution and Stanford University
Rowley, Charles K.	George Mason University
Rubin, Paul H.	Emory University
Ruffin, Roy J.	University of Houston
Sachs, Kevin D.	SUNY at Buffalo
Sailors, Joel W.	University of Houston
Sanchez, Nicolas	College of the Holy Cross
Saues, Raymond D., Jr.	Clemson University
Savas, E. S.	Baruch College, City University of New York
Saving, Thomas R.	Texas A&M University
Schansberg, D. Eric	Indiana University
Schap, David	College of the Holy Cross School of Pharmacy
Schuyler, Michael	Institute for Research on the Economics of Taxation
Schwartz, Markis	Georgetown University
Scott, Frank A., Jr.	University of Kentucky
Scully, Gerald W.	University of Texas at Dallas
Seldon, Barry J.	University of Texas at Dallas
Shah, Parth J.	University of Michigan at Dearborn

Shapiro, Robert	Progressive Policy Institute
Shea, Dennis G.	Pennsylvania State University
Shmanske, Stephen	California State University, Hayward
Showalter, Mark H.	Brigham Young University
Silvers, J. B.	Case Western Reserve University
Simon, Julian L.	University of Maryland
Slesnick, Frank	Bellarmine College
Sloan, Frank A.	Duke University
Slottje, Daniel	Southern Methodist University
Smiley, William Gene	Marquette University
Smith, Vernon L.	University of Arizona
Sollars, David L.	Auburn University at Montgomery
Spencer, Christine S.	Johns Hopkins University
Spencer, David E.	Brigham Young University
Stein, Herbert	American Enterprise Institute
Steindl, Frank G.	Oklahoma State University
Steuerle, C. Eugene	The Urban Institute
Stoddard, Robert B.	Quintiles, Inc.
Stratmann, Thomas	Montana State University
Stroup, Richard L.	Montana State University
Suiten, Mary C.	Center for Economics Education,

	University of Missouri, St. Louis
Sumner, Daniel A.	University of California
Svorny, Shirley	California State University, Northridge
Tanner, Michael	The Cato Institute
Terzq, Joseph V.	Pennsylvania State University
Theroux, David J.	The Independent Institute
Thies, Clifford F.	Shenandoah University
Thompson, Henry	Auburn University
Thornton, Mark	Auburn University
Thurman, Walter N.	North Carolina State University
Timberlake, Richard H.	University of Georgia
Tollison, Robert D.	George Mason University
Tomal, Annette	University of Illinois at Chicago
Tower, Edward	Duke University
Traxler, Herbert	U.S. Department of Health and Human Services
Trejo, Stephen J.	University of California at Santa Barbara
Trivoli, George W.	Jacksonville State University
Troy, Leo	Rutgers University
Tryon, Joseph L.	Georgetown University
Tullock, Gordon	University of Arizona

Ture, Norman B.	Institute for Research on the Economics of Taxation
Twight, Charlotte	Boise State University
Tybout, James R.	Georgetown University
Utt, Ronald D.	The Heritage Foundation
VanBeek, James	Blinn College
Vander Linde, Scott H.	Calvin College
Vitaliano, Donald F.	Rensselaer Polytechnic Institute
Vogel, Ronald J.	University of Arizona
Volpp, Kevin G.	The University of Pennsylvania
Walden, Michael L.	North Carolina State University
Wallace, T. Dudley	Duke University (Emeritus)
Wallis, W. Allen	American Enterprise Institute; Past Chancellor, University of Rochester
Walters, Stephen J. K.	Loyola College (Maryland)
Waters, Teresa M.	Center for Health Services and Policy Research, Northwestern University
Wedig, Gerard J.	The Wharton School, University of Pennsylvania
Weidenbaum, Murray	Washington University
Weier, Andrew W.	Marshfield Medical Research Forum
Welch, Finis	Texas A&M University

Wenders, John T.	University of Idaho
Werner, Herbert D.	University of Missouri, St. Louis
Wessels, Walter J.	North Carolina State University
Westbrook, M. Daniel	Georgetown University
Wiggins, Steven N.	Texas A&M University
Wilensky, Gail R.	Project HOPE; Former Director, Health Care Financing Administration
Williams, Arthur R.	Cookingham Institute of Public Affairs
Willis, Carla Y.	Abt Associates, Inc.
Willis, J. F.	San Jose State University
Wilson, Paul W.	University of Texas at Austin
Wilson, R. Mark	University of South Florida
Wolak, Frank A.	Stanford University
Woodward, Robert S.	Washington University
Wrase, Jeffrey M.	Brigham Young University
Wyrick, Thomas L.	Southwest Missouri State University
Zajac, Edward E.	University of Arizona
Zupan, Mark	University of Southern California, School of Business Administration
Zwanziger, Jack	University of Rochester
Zycher, Benjamin	University of California at Los Angeles, Milken Institute

INDEX